TYNEDALE
From Blanchland to Carter Bar

BOOKS BY THE SAME AUTHOR

Sussex 100 Years Ago
Northumberland and Durham. A Social Miscellany
Bellingham. History and Guide
Hexham. History and Guide
Geordie Pride
Alnwick. History and Guide
Tynemouth. History and Guide
Historic Holy Island
Wooler and the Cheviots
Otterburn and Redesdale
Ovingham, Prudhoe, Bywell and Wylam
Rothbury and Coquetdale
Famous Northern Battles
Historic Northumberland
Historic Newcastle
Bridges of Northumberland and Durham
Corbridge. History and Guide
Sandhill, Newcastle
Northumbria's Lordly Strand
Castle and Town Walls of Newcastle
Berwick. History and Guide
Warkworth. History and Guide
Geordie Song Book
The Farne Islands
Lindisfarne or Holy Island
Old Inns of Northumberland
Old Inns of Lakeland. Two volumes
Old Inns of Cornwall. Two Volumes
Bamburgh, Seahouses and the Farnes
Smuggling in Cornwall
Old Inns of Devon
Smuggling in Devon
Old Inns of Cheshire
Famous Smugglers' Inns
Old Inns of Northumberland and Durham
Cornish Smuggling Tales
Northumberland and Durham 100 Years Ago
North Country Inn Signs
More Smugglers Inns
Lancashire 100 Years Ago
Picturesque North Country
Cheshire 100 Years Ago
Lakeland 100 Years Ago
Yorkshire (N) 100 Years Ago
Famous North Country Women
Cornwall 100 Years Ago
Devon 100 Years Ago
Old Inns of Lancashire
Picturesque Lancashire
Warwickshire 100 Years Ago
Castles of Northumberland
Old Halls of Northumberland

TYNEDALE

From Blanchland to Carter Bar

by

FRANK GRAHAM

Drawings by Susan Martin, Jean Wright and R. Thompson
Photographs by Hylton Edgar and Jack Armstrong
Roman Wall reconstructions by R. Embleton

Published by Frank Graham, 6 Queen's Terrace, Newcastle upon Tyne, NE2 2PL.
Printed by CWS Ltd., Printers, Pelaw, Tyne and Wear

I.S.B.N. 0 85983-115-9

Introduction

In our book on *Tynedale* we have tried to present a comprehensive history and guide to the largest District Council in England. It is our longest book to date and as with all our publications is lavishly illustrated. To present a guide book without illustrations and maps is ridiculous but unfortunately the practice is only too common today.

The last comprehensive guide to Northumberland was by William Weaver Tomlinson and was published in 1888. This book is a Northumbrian classic and with care can be used today. Since then there have been at least twenty surveys of the county which have been pleasant and interesting to read but mostly superficial in content. They have usually been illustrated by a small number of photographs of a limited number of places. Artists have rarely been used.

For twenty-five years I have been working on a comprehensive survey of the county. It is now complete but being, with illustrations, more than two thousand pages in length it would need to be published in three volumes. I will probably publish it in that form at a later date but in the meantime I am publishing seven books which will cover the whole county. Three have already appeared. The first was *Northumbria's Lordly Strand* (272 pages) which described our glorious coast from Berwick to Tynemouth. The second was *The Castles of Northumberland* (360 pages) which included 336 castles and peles. Last year appeared our third book the *Old Halls, Houses and Inns of Northumberland* (312 pages), which was the first on the subject and covered 281 buildings. Tynedale is the fourth volume.

It will be followed next year by a comprehensive, well illustrated, account of the Roman Wall and the camps they built in Northumberland and Durham. The valleys of the Aln and Coquet will be covered in one volume similar to the present book, and Newcastle will be described in greater detail than we have done in *Historic Newcastle*.

There will be a little unavoidable overlap in these seven volumes but where the same places are covered in more than one book, we have tried to vary the illustrations. It is interesting to note that the complete set of books will have well over 2,000 illustrations.

The Tynedale volume covers the whole area of the Tynedale District Council with two or three buildings included just beyond the boundary. The country here is of outstanding beauty and great historic interest. So far it has not been blighted with planner's concrete. The towns and villages have developed and now cater for increasing numbers of tourists but the developments have been well "planned" (if we can use such an obnoxious word today) and have improved the amenities of the area. We hope this book will help Northumbrians and visitors to explore the countless places which can be seen.

Tynedale has been printed by the old method of letterpress. We are the only publisher in Britain today to continue using this expensive method for all our important books. Lithography, which during the past decade has to a large extent replaced letterpress, is a cheaper form of printing but the results are not so crisp and the illustrations tend to be flat. High class lithography can be very effective but poor lithography can be dreadful as unfortunately we can see locally almost every day. All the seven books in this series will be printed by letterpress.

We have arranged the text in alphabetical order. This method, although not perfect, has been used because we have found from experience that it makes possible quick reference to any place visited. If a building or village is not in the alphabetical list a reference to the O.S. map will show the nearest place under which it might appear.

We would be pleased to hear from our readers who notice mistakes in the text or know of places which should be mentioned but have been omitted.

Frank Graham,
October, 1978.

CONTENTS

9

ACOMB

Acomb is sometimes called West Acomb to distinguish it from a hamlet of the same name near Bywell. It consists of one long street running east and west with a small square in which there is an interesting old fountain. On the south side is Acomb House which is dated 1736. It consists of five bays and is two storeys high. The village was once mainly occupied by lead and coal miners but the pits have now closed down.

ALLENDALE TOWN

This large village on the East Allen was once an important lead mining centre but is now dependent on agriculture, small scale industry and the growing holiday trade. The Market Place is surrounded by substantial stone houses with an island of buildings in the middle. It is an attractive village. The church of St. Cuthbert stands high on the river bank. It is first mentioned in 1174. Only one view of the old church has survived, a drawing claimed to be by T. H. Hair (since Hair was probably not born when the church was demolished – he published *Views of the Northern Coalfield* in 1839 – the artist must be someone else). The old church was replaced in 1807 and extensively restored in 1874.

Almost two hundred years ago Allendale was described as "a neat little town, almost every other building of which is a public house for the miners". Bailey and Culley (1805) describe the Friday market there as selling "corn, butcher's meat and considerable quantities of potatoes and garden stuff from Hexham; all for the supply of the mining district to the westward". Another writer, W. Tomlinson, in 1888, describes Allendale or Allenton as "a straggling dreary looking place, situated 1,400 feet above sea level". The Methodists were very active here. John Wesley visited the town in 1748, but on his second visit four years later he wrote:

In the evening we came to Allendale and found the poor society well nigh shattered to pieces. Slackness and offence had eaten them up.

Lead mining started very early in Allendale. It is even suggested that the Romans mined here. In 1320 the Archbishop of York leased to "a Company of miners" a mine within the Regality of Hexham (of which Allendale was part). In 1632 the Manor of Hexhamshire was bought by the Fenwick's of Wallington but in 1689 Sir John Fenwick sold the estate to Sir William Blackett who a few years later bought the lease of the mines in Weardale from the Bishop of Durham. He thus became the sole owner of all the mines in Allendale and Weardale, a control which lasted for 200 years. In the later years of course their successors were the Blackett-Beaumonts. The eighteenth and first half of the nineteenth century were the heyday for mining. The price of lead was high and the market expanding rapidly. Then came the crash. The Allendale mines were partially closed in 1878 and others soon followed.

Allendale Church before 1807

The ore when mined had to be smelted. Half a mile north of Allendale Town was the Allen Mill. We are told:

The Allen smelt mill contained, in 1825, two roasting furnaces, five ore hearths, two refining furnaces, and one reducing furnace. Two flues were subsequently constructed to carry off from the mill the soot and smoke which had previously proved so detrimental to the health of the workmen and to the surrounding vegetation. Two tall chimneys had been erected for this purpose near the mill, but they did not meet the requirements of the case. The first flue originally had its outlet at Cleugh-head, but on the construction of the second flue both outlets were taken to their present position on the moor about three miles west of Allendale Town.

Lead mining and refining were deadly for the workmen but immensely profitable for the owners. Bywell Hall and Wallington Hall are monuments to the wealth derived from the mines of Allendale while the industrial remains scattered around the area tell us of the hard conditions under which the lead was mined and refined.

The pay-bills of the Coalcleugh mines near Allendale in 1793 have survived. 275 miners in one quarter (13 weeks) mined 756 tons of ore and received £2,944 an average of £10 14s per man. The total costs of the mine for that quarter were £3,904 or a little over £5 per ton. The smelting costs are not available and transport to Newcastle was almost £4 per ton but lead was selling at £19 per ton so a handsome profit was available. In the Alston area alone there were 62 mines so the Blackett-Beaumonts were wealthy men. Most of the ore from Coalcleugh went to the Dukesfield Smelting Mill and from there was conveyed to Newcastle. Hubert Dixon in his *Allendale Miscellany*, 1974, describes the methods of transport.

Before the construction of the new highways in the first half of the nineteenth century all transport – of timber for the mines and of lead ore and coal for the smelting mills – was by pack-horses, or, as they were called locally, carrier galloways. These hardly little animals of twelve to fourteen hands high, with loads of up to two hundredweight each, travelled in strings of twenty or twenty-five. They were unbridled, but muzzled to prevent them grazing on lead-tainted grass by the trail, and becoming "bellond" – an incurable form of poisoning, also contracted by drinking water affected with lead washings. A belled and trusted galloway, called the "raker" went in front, set the pace and kept to a familiar route – so much so that the various routes became known as the "carrier ways" – and are currently shown as such on Ordnance Survey maps (six inches to one mile).

Allendale disputes with Hexham the distinction of being the centre spot of Great Britain. To prove their case the inhabitants erected a sundial on the church, which indicates the town's latitude.

However Allendale is nationally famous for its New Year's Eve custom. Twenty-four men, quaintly dressed, with blackened faces, parade through the town with barrels of blazing tar on their heads. A bonfire is lit at midnight in the Market Place and dancing and festivities go on through the night. The custom is undoubtedly pagan in origin since New Year's festivities were usually associated with fire in pagan times.

13

Old Town Bastles, Allendale

Old Town is a farmstead near the River East Allen. Among the farm buildings are two bastles which have been joined together by a later building. The doorway of the east bastle, here shown, has a triangular head and chamfered jambs.

Doorway to Bastle at Old Town, Allendale.

ALLENHEADS

Claimed to be the highest village in England lying seven and a half miles south of Allendale town in a wild and lonely region. Allenheads was for many centuries a lead mining centre. At one time the Allenheads mines yielded one-seventh of the total amount of lead produced in the kingdom. In 1689 the mines were purchased by Sir William Blackett of Newcastle. Due to failure of the male heir the estate finally descended to the Beaumonts of whom Mr. Wentworth Blackett-Beaumont became the first Lord Allendale. In the middle of the nineteenth century Beaumont's mines employed almost 2,000 people, men, women and boys.

Writing in 1811 Mackenzie tells us "this place is inhabited by people engaged in the lead mines. The surrounding country is barren, mountainous, and desolate and offers no inducement to inhabitants except its mineral riches". He mentioned that the village and adjoining mines belonged to Colonel Beaumont. When he visited Hexham in 1832 William Cobbett (*Rural Rides*) made a famous attack on Colonel Beaumont who had just recently criticized Cobbett.

"Beaumont, in addition to his native stupidity and imbecility, might have been drunk when he said this, but the servile wretch who published it was not drunk; and, at any rate, Beaumont was my mark, it not being my custom to snap at the stick, but at the cowardly hand that wields it.

Such a fellow cannot be an object of what is properly called vengeance with any man who is worth a straw; but I say, with Swift, "If a flea or a bug bite me, I will kill it if I can"; and, acting upon that principle, I, being at Hexham, put my foot upon this contemptible creeping thing, who is offering himself as a candidate for the southern division of the county, being so eminently fitted to be a maker of the laws! The newspapers have told the whole country that Mr. John Ridley, who is a tradesman at Hexham, and occupies some land close by, has made a stand against the demand for tithes; and that the tithe-owner recently broke open, in the night, the gate of his field, and carried away what he deemed to be the tithe; that Mr. Ridley applied to the magistrates, who could only refer him to a court of law to recover damages for the trespass. When I arrived at Hexham, I found this to be the case. I further found that Beaumont, that impudent, silly and slanderous Beaumont, is the lay-owner of the tithes in and around Hexham; he being, in a right line, doubtless, the heir or successor of the abbot and monks of the Abbey of Hexham; or the heir of the donor, Egfrid, king of Northumberland. I found that Beaumont had leased out his tithes to middle men, as is the laudable custom with the pious bishops and clergy of the law-church in Ireland."

The Directory of 1827 mentions that "most of the lead miners possess a small plot of land, with the right of common, which privilege renders their circumstances more easy and comfortable than those of the miners in the adjoining parishes."

Walter White (*Northumberland and the Border,* 1859) visited the district.

"It rises higher and higher, and the dale along which flows the East Allen becomes apparently deeper and deeper. The lower slopes are very green; cots are scattered here and there, on small patches of meadow, or struggling gardens sheltered by a few trees; but as we proceed every mile is barer than the last. We pass *St. Peter's,* the mother church of the dale, then the little village of Dirtpot – what a name! – lying in the hollow; then we come to rows of workshops, long rows of bouse-teams and bing-steads on each side of an acre or more of washing-floors, where men and boys are working with noise and activity; a wooden tower, within which is one of the entrances of the lead mines; a row of buildings containing the offices, the library, and reading-room, and we are in Allenheads, one of the most elevated places in England, situate fourteen hundred feet above the sea. It lies, nevertheless, deep within the hollow of the hills, and has all the appearance of a place which has taken to decent ways."

John Murray's *Handbook to Northumberland and Durham* (1873) tells us

"The character of the lead-miners is much influenced by the barren and secluded moorlands in which they live, but beneath a rough exterior they have great kindness of heart and much natural intelligence. There is little poverty amongst them, for the lead-miner, who works only 8 hrs. a day, and works only 5 days in the week, obtains from 15s. to 20s. Still their earnings depend almost entirely on the produce of the mines; and as the productiveness of the lead-veins is precarious, and often of short duration, great care and energy are required in the

15

selection of places for work; and an enormous capital is constantly employed in works which require a great number of years before they can be brought into full operation, or produce any adequate return. The men work in partnerships of 2, 4, 6, or even 8 and 12; and each partnership divides the earnings of the whole among its separate members. In their daily operations, they rely much on their own experience in following out the general directions which are given from time to time by the managers and inspectors of the mine. There is little intemperance among the miners; but bastardy is still very rife, though generally followed by marriage."

The first chapel was built here in 1703 but it was replaced by the church of St. Peter's in 1825.

ALLENSFORD

Allensford on the Derwent is first mentioned in 1382. The bridge here provides one of the main routes into Durham. It is said that Sir Walter Scott refers to this place in his poem *Rokeby:-*

> And when he taxed thy breach of word
> To yon fair Rose of Allenford,
> I saw thee crouch like chastened hound,
> Whose back the huntsman's lash hath found.

The mill here is referred to in 1663.

Lancet window at Aydon Castle

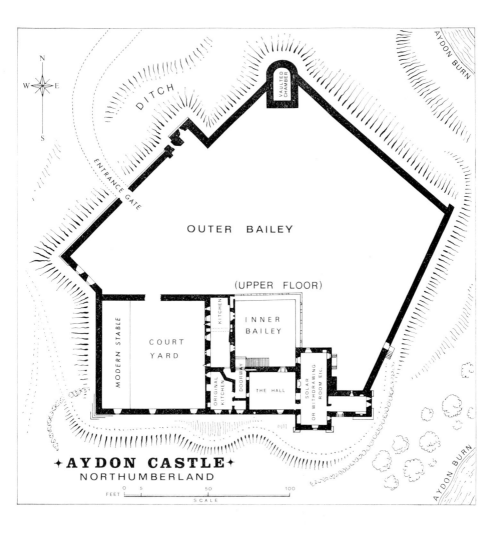

AYDON CASTLE
NORTHUMBERLAND

FEET 0 5   50   100
SCALE

AYDON CASTLE

Aydon Castle, a private residence for almost seven hundred years, has now been taken over by the Department of the Environment. It is an almost perfect example of a fortified manor-house built at the end of the thirteenth century. It stands midway between the large Northumbrian castles like Alnwick and the small towers or peles of which two can be seen in Corbridge. It can be reached by road from Aydon or by foot from Corbridge.

The original house was probably commenced by Robert de Raymes in 1296, and license to embattle and fortify was granted in 1305. Later owners were the Carnabys, the Carrs, the Collinsons, and the Blacketts of Matfen.

Aydon Castle
South Front

The first buildings comprised the house and the inner bailey. Later
(probably in the fourteenth century) the courtyard and outer bailey
were added. The entire defences are still astonishingly complete.
The original main building is cruciform in plan, well built, and two
storeys in height. The hall and chief rooms were on the second floor
and were entered by an external staircase in the courtyard. The main

Court
Yard
Aydon
Castle.

hall is lighted at the east end by two windows each of two pointed lights separated by a decorated shaft and enclosed within a pointed arch. There is no fireplace.

Divided from the hall by a narrow passage or screens is the kitchen with fireplace, locker, kitchen sink and two fine original windows. The fireplace was added by the Carnaby family in the sixteenth century and on it is rudely carved their coat of arms. At the opposite end of the Great Hall was the solar.

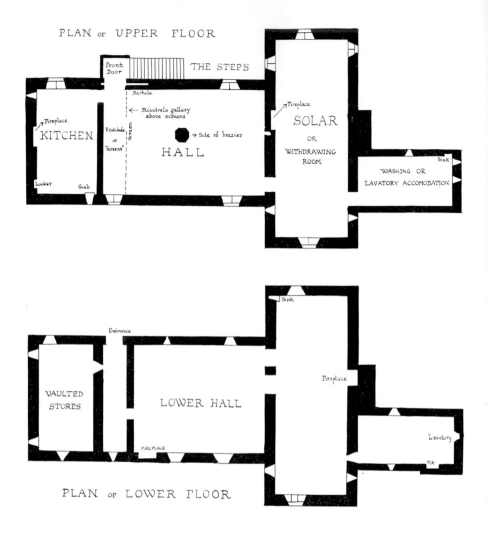

PLAN of UPPER FLOOR

THE STEPS

Front Door

Barhole

Fireplace

KITCHEN

Vestibule or 'Screens'

Minstrels gallery above screens

HALL

Site of brazier

Fireplace

SOLAR

OR

WITHDRAWING ROOM

Sink

WASHING OR LAVATORY ACCOMODATION

Locker

Sink

Sink

Entrance

Fireplace

VAULTED STORES

LOWER HALL

Fireplace

Lavatory

Pit

FIREPLACE

PLAN of LOWER FLOOR

The room below the Great Hall has a fireplace whose jambs are moulded shafts of fine workmanship. But the most striking feature is the chimney which constitutes an architectural gem on the south front of the castle. For about half its height it has the ordinary buttress-like appearance of a projecting chimney. Half way up it becomes semi-circular and terminates at the parapet in a conical cap. Beneath the cap are two slits for the escape of the smoke.

In the basement of the west wing are the stables. The roof is of stone and vaulted, and the mangers are also constructed of stone.

A battlement parapet runs round the whole of the house, except the west wing. The water is carried from the gutters by a series of projecting stone spouts or gargoyles.

20

A rock on the edge of the dene, which the castle overlooks, is called "Jock's Leap". One legend says it was the spot from which a frantic lover threw himself into the dene below. Another tells us that a Scottish mosstrooper, captured during a raid, was condemned by Sir Robert Clavering to be thrown to his death from the castle battlements. He escaped by leaping to a rock on the edge of the dene.

16th Cent. Fireplace. Aydon Castle.

*South Window
in the kitchen*

*Aydon White House
Two views by
Susan Martin*

AYDON HOUSE

The origins of Aydon House, near Corbridge, are uncertain but it was sold in 1798 by John Reed a woollen draper in Newcastle. The newspaper adverts described it as a mansion-house containing two parlors, six bedrooms, cellar, kitchen, dairy with brewhouse, stabling and garden adjoining. It was afterwards bought back by the Reed family. In Dixon's *Corbridge* (1912) it is called "a fine old-fashioned country house, and the farmhouse and cottages surrounding it make it a picturesque little village."

AYDON WHITE HOUSE

The White House is first mentioned in 1568 when the owner was Cuthbert Carnaby whose family sold it in 1682 to John Cook of Aydon. Above the central doorway is the date 1684 and the initials IcM for John Cook and his wife Mary, while above is a sun dial dated 1702. The body of the house is presumably the same as the Carnaby building with the door being added by John Cook. The front, facing south, has a well-moulded doorway with a two light window above. These are flanked by mullioned windows of three lights on each floor. The frames are semicircular in section resembling those in the manor-house of Bockenfield and Swarland Old Hall. The stonework is rather rough and has probably always been covered with lime white-wash, from which the house derives its name, while the roof has stone flags. The interior of the house has been reconstructed on more than one occasion and only one large-panelled door remains of the work done in 1684. The original plan of the house was T-shaped with its head facing south but in the early nineteenth century a wing was added to the bottom of the T, and later extensive farm buildings were constructed to the north.

Ivy Cottage, Bardon Mill, is an old pele tower which has been converted into a modern house.

BARDON MILL

Writing in 1897 Tomlinson describes Bardon Mill as "a quaint little village, which derives its name from the woollen mill established there many years ago. Many of the cottages still retain their old thatched roofs. There is a small inn here, the Greyhound". In 1940 a colliery was opened here but in 1973 (in the middle of the oil and fuel crisis) it was closed down on economy grounds and 240 miners declared redundant. It was the last colliery to operate in West Northumberland.

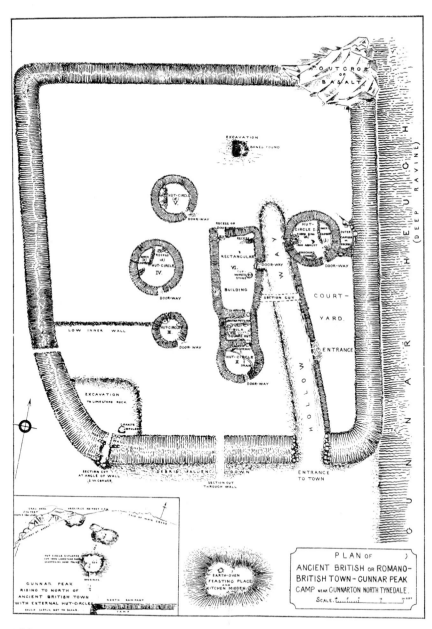

BARRASFORD

Opposite Haughton Castle lies the village of Barrasford where a large sanitorium for consumptives was built late in the last century. The name reminds us that here was an important ford in Saxon times. The area around is rich in prehistoric remains.

Barrasford was a station on the Border County Line which was built in 1856 from Hexham to Plashetts. In 1862 it was extended to Riccarton to link up with the railway into Scotland. A century after building the line was closed to passenger traffic in 1956 and the line was lifted in 1958.

On an escarpment above the Barrasford burn, when the railway cutting was being made the burial of a Saxon chieftain was discovered

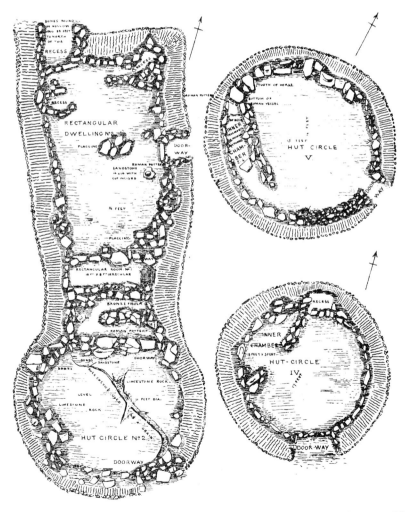

and close to the village until last century three standing stones could be seen. But the finest remains are on Gunnar Peak on the basaltic rocks near Gunnerton. The two plans from *Archaeologia Aeliana* (1885) illustrate the site. The first plan shows the entire village the second shows two of the huts in detail.

The ramparts of the camp are built of rough stones and earth to an average height of twelve feet and were probably crowned with a wooden stockade. The entrance by a hollow way is in the south wall at the eastern angle. The huts are circular, as is usual with British dwellings with the entrances in the south east to catch the early sun. The walls were of wattle on top of a foundation of unhewn stones. The roof would probably be of thatch. All the huts have a recess, probably for sleeping. The excavation a few yards to the north of the huts was probably the communal oven and cooking place as traces of fire and a mound of bones testified. Ninety yards to the east on higher ground is another camp (see *Gunnerton*).

[Gunnar Peak Camp has recently been destroyed by quarrying]

BEAUFRONT CASTLE

Two miles east of Hexham in a well-wooded park stands Beaufront.

Beaufront Tower is first mentioned in the list of castles and fortalices made in 1415. It was the seat of the Carnabys in the reign of Elizabeth. Afterwards it became the residence of the Errington family and a large mansion was built, described by the Rev. John Hodgson in 1810 as follows: "Few places make a finer appearance, or enjoy a larger and better cultivated prospect than this. From the south side of the Tyne it exhibits a long and handsome front surrounded with fine pleasure-grounds, and from its walks are seen towns, towers, and hamlets and the winding stream of the Tyne, sometimes hidden under its banks and at others boldly crossing the meadows in broad and silver looking reaches". At the end of the eighteenth century John Errington spent £20,000 on the gardens, plantations, lawns, and hot houses. Our engraving by J. W. Carmichael shows Beaufront Castle at this period. After the death of John Errington the house was pulled down and the present building erected by William Cuthbert in 1841, from designs by Dobson of Newcastle, in the domestic castellated style. It was his most ambitious work in the Tudor and Gothic manner and he was pleased with the result. It is built asymetrically with south tower facing the Tyne and a tower with main entrance on the west and a projecting wing on the east. The dominating position of the entrance tower was spoilt by the Smoking Room which was built on the south side of the tower about 1870. Of the original Georgian house one room which was incorporated into the new building contains a fine fireplace. The Clock Tower on the north also belongs to the original house. It is a striking and interesting building with some of the figures which were found all over the early house. Today Beaufront would not be considered one of Dobson's best buildings.

Beaufront Castle by J. W. Carmichael

Beaufront Castle by J. W. Carmichael. Water Colour. Laing Art Gallery

BELLINGHAM

Bellingham is a small market town on the North Tyne at the foot of some of the wildest and most barren fells in Northumberland. Although the parish took its name from Simonburn, Bellingham has always been the most important centre. There are medieval references to Bellingham castle as belonging to the King of Scotland's Forester, one Bellingham of Bellingham, but no trace remains. It may have been on a green mound near the Hareshaw burn and was probably a motte and bailey fortress. Nearby was the mill from which the De Bellinghams in 1263 paid the enormous rent of ten pounds yearly. The wool fair at Bellingham used to be the largest in the country. Mugger's Hill received its name from the muggers or potters who used to attend the fair and used that place for the display of their wares.

BELLINGHAM CHURCH,
North.ᵈ
Published 1.Nov.1823. by W.Davison Alnwick.

The church is dedicated to St. Cuthbert. The original church was completely demolished in the twelfth century and a new church erected. Its principal feature (almost unique in England) is the massive stone roof which consists of six-sided stone ribs overlaid with heavy stone slabs. This was a protection against fire (the chancel, with a wooden roof, was twice burnt by the Scots). The extremely narrow windows of the nave were built for defence. In 1607 we are told the church had a small attendance, the font was broken, the religious books had disappeared, and the clerk was illiterate. In 1709 William Charlton of Reedsmouth, called Bowery Charlton from his estate of the Bower, killed Henry Widdrington of Buteland in a duel near Bellingham. The body of the victim was buried before Charlton's pew-door in the church, and according to tradition Charlton never entered the building again.

Lee Hall, three miles south of Bellingham, is a Georgian house of five bays and two and a half storeys. It has an arched doorway in the middle and an arched window above. It occupies the site of an earlier building. It was the ancient seat of a branch of the Charlton family. The misdeeds of William Charlton of Lee Hall who was county

Lee Hall of "Long Pack" fame

keeper at the end of the seventeenth century were long remembered in the district. "He is said to have been closely connected with an organised gang of horse-stealers, who made their raids on both sides of the Border. His feuds with Lowes of Willimoteswick, the county-keeper of South Tynedale, were long remembered in the district. After several narrow escapes from his bold and implacable enemy, Lowes was at length taken prisoner in a fight near Sewingshields, and conveyed to Lee Hall, where he suffered, it is said, the greatest indignities, having been actually fastened to the grate of the kitchen fire, with just enough length of chain to enable him to get his food at the table with the servants. He was subsequently rescued by Frank Stokoe, of Chesterwood".

On one occasion they fought together and Charlton killed his opponent's horse, on which the local people made a rhyme :-

Oh had Lee Hall but been a man,
As he was never nane,
He wad have stricken the rider
And letten the horse alane.

A writer in 1715 tells us that "at ye Lee Hall a excellent spring, ye vertue is such yt if ye lady of ye Hall dip aney children yt have ye rickets or any other over groone destemper, it is either a speedy cure or death. The manner and form is as followeth:- The days of dipping are on Whitsunday Even, on Midsummer Even, on Saint Peter's Even. They must bee dipt in ye well before the sun rise, and in ye River Tine after ye sun bee sett: then ye shift taken from ye child and thrown into ye river and if it swim, child liveth, but if it sink dyeth".

Of the village of Shitlington, two miles west of Lee Hall, nothing now remains but the socket stone and broken shaft of a wayside cross. There is a tradition that fairs used to be held here.

A corner of Bellingham in 1891

At Bellingham the Hareshaw Burn joins the North Tyne and there is a delightful walk up the burn to Hareshaw Linn where

> With sudden dash and bound and splash,
> With rout and shout and roar and din,
> The brook amazed, alarmed, and crazed,
> Is sprawling into Hareshaw Linn.
> 'Tween wooded cliffs, fern fringed, it falls,
> All broken into spray and foam.

Gun at Bellingham.

Clock Tower
Town Hall
Bellingham

Rustic Bridge o'er the Hareshaw Lynn
Bellingham.

Rustic Bridge
near Bellingham

Bellingham

Views in Bellingham and up Hareshaw Lynn. Drawn and engraved in 1891.

St. Cuthbert's Well

The wells named after St. Cuthbert (Cuddy) are usually in different places from those of St. Ninian (Ninny or Nine Wells). Ninian's wells are usually near Roman roads while those of St. Cuthbert are in remote places. This is because St. Cuthbert preached in out-of-the-way spots. The well is half way between Bellingham church and the river. It has a stone pillar called a pant, the water coming through a spout, probably built in Georgian times. Stories are told of its miraculous properties but no pilgrims visit it today.

St. Cuthbert's Well, Bellingham.

Hareshaw Ironworks

A picturesque dam a short distance below Hareshaw Linn and heaps of shale are all that is left of the Hareshaw ironworks established in 1838. It had a brief life closing down in 1849. There were two blast furnaces, later increased to three. The ironworks relied on local supplies of coal limestone and iron ore but it never prospered and in 1846 was bankrupt being taken over by the Union Bank of Newcastle (see *Ridsdale Ironworks*).

Bellingham Bridge

In the early Middle Ages the bridge is referred to in a miracle supposed to have occurred at the Bridge Ford in which a man lost an axe which was restored by St. Cuthbert. This bridge later disappeared and for centuries there was none over the Tyne above Chollerford. In 1760 Bishop Pococke wrote: "There is not one bridge over North Tyne, but they have a summer ford at the town, and a winter ford a mile lower called Bridge Ford". In 1834 the present bridge was built by John Green, the Newcastle architect.

The Long Pack

The Long Pack is the most famous of Northumbrian tales. The story is a common tradition, told of other places. It was written by James Hogg, the Ettrick Shepherd, who said that the incident occurred in 1723 at Lee Hall whose owner was "Colonel Ridley". The story is also told by Mrs. Gaskell (who had friends in Newcastle) in Cranford with very different details. The story tells how, in the year 1723, Colonel Ridley and his family being away in London, his country seat, on the banks of the North Tyne, was left in the charge of a maid-servant named Alice and two male servants. One afternoon, in the middle of

THE HISTORY OF THE LONG PACK:

A NORTHUMBRIAN LEGEND.

BY THE ETTRICK SHEPHERD.

YORK: T. ARTHUR.

winter, a handsome-looking pedlar called; and after having been properly refused a night's lodging, asked permission to leave his heavy pack till the next morning. The request was granted, and the pedlar went his way, wishing Alice a good-night. Left alone, the girl could not help feeling uneasy about the pack, and after a while took up a candle to have a careful look at it. What was her horror to see it move! She at once called in a fellow-servant, old Richard, who, however, assured her the pack was right enough. While they were talking, a lad named Edward, who herded the cattle, came in with a large old military gun named Copenhagen, and proposed to empty the contents of the barrel into the pack. This he accordingly did, with a hideous result, for a stream of blood gushed on to the floor, and a dreadful roar, followed by the groans of death, issued from the pack, where a man had been concealed in a very ingenious way. As it was quite evident that an attack would be made on the house by the man's confederates, a number of the colonel's retainers were called in to guard the house. About midnight it occurred to Edward to blow the thief's silver wind-call. In less than five minutes several horsemen came up at a brisk trot and began to enter the court-gate. Edward, unable to restrain himself any longer, fired Copenhagen in their faces. This was the signal for the other guns to fire, and when the smoke had cleared away four men were found to have fallen. During the night the corpses were removed

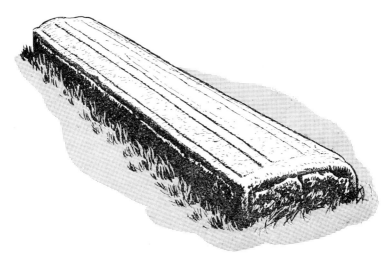

Bellingham Long Pack

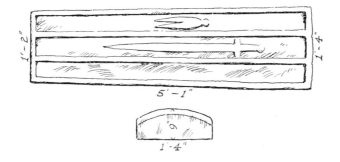

by the robber-gang, and though large rewards were offered for the apprehension of any of the culprits, no one concerned in the affair was ever discovered.

In the churchyard can be seen the famous Long Pack tombstone where legend says the pedlar was buried. The tombstone, however, is probably medieval. We here show a drawing of the stone and a plan.

Bellingham Show

The annul September Agricultural Show at Bellingham is well known in the North. It attracts great crowds. It has even been recorded in poetry.

A's an auld shepherd an A' live oot-bye,
An a' seldom see out but the sheep and the kye,
So a' ses to wor Betsy "a' think a' will go,
And hev a bit look at the Bellingham Show".
"A weel," says the auld wife "if thou's money to spare,
Nae dout its a lang time sin ye hae been there".
But the pack lambs selt weel, they've a lang time been low,
So a' think a' will gan to the Bellingham Show.

The visit however proved unfortunate. The shepherd got drunk and finished up in the Police Station.

BELLISTER CASTLE

BELLISTER CASTLE

Opposite Haltwhistle on the south side of the Tyne is Bellister Castle. It is a pile of grey ruins with a large farmhouse attached built in the castellated style. It stands on a mound partly natural and partly

36

Bellister Castle. Print 1840

artificial, with hardly a trace of the moat that once surrounded it. The origin of the castle is not clearly known but in 1541 it is described as a "bastell house, in thoccupac'n of one Blenkensoppe, in measurable good repacs'ns". The attached house has a date-plate 1669. It is three-storeyed with mullioned and transomed windows and two towers at its angles. The entrance is by a doorway with an oddly shaped lintel. John Dobson carried out some alterations here in 1826.

Bellister has its legend. Many centuries ago, we are told, a wandering minstrel came to the castle seeking hospitality for the night. He was welcomed by the Lord of Bellister. However, before the night had passed suspicion grew in the mind of the host that the minstrel was a spy; his distrust was noticed by his guest who, when the time for withdrawal came, decided to leave the castle secretly. The baron noticed his disappearance, a fact which seemed to confirm his suspicions. The bloodhounds were sent in pursuit and on the banks of the Tyne came up with the unfortunate minstrel and killed him. Before long his ghost, called the "Grey Man of Bellister", began to haunt the castle and many uncanny tales were told about the doings of this restless spirit.

BELTINGHAM

This picturesque Northumbrian village lies in an angle formed by the meeting of the South Tyne and the River Allen. Its stone-roofed cottages are built around the village green close to a fine Georgian three-bay house with a fine doorway and entrance gates. The church was extensively restored in 1884. It dates from the early sixteenth century. It is the only church in Northumberland built entirely in the perpendicular style. It was a chapel of ease of Haltwhistle. On the priest's doorway, now blocked, there is a date 1691. Some of the south windows have in their voussoirs crude carvings, an ox, two suns, a flower and a human head. The print below is dated 1840.

BIRTLEY

The church is said to be Norman but was extensively rebuilt in 1884. Inside is an inscribed stone c. 700. In the vicarage gardens are the ruins of a Tower, the walls standing up to ten feet high. No historic notice can be found of this ancient stronghold, which, at a later period, was known as Birtley Hall. No decorative features survive but in the east face is a stone carved with the letters JH and the date 1611. The stair was in the north-west corner.

The church of St. Giles has a fine pointed arch and a chancel doorway which probably survive from the twelfth century building. The pre-conquest stone found in the last century suggests a Saxon church on the site. It may have been of wood since no remains have ever been found. The letters on the stone O R P E probably stand for [OR]ATE [P]RO [E]DMUND or some other name beginning with E. The large round font is probably of Norman origin and built into the porch are six medieval carved gravestones. The old inn is called the Percy Arms.

To the north of the church beside Holywell Burn is a chalybeate spring called the Holy Well. It issues from a high rock beneath a picturesque waterfall called the Male Knock. Nearby above the spring is the Devil's Stone a massive rock standing twelve feet high and weighing several tons. Legend tells us that a demon once tried to leap from it to the opposite side of the river a mile away. He failed and was drowned in Leap Crag Pool said to be the deepest in the North Tyne. The demon's hoof marks can still be seen on the top of the rock.

Magnificent views of the valley of the North Tyne can be seen from Birtley.

BLACK HEDLEY

The old house of the Hopper family of Black Hedley was rebuilt and extended by Humphrey Hopper about the year 1750. It is a plain Georgian house of five bays with a fine doorway. The striking features are the outbuildings especially the castellated gatehouse adorned with life size figures in stone (see Shotley Church). John Graham Lough the famous local sculptor was born here in 1798.

GREENHEAD—LOUGH'S BIRTHPLACE.

Typographic Etching Co., Sc.

BLACK MIDDINGS

In the upper reaches of the Tarset burn there are some particularly interesting strong houses, Black Middings is a Castle house of similar plan to those of Gatehouse. There is the usual narrow door at one end of the lower storey – two feet three inches wide. There is an outside stair to a door in the middle of the south wall. The two doors on the ground floor of the same wall

Black Middings.

are eighteenth century additions. To the east are the remains of the eighteenth century cottage which stands upon the massive foundations of an earlier house which was probably built before the pele tower.

Blanchland, The Gateway

BLANCHLAND

Blanchland is a delightful village of fine stone built houses, well laid out, and a fine collection of medieval monastic remains. It is in a glorious setting on the river bank and is surrounded by wild and picturesque moors. Two streams (the Knucton and Beldon burns) unite to form the Derwent, a mile above Blanchland at a high imposing cliff called Gibraltar Rock.

Blanchland in 1162 was called *Blanchelande* although the Latin form *Blanca Landa* or *Alba Landa* is also used in early documents. It was probably named after the abbey of Blanchelande near Cherbourg. In Norman the word *lande* means "untilled land". Blanche of course refers to the white habits of the monks of the Praemonstratensian order who came here in 1165. The founder was Walter de Bolbeck III. He granted the twelve monks large stretches of land around Blanchland together with the churches of Harle, Bywell St. Andrew, Styford, Shotley and Appletree. Later they were granted the church of St. Andrew at Heddon on the Wall. Blanchland is rarely mentioned in historical records. Edward III stayed here in 1327. He had come north to counter a large Scottish raid into England in which the abbey of Blanchland had been burnt by the Scots. The Scottish army however gave Edward the slip and retreated into Scotland. While at Blanchland the English army had consumed everything in the district: the people suffered greatly but later received compensation from the king. Blanchland suffered many times from Scottish raids.

The abbey was dissolved in 1536 but was soon refounded by Henry VIII, a very rare occurrence. It was dissolved a second time in 1539 and the

41

canons received liberal pensions. In 1545 most of the property and lands, together with extensive estates which once belonged to the Priory of Holystone, were purchased by John Bellow and John Broxholme for the sum of £2,371. They resold Blanchland in the same year to William Farwell for £200. Late in the sixteenth century through marriage settlements the Forsters of Bamburgh became the owners. They turned the domestic buildings of the abbey into their home.

The last male heir of the Forsters of Bamburgh was murdered in 1701 by John Fenwick of Rock. The estates were in debt and in 1704 and 1709 were purchased by Nathaniel Lord Crewe, bishop of Durham. It is sometimes stated that the Forster estates were forfeited after the rebellion of 1715. This is not true. The estates were lost through reckless extravagance. Therefore when General Forster joined the rebels he had nothing to lose, his estates having been sold six years earlier.

Lord Crewe was married to Dorothy Forster one of the large Forster family. He was sixty-seven when he married her in 1703. She was only twenty-four years of age and a noted beauty. When Lord Crewe died in 1721 at the ripe age of eighty-eight years he left his estates in trust for charitable purposes and they are now controlled by the Ecclesiastical Commissioners.

In spite of his charitable work Lord Crewe won the contempt of his contemporaries. The historian Surtees says: "The meanness of Bishop Crewe's political conduct is well known to have thrown a deep and lasting shade over his many splendid qualities; he is alike excluded from the palm of the patriot, and from the faded but perhaps not less honourable wreath due to the fidelity and constancy of the devoted loyalist, who adhered in poverty and exile to the blood of his ancient masters". His own chaplain said that "when King James's declaration (for liberty of conscience) was appointed to be read, the most condescending thing the bishop ever did me was his coming to my chamber to prevail with me to read it at his chapel at Auckland, which I could not do, having wrote to may curate not to read it at Long Newton; he prevailed, however, with the curate of Auckland to read it in his own church, when the bishop was present to countenance the performance."

However after the Revolution, under William and Mary he once again became a true pillar of the Protestant church. John Wesley visited Blanchland in 1747 and describes "the little town as little more than a heap of ruins". He preached to the leadminers, from all over the district, from a large tombstone in the churchyard. On his visit in 1776 the historian W. Hutchinson was not impressed.

"By a disagreeable road", he wrote, "in a desolate country we travelled to Blanchland, seated in a narrow deep vale, on the river Derwent; a few strips of meadow ground lay along the margin of the stream, and some cultivated lands skirt the feet of the hills, whose summits are covered with heath. This is a very different situation from others I have seen, chosen by the Religious for the foundation of their houses; the country around is barren and mountainous; the narrow vale in which the abbey is placed, seems in no-wise suited to the maintenance of its former inhabitants – poverty for ages past has reigned over the face of the adjacent country. The sites of religious houses are generally in well-sheltered and warm situations where the retirements are surrounded with rich lands. This place looks truly like the realm of mortification.

"The west and tower of the church and the fourth aisle of the cross remain; the latter neatly fitted up for parochial duty. The gateway entering into the square, where formerly the houses of the Canons stood, still remains; the towers on each hand converted into ale-houses: the buildings which are standing are now inhabited by poor people who are perhaps employed in the leadworks; the distress and ragged appearance of the whole conventual buildings, being most deplorable; no one relique of church pomp remaining."

The Crewe trustees gradually changed this, improving the village and restoring the church. In 1802 the Reverend Richard Wallis published a poem about Blanchland called *The Happy Village*. The title page was engraved by Thomas Bewick and is here reproduced. Archbishop Singleton's visitation of 1828 records:

BLANCHLAND CHURCH IN 1802.

Being the title page to " The Happy Village," by the Rev. Richard Wallis.

A horrid road over moors ten times more dreary than Rimside or Harewood to a very beautiful spot. Blanchland is the very gem and emerald of the mining district. Its old conventual and abbey shaped church, its verdant inclosures, its neat dwelling houses, and its abundant wood are seen to great advantage in contrast with the circumjacent lands. It seems to have been a pet place, a sort of hobby horse of Lord Crewe's trustees, and barring some detestable improvements in the ante-church, their labours and expenditure tell well . . . The general character of the population is good, they are moral and sober, and neither the registers nor public fame give any credit to the idea that the average of human life is shortened in mining societies. In spite of all that is done for them in the way of church and schools, there are some ranters and more methodists. The inn is large and good, and there is a good picture of Lord Crewe. The vestry is distinct from the church, and is at present occupied by an old woman with a crockery shop.

Of the monastic buildings only the gateway, and remnants of the refectory, Prior's lodging, and church survive. The Lord Crewe Arms is part of the refectory which stood on the west side of the cloister garth (now the inn garden). It has been altered and added to at various times. The upper portion of the inn is clearly Georgian with its ogee-headed windows but original pieces of the monastery can be seen as for example the pointed trefoiled head of the entrance door, the 12th century piscina in the west wall, and the large thirteenth century segmental arch in the east wall, originally forming a recess for a lavatory. Inside the hotel is a large original fireplace with its Priest's Hole, a cunningly concealed sanctuary, made probably in the sixteenth century. The walls of the ground floor are all of medieval masonry.

The Prior's lodging lies to the north of the monastic refectory. Its mediaeval stone vaulted chamber has been tastefully converted into a bar. The upper floors are post-mediaeval. The windows are square-headed enclosed by a square labels, probably made after the Dissolution and the battlemented parapet is even later. From the present bar a stone staircase leads to the gateway and another one to the Dorothy Forster sitting room. In the fine drawing room of the inn, said to have been the ballroom of the Forster mansion, hangs a portrait of Lord Crewe, who was notorious for the way in which he changed his religious and political opinions to suit his own ends.

When, following the Jacobite revolt of 1715, Thomas Forster was captured and taken to Newgate for trial his sister Dorothy Forster contrived his escape and eventual exile in France. One story says that while awaiting an opportunity to cross the water he used the secret room in the kitchen chimney as a refuge. Walter Besant's novel "Dorothy Forster" tells of her adventures. It was her niece and name-sake who married Lord Crewe. A portrait of the niece hangs in the sitting room named after her and a portrait of the aunt, said to be by Lely, looks down the stone staircase to haunt part of the hotel. The rooms called Dilston, Radcliffe and Bamborough are named after people and places connected with the Forsters. Dilston was the home of the Earl of Derwentwater, the mainspring of the 1715 revolt; the Radcliffes married into the Forster family whose ancestral home was Bamborough.

Some historians consider that the Lord Crewe Arms occupies the site of the monastic guest house and the refectory or frater they place to the south of the inn where a line of cottages now stands. Such a large guest house might have been needed to house the wayfarers passing north and south between the two kingdoms in an area where accommodation was sparse. If we accept this suggestion we could describe the Lord Crewe Arms as originally a true monastic hostel.

The lead mines of Blanchland have been worked for centuries. The mine at Shyldeyn (Shilden) is mentioned in 1475. Tradition says that Old Shilden mine was wrought when only four lead mines in England were open. It was working in 1804 when John Hodgson visited it. Shilden was the name of a brook and narrow valley running north from Blanchland. On Bell's hill is an ancient heap of lead scoriae.

The Abbey of S. Mary Blanchland, Northumberland.

Ground Plan. May 1879.

Charles C. Hodges, del.

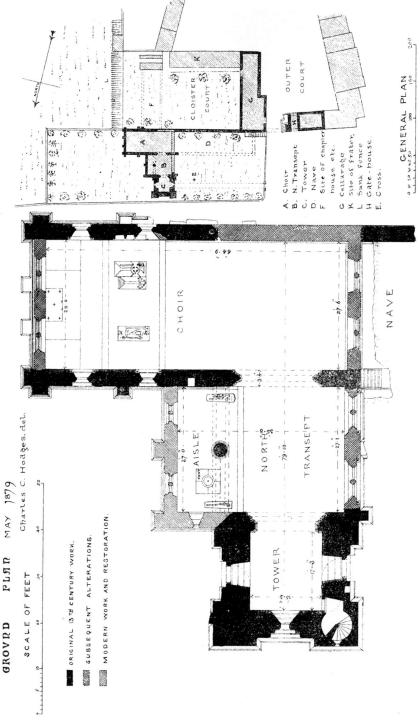

SCALE OF FEET

ORIGINAL 13TH CENTURY WORK.

SUBSEQUENT ALTERATIONS.

MODERN WORK AND RESTORATION.

CHOIR

NAVE

AISLE

NORTH TRANSEPT

TOWER

A. Choir
B. N. Transept
C. Tower
D. Nave
F. Site of chapter house etc.
G. Cellarage
K. Site of Frater.
L. Sunk fence
H. Gate house.
E. Cross.

CLOISTER COURT

OUTER COURT

GENERAL PLAN

At Acton was an old smelt mill which closed before Hodgson's visit (a detailed account of the Blanchland lead mines is given in Mackenzie's *View of the County of Northumberland* 1811).

Blanchland Church

From the dissolution of the religious houses to 1752 the abbey church was allowed to become ruinous. Of the original monastic church nothing is known. But parts of the choir walls can be dated to about 1225. The choir was restored in 1752 and made into the parish church. The nave of the monastic church has gone entirely and its position west of the choir can only be guessed at. Next to the north transept is a strong tower, the two lower stages dating from about 1300 and the upper from 1400. The tall pointed tower arch is an attractive feature. In the chancel east and south windows are two examples of fifteenth century glass showing figures of Premonstratensians. There are five interesting grave covers in the church. The one with a cross on steps is the earliest from about 1300, a more elaborate one of about 1350 also shows a crozier and chalice: these are abbot's stones. The smaller one probably commemorates a canon. There are two grave covers of foresters of the abbot. One showing a sword, arrow and horn commemorates Robert Egylston, the other with the same decorations is to T(HOMAS) E(GGLESTON). In the churchyard is a fine cross of millstone grit still with its traceried head which is usually damaged or removed.

Grave covers
of a canon
and
forester

Blenkinsopp Castle, c. 1890

Blenkinsopp Castle today

was as avaricious as he was bold. At a festive gathering, when being taunted with still being a bachelor he said he would never marry until he met with a lady possessed of a chest of gold heavier than ten of his strongest men could carry into his castle. Shortly afterwards he went abroad, probably to the Crusades, and after some years he returned with a wife and a large chest of gold. Bryan Blenkinsopp was now the richest man in the north of England but his marriage was not a success. He and his lady quarrelled continually. After one bitter argument Lady Blenkinsopp arranged with her foreign servants to have the chest of gold secretly buried to spite her husband. In a rage he left the castle, never to be seen again. It is said the lady, filled with remorse, went forth in search of the baron but she likewise never returned. It is claimed that she cannot rest in her grave but must wander back to the old castle to mourn over the chest of gold, the cause of all her suffering. Here she must continue to wander until someone finds the gold and so allows her spirit to rest.

We are told that the "White Lady" was an infidel and never went to church. This probably explains the legend. To a superstitious and bigoted people any deviation from established religion would appear strange and distasteful.

BLENKINSOPP HALL

Originally it was called Dryburnhaugh and in 1663 was the home of John Blenkinsop. Early in the nineteenth century it was largely rebuilt with a long two-storeyed front of five bays. "Seated on rich ground, at the opening of a woody glen it smiles sweetly on the eye of day, and stretches out its towered walls and long-extent of front to the noon-tide sun. The entrance hall and dining room occupy the ground floor of the centre of the front". (John Hodgson, 1840).

A south east tower was added in 1835, probably by John Dobson, but was pulled down some years ago. The back of the house is largely Victorian built about 1877. A new entrance porch on the east was added at the same time. The stable block at the rear was built in 1902.

Our view by J. W. Carmichael was published in 1838 in his *Views on the Newcastle and Carlisle Railway*. He describes the hall as "the seat of Hospitality and of Colonel John Blenkinsop Coulson situated about threequarters of a mile north of the Railway. The grounds in front of the hall are laid out with great taste they are bounded on the south by the River Tippal, which at this place runs nearly parallel with, and separates them from the Railway . . . About a mile to the westward of the hall is an extensive colliery, belonging to Colonel Coulson, but leased to a company of Gentlemen, under the title of the Blenkinsopp Coal Company. The coals from this colliery are of a superior quality, and are conveyed in large quantities a distance of twenty miles by the Railway to Carlisle."

Here was once a fortified medieval tower which has completely disappeared. There is a tradition here of a black dog which always appears as a warning before death.

BRUNTON GATE

There are very few tollhouses left in Northumberland. Road improvements have destroyed most of them. The one called Brunton Gate, on the Military Road a few miles east of Chollerford, is typical of the dozens that once existed. Basically it is a two-roomed cottage, The interior dividing wall once had an opening in line with the small window in both gables. The toll collector could thus see the road in both directions irrespective of which room he was in.

BRUNTON TURRET

The turret here (26b) is one of the best preserved on the line of the Wall. It is reached by a signposted path from the Hexham-Chollerton road (A6079). The turret internally measures 12′ 9″ by 11′ 6″ and stands fourteen courses high. The wall on the east side running towards Planetrees is six feet wide while on the west a magnificent stretch ten feet wide can be seen. The core of the Wall is now mortared for preservation but originally was set in puddled clay which was still resilient when uncovered in 1950. In front of the Wall the ditch here is very bold.

BUSY GAP

A mile west of Sewingshields a broad break in the mountain ridge is called *Busy Gap*. The name was probably originally *bushy-gap*, that is a gap with plenty of bushes. A drove road passes through here. The spot was much frequented by the mosstroopers and thieves of the Middle Ages. When Camden and Cotton visited here in 1599 they dared not go to Busy Gap. "The Wall," Camden wrote, "goeth forward more aslope by Iverton, Forster, and Chester-in-the-Wall, near to Busy Gap – a place infamous for thieving and robbing; where stood some castles (Chesters they call them) as I heard, but I could not with safety take the full survey of it, for the rank robbers thereabouts."

The term a "Busy Gap Rogue" was one of abuse down to the seventeenth century.

Hutton visited the area in 1801. "A more dreary country than this in which I now am, can scarcely be conceived. I do not wonder it shocked Camden. The country itself would frighten him, without the Troopers".

Byrness Church

St. Andrew's Church, Bywell, in 1824

Simeon of Durham says Ecgberht was consecrated Bishop of Lindisfarne at "Bigwell" in 803. The church was almost certainly St. Andrew's. No earlier documentary evidence is available for either church. St. Peter's is the larger church but its Saxon origins is not certain. At one time St. Andrew's belonged to the White Canons of Blanchland and St. Peter's to the Benedictine monastery of Durham (The Black Monks). Hence they were known as the Black and White churches.

St. Andrew's has to a large extent been reconstructed in modern times but the ground plan has been preserved. The tower and west wall of the nave are Saxon. The tower is the finest in the county. It is fifty-five feet high and consists of four stages. The first stage has no western doorway but is entered from the nave by a thirteenth century arch. The dominating feature is the fine belfry.

Eighteen early English coffin lids, many with incised crosses have been built into the north wall of the church. An inventory of 1552 describes two "belles in the stepell" which are probably the same as those used today. The church also possesses a fine chalice made at Newcastle in 1642.

St. Peter's Church, Bywell, in 1824

In St. Peter's Church the north wall of the nave with its four original windows is eleventh century work but whether before or after the Conquest is not certain. The windows are similar to those in the nave of Monkwearmouth. The rest of the church is essentially thirteenth century work.

An interesting relic of medieval times is the low-side or leper window, on the south side of the chancel, through which the sacrament was administered to lepers or sick persons, during the time of the plague. The church was badly damaged during the great flood of 1771. The horses of Mr. Fenwick were taken to the church and were saved from drowning by holding on to the tops of the pews, one even taking refuge on the altar.

In the tower are two very old bells. One is inscribed TU ES PETRUS followed by the complete alphabet in Lombardic letters. On the other bell (cast c. 1600) is a monkish hexameter verse in Gothic capitals UT SURGANT GENTES VOCOR HORNET CITO JACETES (I proclaim the time for people rising, and summon those still in bed).

In the south wall of St. Peter's Church outside, near to its easternmost buttress, is a *Scratch-Dial* or *Mass-Clock*. It was probably cut early in the twelfth century.

These clocks showed the time when service was to begin, the markings being intended as indications for the tolling of the bell. It appears that three services are indicated and two contiguous lines at noon mark the dinner-hour. Although these dials are often found in the south only two are to be seen in Northumberland, the other being at Rothbury.

Scratch-Clock, Bywell.

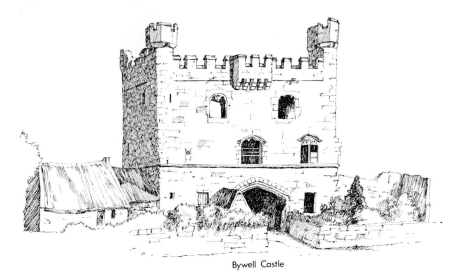

Bywell Castle

From a Drawing by S. H. Grimm c. 1786

Bywell Castle

In 1464 Henry VI, fleeing from the battlefield of Hexham, found shelter in Bywell Castle, but only for a brief period, since it was quickly surrendered to the victorious Lord Montagu who found there the king's sword, helmet and crown and the trappings of his horse. This is the earliest reference to a castle at Bywell which was built by Ralph Neville, the second earl of Westmorland, in the first half of the fifteenth century. The Nevilles held the barony from the days of Edward III to the time of the Rising of the North when their estates were forfeited.

The situation of the castle is unusual. It did not guard the old bridge, nor take advantage of the high ground, but stood at the end of the village and enclosed a large barmkin which provided protection to the cattle of the villagers. Bywell was then a place of importance which is difficult to appreciate when we visit this beautiful and secluded sylvan retreat today. A survey made by the royal commissioners in 1570 tells us:-

"The towne of Bywell ys buylded in lengthe all in one streete upon the ryver of water of Tyne, on the northe and west parte of the same and ys devyded into two severall parysshes and inhabyted with handy craftesmen whose trade is all in yron worke for the horsemen and borderers of that countrey as in makyng byttes, styrappes, buckles, and suche othere, wherein they are very experte and conyng, and are subject to the incursions of the theaves of Tynedale, and compelled wynter and somer to brying all their cattell and sheepe into the strete in the night season and watche both endes of the strete and, when th' enemy approchith, to raise hue and cry wherupon all the towne preparith for rescue of there goodes which is very populous by reason of their trade, and stoute and hardy by contynuall practyse ageynst th' enemy . . . . Also in Bywell towne on the north syde of the ryver

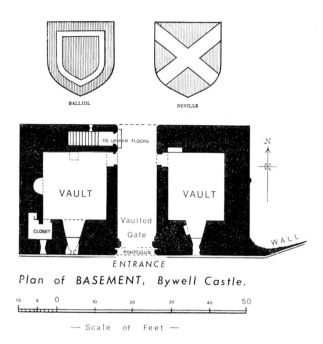

BALLIOL NEVILLE

Plan of BASEMENT, Bywell Castle.

— Scale of Feet —

th' auncestours of th' erle of Westmorland buylded a faire towre or gate house all of stone and covered with leade, meanyng to have proceded further, as the foundations declare beyng the heyght of a man above the ground, which were never fynyshed and the said towre is a good defence for the towne and will sone decay yf yt be not mayntened''.

Bywell, like Dunstanburgh, Bothal, Tynemouth and Willimoteswyke is a stronghold in which the gatehouse is the dominant feature. Part of the curtain wall, with two slits, remains between the tower and a comparatively modern house which is built on the site of the castle Gun-house and retains its vaulted basement. Writing in 1810 Sir David Smith described this Gunhouse as being "in the S.E. corner and the Dungeon in the S.W. corner of the Courtyard. The Dungeon is about twenty-six links square and the curtain wall between the square tower and the Gunhouse is 125 links".

The gate-tower is a rectangle of fifty-nine feet by thirty-eight feet. The gate was protected by a portcullis, as may be seen from the groove, with machicolations over the entrance. The passage through the tower is ten feet eight inches wide with a doorway in each side at the inner end leading into the vaults. A little further on is the door of the stair which leads to the first floor. The two drawings from Bates's *Border Holds* show this door from both sides as it was at the end of the last century. It is a fine example of an ancient iron gate.

Behind this grille the straight stair leads to the first floor and is protected by a meutriere in the window recess. A newel stair leads to

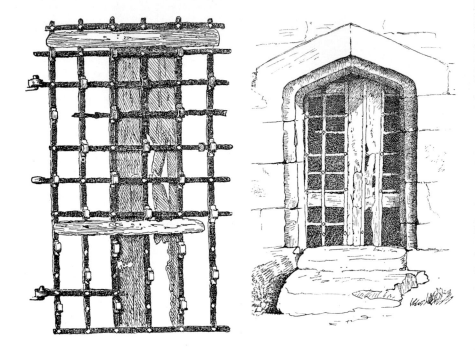

the second floor. The turrets and battlements are of great interest. The four square turrets are converted into octagonal angle projections and are entered by straight external staircases on the east and west walls whose battlements are carried to a great height to screen them. All the turrets have meutrieres in their floors.

Bywell Hall

Bywell Hall was built in 1766, from designs by John Paine out of an older house. John Paine was a well known local architect who built many houses in the county including Belford Hall and Gosforth House. Wallis, writing about 1769, says it is situated *"in a bounded, low, but delightful situation, beautifully rural, by the banks of the river Tyne, having a grass lawn before it to the south, with a dwarf wall and a high road between it and the river, the south borders of which are adorned with stately oaks and other forest trees, and some pieces of statuary, which on a sunny day are finely imaged by the water. To the east it has in view not only a pleasant garden noted for early productions, but also two churches within so small a distance almost as a stone's cast from each other, a salmon weir, two pillars of stone in the river which formerly supported a bridge."*

It is built in the Ionic style; the ground floor is rusticated, and the front facing the lawn adorned with pilasters, supporting an architrave and pediment. The hall contains wood carvings by Grinling Gibbons,

62

*Bywell Hall by J. W. Carmichael 1830.   The Seat of T. W. Beaumont M.P.
Published by W. Davison, Alnwick*

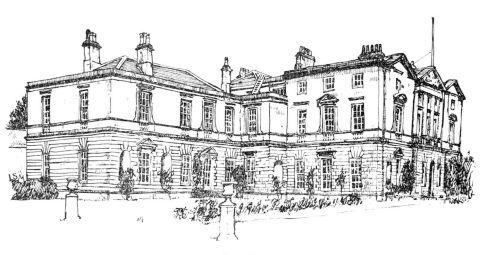

Bywell Hall today

CARRAWBURGH (BROCOLITIA)

Little can be seen of the fort here which stands on a bare flat moor. The north rampart and the wall are covered by the road while the east, west and south ramparts are only mounds in the fields. It covers about three and a half acres. In the second century the garrison was the first cohort of Aquitanians, later the first cohort of the Cugernians and in the third and fourth centuries by the first cohort of Batavians. Little excavation has taken place here although the walls would be impressive if cleared of debris. The position of the vallum is of great interest. It can be seen as though passing through the fort. Clearly the fort was built later than the vallum and was built over it. This makes Brocolitia either contemporary with or later than the Narrow Wall which formed the north rampart.

The western and southern slopes outside the fort were occupied by the *vicus* in which was a bath-house excavated by Clayton in 1873. In plan it was similar to the one at Chesters. Nothing can be seen of it today.

Outside the south west corner of the fort in boggy ground are the remains of the most important Mithraic temple to be found in Britain. It was discovered in 1949 during a very dry summer. Three altars to Mithras, still standing in position, were seen protruding through the grass. The following year it was completely excavated. Building was early in the third century and alterations were carried out several times before its destruction in 297 A.D. It was rebuilt shortly afterwards but before many years had passed it was demolished early in the fourth century, probably by Christians.

The pilgrim entered the ante chapel (Narthex) by a door in the south wall. On his left was the hearth where food was prepared and nearby was the ordeal pit. To the right, in front of the wickerwork screen is the statuette of a mother goddess. On entering the nave raised benches could be seen on either side. Here were four small altars especially the twin statues representing on the east CAUTES (torch upright to represent the rising sun) and on the west CAUTOPATES (torch downwards to represent the setting sun). At the far end was the sanctuary with its three main altars dedicated by officers from the fort. The western one depicts Mithras as charioteer of the sun (dedicated to Marcus Simplicius Simplex), the central altar is dedicated by Lucius Antonius Proculus, and the eastern altar is dedicated by Aulus Cluentuis Habitus. Behind the altars in a recess would have been a relief showing Mithras slaying the bull, but it was probably destroyed by Christians. (The altars to be seen in the Temple are replicas. The originals are in the Museum of Antiquities at Newcastle University.)

North west of the Mithraeum on the edge of the vallum is Coventina's Well. It was discovered in 1876 but had been recorded by Horsley in 1726.

"they discovered a well. It is a good spring, and the receptacle for

The Temple of Mithras today

the water is about seven foot square within, and built on all sides, with hewn stone; the depth could not be known when I saw it, because it was almost filled up with rubbish. There had also been a wall about it, or an house built over it, and some of the great stones belonging to it were yet lying there. The people called it a cold bath, and rightly judged it to be *Roman*."

Here was found the richest collection of Roman coins and altars ever discovered on the frontier. There were 13,487 coins (apart from many carried away in a raid on the site) and numerous altars and native objects now to be seen in the Chesters Museum. The water goddess worshipped here was the Celtic *Coventina*. The whole shrine measured forty feet square internally with the sacred spring in the centre. Among the coins found were over three hundred brass *"as"* of Antoninus Pius. They commemorated the pacification of northern Britain after the revolt of 155. They show Britannia sad and disconsolate with her head bowed unlike her usual portraiture.

Reconstruction by R. Embleton of Temple of Mithras at Carrawburgh

Coventina's Well. 1878

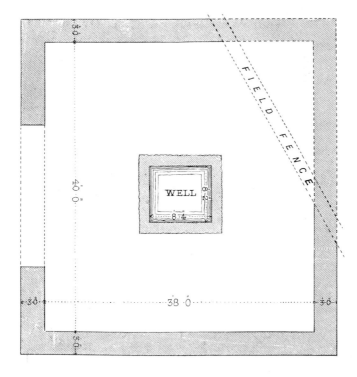

Reconstruction of Temple of Coventina by R. Embleton

Of the 13,487 coins recorded in the well four were of gold, one hundred and eighty-four of silver (denarii), and the rest were bronze and copper. The earliest coins are three silver ones of the time of Marc Antony and the last were of the reign of Gratian. The coins found here are "a fair representation of the money circulating at Brocolitia at the close of the reign of Gratian".

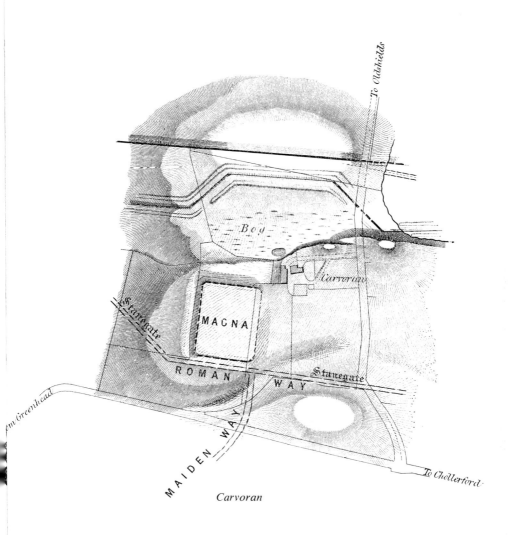

Carvoran

CARVORAN

Carvoran was situated on the Stanegate at its junction with the Maiden Way from the south. It is the MAGNA of the *Notitia* where the second cohort of the Dalmatians was stationed. It is to the south both of the Vallum and Wall, having probably been erected before them to command the valley of the Tipalt and guard the road junction although no remains of a pre-Hadrianic fort have been discovered. The fort measures 440 by 360 feet containing an area of $3\frac{1}{2}$ acres. The north-west angle-tower is visible but little is known of the internal buildings which have not yet been excavated. There have been casual discoveries made in the civilian settlement, the cemetery and the bath house some of which are reproduced here.

But the most important discovery was made in 1915. A postman, delivering to the neighbouring farmhouse, noticed what appeared to

Lithograph by J. T. Kell

Castle-Nick Mile Castle

CASTLE NICK MILECASTLE

Castle Nick receives its name from Milecastle 39. The milecastle measures internally 50 feet from east to west and 65 feet north to south. Its well-preserved walls are seven feet thick. On the west side the foundations can be traced. Examination of the south gateway shows that in the Severan reconstruction it was reduced to a postern. Both gateways were built of small masonry perhaps because it was difficult to transport large blocks to such a difficult site. The military way can be seen here very clearly, in some cases both kerbstones are visible. The terra-cotta lamp here reproduced was found in the milecastle.

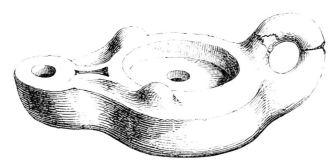

Terra-cotta Lamp, 4 inches in length, discovered in the Mile-castle, Castle-Nick.

CATCLEUGH HILL (1,586 feet)

Here are some stone circles. There are eight or nine fallen stones called *"The Border Line"* and a smaller circle of four stones, of which three are standing, called THE THREE KINGS.

Four miles from Catcleugh is *Whitelee* the last house in England. The name was originally White Law, the term *white* meaning *whiteish grass* as opposed to Black Hill which was a hill covered with heather. On the stone-lintel over the front door is the inscription "Pax sit hiuc domo intrantibus" (Peace to all that enter here). The inn which was once here has unfortunately been closed for almost a century. In its day it must have been a welcome sight to travellers from Jedburgh into England.

Two miles further on we come to Carter Bar, 1,370 feet above the sea. The Bar comes from the tollhouse which once stood on this spot when the turnpike was built in the eighteenth century. The word Carter comes from the Celtic "cart" meaning a hill. Carter Bar is a *swire,* or neck of land, connecting Catcleugh Shin and Arks Edge and was anciently called the Reidswire. The land up here is bleak indeed. Tomlinson relates how an old carrier who was asked what he thought of the weather up there replied "Hoot, man, hoot; the very de'il himsel' wadna bide there half an hour unless he was tethered!"

In 1575 the last battle between England and Scotland took place here a fight commemorated in the famous ballad 'The Raid of the Reidswire".

Rede through a deep gorge above Catcleugh, is celebrated for its jasper. The pebbles fall from the face of the crumbling rock into the stream below, and are sometimes beautifully polished by the action of the water. The colours are good – yellow, red, and a bluish white chalcedony, spotted with red – but the stone, although it takes a good polish, is much traversed by cracks."

Catcleugh Reservoir stretches a mile and a half beside the main road to Scotland. It holds 2,300 million gallons and provides 13 million gallons a day plus 3 million gallons for compensation. Its maximum depth is 78 feet, surface area 270 acres.

CATTON

At the foot of the moors on the east side of the East Allen is the long straggling stone-built village of Catton. It was called "Catteden" in 1295. Apart from being raided in 1589 it has little history. A mile to the north at an elevation of 1,700 feet is Catton Beacon. "Upon the moor," wrote Wallis in 1769, "is a hillock of stones whereon about fourteen years ago stood an upright piece of timber or pole called Catton beacon, to which was affixed a vessel with fire in it to alarm the country on any public danger. The alarm was communicated from it to another beacon on Whitfield fell, visible both from it and from the mount of Stony Law." A mile to the west is Old Town which is reputed to be of Roman origin, but only fragmentary Roman remains have been found in the neighbourhood.

CAWFIELDS MILECASTLE (No. 42)

This milecastle stands about a mile east of Greatchesters Fort. It is well preserved with the walls standing seven or eight courses. Internally it measures 63 feet from east to west, and 49 feet from north to south with walls 8 feet thick. Both gates are of massive masonry. The pivot holes and bolt holes can still be seen in the south gateway. It was built by the Second Legion. The milecastle is built in broad gauge although the wall itself is narrow gauge.

To the east of Cawfields is Thorney Doors and Bloody Gap. Then comes Caw Gap to the north of which was a lonely "house called Burn Teviot, formerly the resort of smugglers and sheep-stealers, and now inhabited, it is alleged, by the spirits of the persons murdered there." (Tomlinson). To the south are two stones called the *Mare and Foal*. They are part of a Druidical cerele. When Armstrong made his map three were standing.

CHESTERS

The estate of Chesters came into the hands of the Errington family in 1555 and remained with them until it was sold in 1792 to Adam Askew of Redheugh who resold it in 1796 to Nathaniel Clayton. The fine house was built in 1771 by John Errington of Walwick Grange. Recently Robert Wragg has shown quite clearly that the architect was John Carr of York (1723-1807). He discovered his original sketch in the Soane Museum. Additions to the house were made in 1832 and 1837 by John Dobson. The photograph of about 1840 clearly shows Carr's original house. It was a square plan of two-and-a-half storeys with the entrance porch on the south flanked by hipped bay windows rising the full height of the building. The two wings, standing well back from the main house can only be seen at a distance. The windows in the wings are altered from the original plan and are probably the work of John Dobson.

In 1891 the house was enlarged and extensively rebuilt by Norman Shaw (1831-1912). Although externally the centre block remains as it was designed by John Carr the interior was gutted and the entrance

The Mansion at Chester about 1840

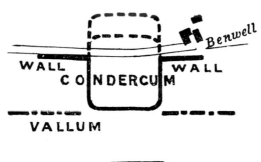

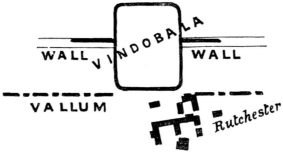

The Gateways

The gateways at Chesters were all of the same type. The main gate-way the *porta decumana* shows what they were like. The double gate has towers on either side with guard chambers. The *spina* separating the two portals is built of massive masonry. The rest is in stone similar to the wall itself. The doors would be of oak reinforced with iron. The doorways of the guard rooms opened into the gate-passage.

North Gate (Porta Praetoria)

The visitor enters the fort by this gateway. It is a double portal gateway but its west portal was blocked very early since its threshold is almost unworn. Its east portal however is of great interest since the stone channel of an aqueduct enters here, fed by one of the springs to the north of the fort.

Main West Gate (Porta Principalis Sinistra)

This also has twin portals and guard chambers. However, both sills are unworn suggesting the gate was walled up at an early date. The northern guard chamber has a large stone storage tank fed by an aqueduct to the west. Whether there were one or two aqueducts we don't know but the bringing of water (aqua adducta) is recorded in an

82

CHESTERS-CILURNUM

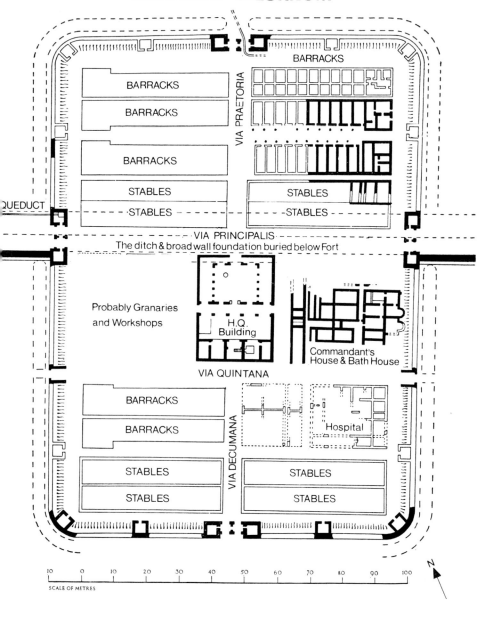

BARRACKS

VIA PRAETORIA

BARRACKS
BARRACKS
BARRACKS

STABLES
STABLES
STABLES
STABLES

AQUEDUCT

VIA PRINCIPALIS
The ditch & broad wall foundation buried below Fort

Probably Granaries
and Workshops

H.Q.
Building

Commandant's
House & Bath House

VIA QUINTANA

BARRACKS
BARRACKS

VIA DECUMANA

Hospital

STABLES
STABLES

STABLES
STABLES

```
10    0    10    20    30    40    50    60    70    80    90    100
SCALE OF METRES
```

N

inscription (to be seen in the Museum) probably of the early third century when the governor was Ulpius Marcellus. The Narrow Wall on a broad base comes up to the south tower. Originally the wall crossed the fort and in 1945 Turret 27A was found near the north east corner of the headquarters building.

Smaller West Gate (Porta Quintana Sinistra)

About 50 yards to the south is a single portal gateway with little to be seen. Travelling round the fort we meet traces of the angle tower and half-way between the angle and the south gate is a fine interval tower. The doorway at the back led on to the street called the INTERVALLUM. The gutter can still be seen. There were eight interval and four angle towers at Chesters. They were all probably raised 10 feet above the rampart walk like the gate towers.

South Gate (Porta Decumana)

Has the usual twin portals and towers. The western portal was blocked when still new. The eastern portal was restored on more than one occasion, after the fort had been overrun, so the level of the portal is much higher. In the east guard chamber of this gate a remarkable bronze tablet of 146 A.D. was found. It is a *diploma* or *tabula honestae missionis*. This was given to an auxiliary soldier when he had served for twenty-five years and received an honourable discharge. It legalised his marriage past or future. The original is in the British Museum but a copy can be seen in the Chesters Museum.

Smaller West Gate (Porta Quintana Dextra)

Of the eastern wall only the gateways can be seen. This gate is a single portal and the MILITARY WAY, leading from the bridge across the Tyne enters the fort here.

Main East Gate (Porta Principalis Dextra)

In a fine state of preservation with walls standing twelve courses high. It was never used by wheeled traffic and was walled up about 300 A.D. Each portal had an arch at back and front and the south near pier still has the slots on top of the upper course which held the shuttering for the arch.

Headquarters (Principia)

This is the most important building in the fort, almost twice the size of that at Housesteads, and the finest on the line of the Wall. It was the nerve centre of the fort. Here in the various rooms all the business of the regiment was transacted. The entrance was on the north through a monumental gateway (although there are two side entrances as well) into an open courtyard. From here the visitor could look straight ahead through the Cross Hall to the chapel. The courtyard was paved with a verandah on three sides whose supporting columns can still be seen. In the north west corner is a well and nearby on one of the paving stones is a large phallus. From the courtyard the spacious Cross Hall is entered. The south side is occupied by five rooms. The central one is the *sacellum* which housed the regimental colours and a statue of the emperor. The chapel gave access to the strongroom which was under one of the rooms of the standard bearers. It was used for the money and valuables of the regiment. The two rooms to the west of the chapel were the offices of the adjutant who looked after the regimental records. The two rooms to the east were used by the standard bearers who looked after the company records and the individual savings of the soldiers. The strongroom (*aerarium*) is

illustrated here from an old woodcut. It was found by accident in 1803 but only excavated in 1840. We are told that "a tradition existed in the country that the station had been occupied by a cavalry regiment and that the stables, which were capable of accommodating 500 horses, were underground. The rustics when they came upon this vault naturally enough thought that the later part of the legend was about to be verified and that they would soon enter the stables; it was not to be so, however. An oaken door, bound and studded with iron, closed the entrance into the chamber, but it fell to pieces shortly after being exposed. On the floor were found a number of base denarii, chiefly of the reign of Severus. The roof of the apartment is peculiar. It consists of three separate arches, the intervals between them being filled up by the process called 'stepping over'."

The Stables and Barracks

Cavalry regiments were divided into 16 units called *turma* and each consisted of 30 men commanded by a decurion, and two N.C.O's. Ronald Embleton's reconstruction, in Russell Robinson's book *What the Soldiers wore on Hadrian' s Wall,* shows a decurion with two troopers of an *Ala* in the third century. Almost nothing is known of the stables at Chesters apart from their sites which are partially conjectural. Since there were at least 500 horses in the fort and since in the winter they would consume large quantities of hay and straw it is difficult to visualize how they could have been accommodated in the eight blocks suggested for stabling. (It is noteworthy that the cavalry fort of Hunnum had to be increased in size.)

Some of the barracks can, however, be seen. Cavalry were given more ample accommodation than infantrymen, probably because they kept their harness and equipment where they slept. There were eight barrack blocks. Each housed two *turmae* and at the ends near the fort walls were the rooms of the unit commanders. The 60 men were probably equally divided among the remaining ten rooms. The barracks had a veranda on which the cooking was done. Some of the pillars which supported this veranda can be seen.

Commandant's House

This building is very confusing but was obviously an elaborate and luxurious house with the normal Roman central heating and a private bath-house attached. The commander of a cavalry unit (*praefectus equitum*) was a man of importance in the Roman army.

There were probably two granaries to the west of the headquarters but the area has not been excavated. The fragments of a large building to the south of the Commandant's house probably contained the regimental hospital.

The civil settlement was to the south and east of the fort. Excavations have not been carried out but aerial photography suggests there was a large population here with several important houses. Excavation at some future date will probably provide valuable information about civilian life on the frontier. The vicus here was almost a military town.

Bath-house

The large military bath-house outside the fort is one of the sights of Chesters. Due to the damp air and changes of heat bath-houses needed constant attention to prevent deterioration. The bath-house at Chesters has undergone several alterations. So today it is difficult to follow exactly the route the bathers would take through the various rooms.

They entered by a flight of steps from the military way leading to a porch which gave access to the Dressing Room. This was the largest

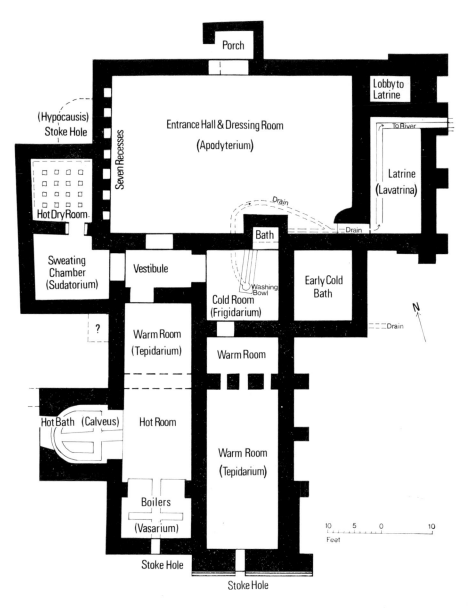

Porch

Lobby to Latrine

(Hypocausis) Stoke Hole

Entrance Hall & Dressing Room

(Apodyterium)

To River

Seven Recesses

Latrine
(Lavatrina)

Hot Dry Room

Drain

Bath

Drain

Drain

Sweating Chamber
(Sudatorium)

Vestibule

Washing Bowl

Early Cold Bath

N

Cold Room
(Frigidarium)

Drain

?

Warm Room
(Tepidarium)

Warm Room

Hot Bath (Calveus)

Hot Room

Warm Room
(Tepidarium)

Boilers

(Vasarium)

10   5   0   10

Feet

Stoke Hole

Stoke Hole

room in the baths as was customary. Going to the baths was a social
function where you met friends and had a chat, almost like a club, so
this main room needed to be substantial. In the west wall are seven
niches. Their use is a matter for argument. Alcoves for statues, for
clothes, for ointments, etc., have all been suggested. To the east of the
changing room was a latrine. Leaving the main room the bather
entered the vestibule. From here three rooms opened. On the left was
the cold room with a washing basin in the centre. To the right were two

87

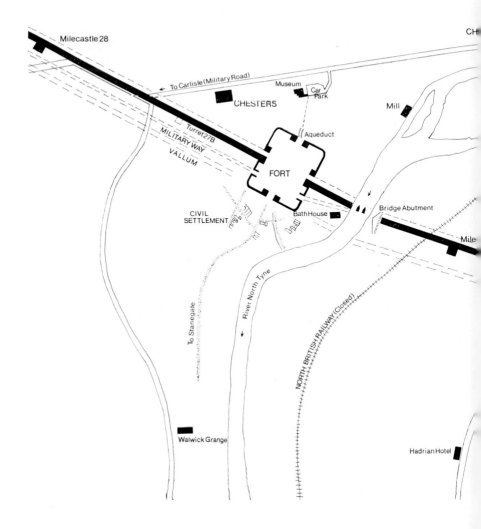

To Carlisle(Military Road)

Museum

Car Park

CHESTERS

Mill

Turret 27B

MILITARY WAY

Aqueduct

VALLUM

FORT

CIVIL
SETTLEMENT

Bath House

Bridge Abutment

Mile

River North Tyne

To Stanegate

NORTH BRITISH RAILWAY (Closed)

Walwick Grange

Hadrian Hotel

rooms for dry heat, the inner one being the hottest. Straight ahead were the warm and hot rooms with moist heat. Off the hot room was a room containing a hot bath. This room was lighted by a window the broken glass of which was discovered when excavating. Parallel with the *tepidarium* and *caldarium* are two extra warm rooms entered from the cold room to the north.

The rooms were heated by a complicated system of hot air channels which ran under the floors and through the walls, the heat being provided by three stoke holes.

To keep in the heat the various warm rooms had barrel vaulted ceilings composed of blocks of tufa, which were light and so avoided

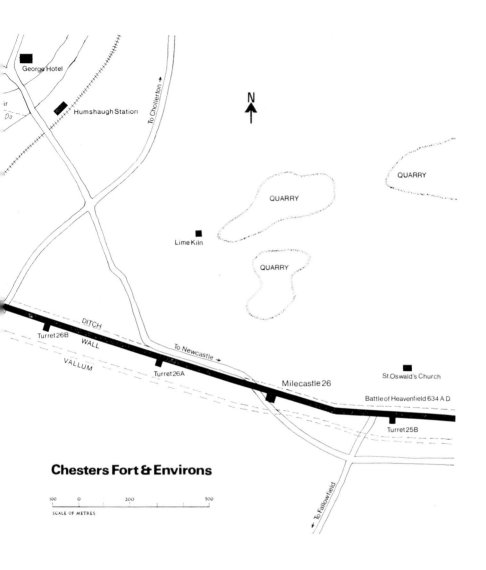

Chesters Fort & Environs

SCALE OF METRES

the necessity of heavy buttresses on the walls. The rest of the baths had the conventional roof of red times.

The Bridge

There were two Roman bridges here. The first was a narrow bridge arched in stone which carried the wall or rather its walk across the Tyne. Much later a new wider bridge was built to carry the Military Way. This bridge had a wooden superstructure. The bridge at Chollerford was built in medieval times, destroyed in the Tyne flood of 1771 and rebuilt in the form we see today. Between Chollerford and the Roman bridge was an old crossing called the Island Bridge. We

Hypocaust at Chesters, E. B. Richardson. 1867

know nothing about this bridge and it could have been Roman carrying a road north east to join Dene Street. So there have been five bridges across the Tyne here. (The Official Guide by Eric Birley suggests there was an earlier wooden bridge down river to carry the lateral service road. He dates the two stone bridges as late as the beginning of the third century).

The abutment of the second Roman bridge on the east bank is an outstanding example of Roman workmanship. Massive dressed stones joined together by iron cramps embedded in lead can still be seen. The river has altered its bank since Roman times so the east abutment is now 50 feet from the bank while the west abutment is submerged. The second bridge had three water piers two of which can be seen when the river is low. The eastern abutment carried a tower which the wall joins on the north side. Beneath it is a mill race which worked an under-shot water-mill similar to the one on the Irthing bridge. There is no evidence that there was a tower on the west abutment.

Remains of the early bridge can be seen on the east abutment and the middle water pier. It had four piers, was 10 feet wide, and longer than the second bridge. The second bridge is 190 feet from abutment to abutment with a width of just over 20 feet.

Abutment of Bridge, Chesters. 1867

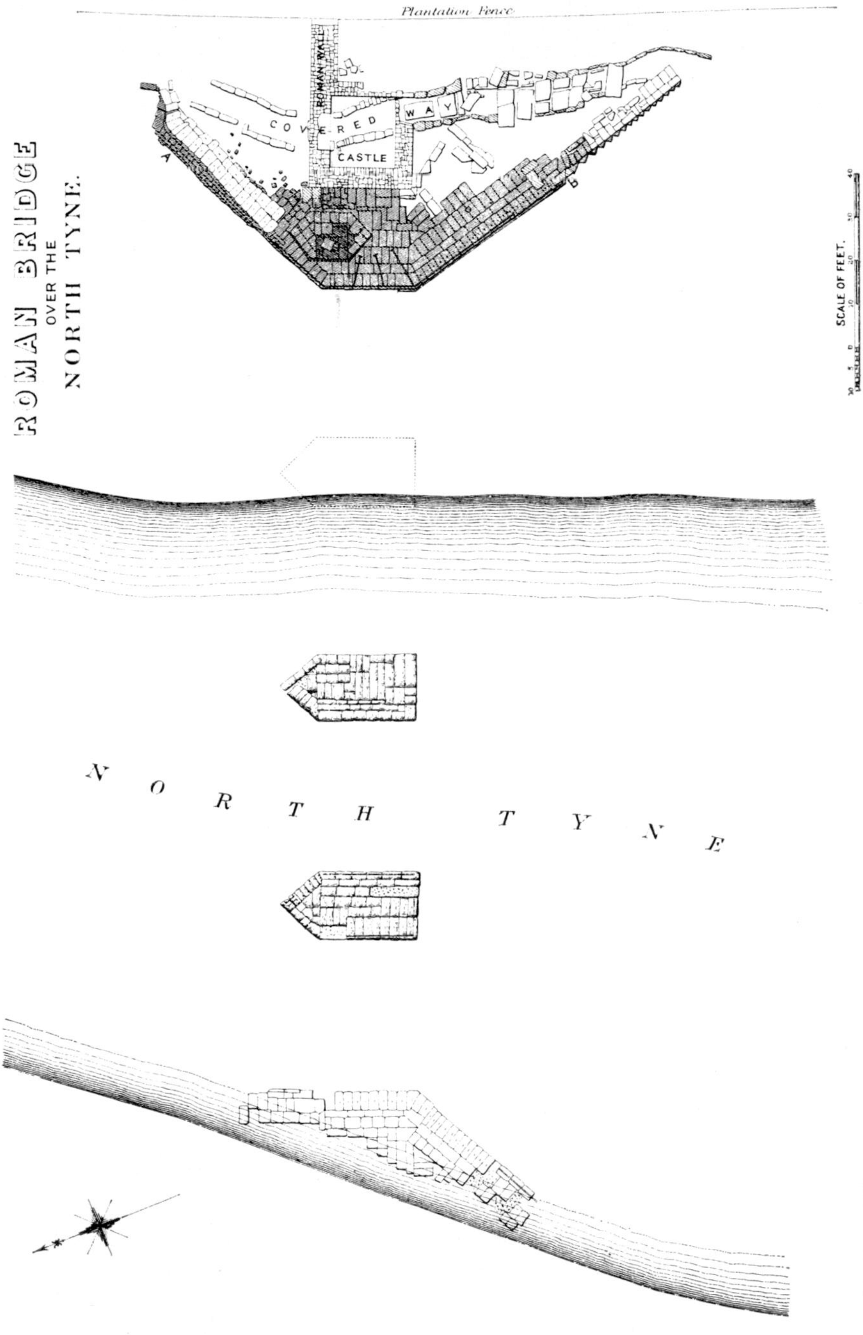

ROMAN BRIDGE
OVER THE
NORTH TYNE.

Plantation Fence

ROMAN WALL

COVERED WAY

CASTLE

SCALE OF FEET.

Andrew Reid. Newcastle.

N O R T H   T Y N E

CHESTERWOOD

This small village, a mile to the north of Haydon Bridge, once contained a number of pele houses. In the eighteenth century Tomlinson tells us one Frank Stokoe lived in one of these houses. He was a man of gigantic stature, a bold and determined character, of whom many stories are told. One winter night he was awakened by a noise, and found that someone was trying to draw back the bolt of his door with a knife. He instructed his daughter to stand behind the door, and as the knife was withdrawn, to push the bolt quickly back again, but without alarming the party. He then took his musket, and loading it with slugs, descended through the trap-door into the cow-house below, and cautiously unbarred the door. At the top of the heavy flight of stone stairs leading to the dwelling apartment he saw four or five men with a dark lantern. After carefully surveying them for a few minutes in order to satisfy himself as to who they were, he broke silence in a thundering voice – "You d—d treacherous rascals, I'll make the starlight shine through some of you!" and discharged his weapon at the same moment. The holder of the lantern staggered across the stair-head, and fell headlong down the steps, shot through the heart. His terrified companions jumped over the wall and fled in all directions. Stokoe hastily entered the house, closed the door, and retired to his bed, as if nothing particular had happened. He was out with the Earl of Derwentwater in 1715, but escaped from Preston by clearing a high wall with his horse. He was one of those who helped to convey the body of the decapitated earl to Dilston.

CHIPCHASE CASTLE

Chipchase Castle is situated on the left bank of the North Tyne and is one of the most picturesque of Northumbrian mansions. The name is probably derived from "cipp", a log, and "kos", a heap, meaning "a heap of logs" or "a trap for animals made of logs". In the reign of Henry II Chipchase was a hunting ground of the Umfravilles, Lords of Prudhoe. In the fourteenth century the manor passed, by marriage, into the Heron family. Sir George Heron, keeper of Tynedale, was killed in the border fight called the "Raid of Redeswire" in 1575. The Scots afterwards made presents of falcons to the prisoners saying that the English were nobly treated, since they got live *hawks* for dead *herons*.

The castle really comprises two buildings – the old fourteenth century pele and attached to it a Jacobean mansion. The tower of Chipchase is one of the most imposing and best preserved in Northumberland being unusually well built. The plan is oblong measuring fifty-one and a half feet by thirty-four feet. It is fifty feet high with an extra ten feet for the angle turrets. The ground floor is vaulted and the three upper floors were of timber supported on corbels. The main area of each floor was a single apartment with a number of smaller

The Porch, Chipchase Castle

rooms, well lighted, arranged in the thickness of the walls. The entrance doorway is on the east side with part of the original oak portcullis remaining in its seat. The tower has a fine corbelled and machicolated battlement with four overhanging angle turrets similarly machicolated.

The manor house, built by Cuthbert Heron, to the south-east of the tower in 1621, is the finest example of the architecture of its time in Northumberland.

The library, or "music room", as it is called, is one of the most interesting apartments in the castle, on account of the richly-wrought cornice around the ceiling, and more especially on account of the elaborately-carved mantelpiece of black oak, representing "The

Chipchase Castle   *Photo Philipson Studios*

March of Time, or the Four Seasons". The original whereabouts of this mantelpiece are unknown but it is probably of Flemish workmanship manufactured in England.

The porch is a very fine entrance to the castle. Tomlinson tells us – "On each side of the steps in the prediment of each column is a sculptured panel. That on the right hand bears the representation of a heron in a very conventional oak, and is said to symbolise the prosperous times of the Heron family. But it seems there was a local prophecy, that when the heron should be seen charging through a fence instead of flying over it, the extinction of the family was near at hand: and so, according to tradition, the last owner of the name is stated to have caused this ill-omened symbolism to be carved on the left-hand panel, before he parted with his last ancestral acres". The account is pure invention. Of the panel on the left we can only say it is a bird of some sort but definitely not a heron.

From the basement of the tower an underground passage has been traced for some distance to the south. Whether this was an emergency exit is extremely doubtful. Like all castles it has its ghost. In this case a knight Sir Reginald Fitz-Urse who was starved to death in the prison of the Great Keep and returns to haunt the scene of his suffering.

CHIPCHASE CASTLE

Chipchase Chapel

The early chapel of Chipchase was dependent on Chollerton church and is said to have stood near the castle. A report of 1723 tells us – "Here is a little chapel in which the sacraments have been formerly administered, and where at present there is service performed four times in the year. It hath neither books, vessels, or vestments belonging to it. There is a bell lying in the chapel, but it hath never been fitted and hung up. The chapel hath never been either plaistered or floored."

The present chapel is about 100 yards east of the castle and was built in the middle of the eighteenth century. Above the arched entrance is a heavy bell cot. Inside are old box-pews and an interesting octagonal pulpit.

Chollerford Bridge and Inn.
Courtesy of Tyne and Wear Museums (Laing Art Gallery)

CHOLLERFORD BRIDGE

The medieval bridge here is first mentioned in 1333 when Bishop Skirlaw of Durham granted an indungence to all who should by labour or money contribute to its repair.

If we can accept as genuine the ballad "Jock o' the Side" there was no bridge here in his time (c. 1569).

> But when they cam' to Chollerford,
>   There they met with an auld man;
> Says – "Honest man, will the water ride?
>   Tell us in haste, if that ye can."

"I wat weel no," quo the gude auld man;
I hae bided here threty years and thrie,
And I ne'er yet saw the Tyne sae big,
Nor running once sae like a sea."

The Grand Jury at the Northumberland Sessions of 1718 reported Chollerford Bridge "to be fallen downe and out of repaire, and that the same lyes upon the King's High Street or way leading from Carlisle to Newcastle, and is very necessary and convenient to the said county, and that the ford which lyes nigh the said bridge is very dangerous almost att all times to be ridd." This bridge had four arches but whether it was the bridge referred to in 1333 we do not know. It was damaged in a flood in 1733 and destroyed in the great flood of 1771. It was replaced by the present fine bridge of five arches with big cu-waters in 1775. It stands half a mile north east of the Roman Bridge.

The fine illustration we reproduce is from a water colour by T. M. Richardson, Junr. It shows the old inn as well and was painted in 1839. It belongs to the Laing Art Gallery.

The George Hotel ~ Chollerford

CHOLLERFORD. The George Hotel

Little is known of this famous inn. The first reference to it is in Wallis' *Natural History and Antiquities of Northumberland* (1769).

Chollerford. 1889

Describing a thunderstorm in the Tyne valley he wrote:

Thunder-storms are not very frequent. A little before Midsummer in 1756, we had a very remarkable one; the lightning and explosions dreadful. It entered and demolished all the windows of the New Inn at Chollerford-Bridge, upon the banks of the North Tyne.

The name suggests the inn, now the *George*, had been recently built. The inn was closely associated with the history of the bridge. Although a medieval bridge is referred to in 1333 it has certainly been replaced before the eighteenth century. In 1718 Chollerford Bridge had "fallen downe". It was replaced shortly afterwards and the *George* was probably built about the same time. In 1826 the name George Inn is used and the innkeeper was William Bell.

W. Hutchinson in his *View of Northumberland* in 1778 writes:

"The Inn at Chollerford tempted our stay; a spacious room built for the resort of the neighbouring gentlemen afforded us a pleasing view upon the river; whilst excellent accommodations indulged us with that degree of satisfaction, which truly constitutes the traveller's ease."

Bulmer's Directory of 1886 describes it as a "commodious inn and posting house occupied by Mr. Thomas Black." Our illustration is from a water colour by T. M. Richardson, Jun. It shows the inn and bridge and was painted in 1839.

Strange birds have been found in strange places. A newspaper report of 1776 tells us that a stork was shot at Chollerford. Its skin was nailed up on the wall of the George and crowds came to see it.

CHOLLERTON

The township of Chollerton was a manor within the barony of Prudhoe and was held by the family of Umfravill. In the thirteenth century it came into the hands of William Swinburne who also held property at Haughton. To make communication easier between the two places he established a ferry on the North Tyne. In the late seventeenth century Chollerton was farmed by the Carnaby family who lived in a house which before the Dissolution of the Monasteries belonged to the Priory of Hexham. When Ralph Carnaby died in 1693 his will gives a fascinating account of the contents of a farmhouse belonging to a wealthy tenant. Here is the inventory of his possessions:-

In the hall, one long table, valued at £1 15s; in the out-rooms, another table, 5s.; in the dairy, bowles, a chirnn, chesfatt and suchlike, £3 10s. Potts, panns, and little things as trenshare, £1; three kettells and a fish pann, £2 14s. Fowerteen pewter dishes, most of them little ones, 3 douzen of plates, 2 pair of candlesticks, 2 pair of brass candlesticks, with snuffers and snuffe pans for both, one dish cover, one cullinder, 1 douzen of petty panns, a little ring for sallett, 2 brass rings, 30 glasses, jugs and cups, with a latting pudding pan, a big earthen pot, all at £5. One fine new tick for a bed, £2; one webb of unbleached cloth, £1 6s.; 17 yards of unbleached harden, 14s. 6d; 9 spindle of yarne, £1 2s.; 2 spitts and a pann, 6s. The linning; 8 paire and one sheet, most of them thinn, £2 15s.; seaven paire of a courser sort, more worn, £1 18s.; nine paire and one of course sheets, £1 18s.; nine paire of good pillowbers, one paire more, very cours, £1 2s.; one window curtain of course cloth, and clother (sic) for another, 8s.; 13 table cloths of linning, dyper and huggaback, and one more, £2 5s.; 9 douzen and a half of linning dyper and huggaback napkins, with fower dyper towels, £2 15s.   Two barrells, 3s., one new-booke, 6s.; one old green bed, 10s.; a browne bed and bedstead, £2 10s.; three feather beds, 3 paire of pillows, 2 bowlesters, one piece of course ticking for a bowlster, £4 10s.; five paire of blanketts, £1 15s.; 2 pieces of wooling cloath for blanketts, 10s.; 2 ruggs, 4 coverlitts or happins, 3 more all very bad, £1 2s. A prospect glass, a runner to cut paste, and a sause pann, 5s.; 2 coverlitts, and two paire of more blankets, £1. There was one broune bedd and bedstead, fether bedd, bowlster and pillows, blanketts, rugg, and one looking glass, which was left Mrs. Troath Swinburne by Mr. Carnaby's will, and which the said Troath Swinburne had, the same were vallued at £4 5s. There was chaires, virginalls, trunks, with Mr. Carnaby's cloathes in them, severall boxes, chists and cupbert of drawers, 2 iron boxes, and a dish, a warmeing pann, the fether bedd, bowlster, and pillows, bedstead, curtaines, and table (and the kitchen racks) that was in Mr. Carnaby's chamber, and other fether bedds with blanketts, and one looking glass, that Mr. Bury had and disposed of, £— —s. The particulars of plate: One little silver tankard valued at £3; one silver tumbler, 15s.; tenn silver spoons, £3; a little teapott of silver, 15s.; one silver salt, £2. These particular peices of plate Mr. Bury had and received the same to his owne use without allowing my Lady Swinburne, the other legatee, her moyety or share thereof. The beasts and other cattell at Chollerton upon the lands at Mr. Carnaby's death valued: 23 draught oxen at £3 15s. per beast, £86 5s.; 17 fat oxen at £7 per beast, £119; 28 milk cowes, £3 per beast, £84; 10 steers at £5 per beast, £50; 12 steers and quies at £1 5s. per beast (these were two years old), £15; 12 steers and quyes more at £1 15s. per beast, £21; 16 one year old stirks at 15s. per beast, £12; 1 bull at £3; one bull segg at £4. 15 score of ewes at £7 10s. per score, £112 10s.; 6 score of hogge at £4 per score, £24; 11 score of wethers and seven dinments at £7 per score, £79 9s. The swine: one sowe at 14s.; 3 piggs at 8s.; 2 hoggs at £3; 2 braunes at £1 2s. The horses: 4 maires at £2 each, £8; 3 old work horses at 10s. each, £1 10s.; the husband geare valued at £11 9s. 4d. The corne in the garth valued to £70; the cropp upon the ground at £20; reedy money in the house, £350.

The pleasant village of Chollerton lies less than two miles north east of Chollerford. The church of St. Giles is of early Norman origin but as seen from outside it is entirely modern. The tower is square and battlemented with a strange Victorian spire. The thirteenth century north aisle has pointed arches on eight sided pillars but the south aisle is the most interesting. Here the five round pillars are of Roman work probably from the Roman camp at Chesters.

Chollerton has three interesting fonts. Inside the entrance door is a massive Roman altar made into a font. The Roman sacrificial instruments can still be traced on the stone. There is also a shallow octagonal bowl which once belonged to the old chapel at Gunnerton. The one now in use has a round bowl on clustered columns dating from the thirteenth century. The Jacobean oak cover is very ornamental with flying buttresses and a plain pinnacle.

CHOLLERTON CHURCH,
North
Published 3, Oct. 1823 by W. Davison Alnwick,

The parish church occupies high ground which falls away to the river on the south. It originally belonged to the Priory of Hexham. The exterior is fairly modern and not impressive. The quoined tower is the oldest part and was built some time before 1769. A strange wooden spire was added in Victorian times. The church was originally Norman and fragments of Norman work can be seen inside and the present church is based on its Norman predecessor. When the south aisle was added the columns, and the respond shafts at the two ends of the arcade were taken probably from the Roman fort of Cilurnum. The original font was also once a Roman altar. It can be seen just inside the door. The eastern wall of the chancel has some richly carved Jacobean panelling and the backs of the choir stalls are of the same date. They are all probably reused carving.

The Elizabethan organ by the famous Father Schmidt, with its twenty-three gilded pipes was given to the church just over a century ago. Among the church plate is a fine chalice by Eli Bilton, 1687, the Newcastle goldsmith.

However the most interesting building stands at the entrance to the churchyard. It is a picturesque low stone – roofed building with narrow slits for windows and a mounting block in front. It was used as a stable for those who travelled long distances to church.

The bridge here was built by Robert Mylne in 1785.

Stable at Chollerton Church

CLOSE HOUSE, WYLAM

Close House lies south of Heddon-on-the-Wall a few hundred
yards from the bank of the Tyne. It was built in 1779 but the site has
been occupied since the thirteenth century. We read of the Close House
Chantry in 1414. It was knocked down when the house was built.
Close House is a fine building with a five-bay front of two-and-a-half

storeys, with a doorway with Tuscan columns. One of the rooms has some fine stucco work.

To the south of Close is Stanner Ford, the first safe crossing on the river Tyne and nearby were once the remains of two standing stones. It will be noticed from the map that the road along the Tyne is here called the "Fisher Way".

COCKLAW TOWER

Cocklaw Tower is four miles north of Hexham. It is well preserved and of excellent masonry, probably built in the fifteenth century.

Entrance Passage, Cocklaw Tower, from the inside

The plan is oblong with one large room in the basement and one each on the two floors above. The entrance is on the south leading into the basement which has a pointed vault. On the right of the entrance passage is a newel staircase leading to the upper floors and battlements. There were turrets at all four corners and machicolations above the entrance door. The chief apartment is on the first floor, lit by four windows two of which are large with double lights. A pointed doorway in the south wall leads to the famous "painted chamber". Here is a coloured frieze decorated with a crude acanthus design. Our drawing of it is based on a painting by Mr. Archer about 1862 made for the fourth duke of Northumberland. A doorway opens from the staircase between the first and second floors into a vaulted room 15½ feet long and 5½ feet wide. It is lit by a loop in the south wall.

Cocklaw Tower, 1882

Interior   *drawing by Susan Martin*

COLWELL

Only fragments remain of the ancient chapel here. The village stands on Watling Street where it is crossed by the Cambo road.

The County History tells us that "the old house or hall at the west end of the village may have been the home of that cadet line of Widdrington which for some generations resided at and owned part of Colwell". A "dove cote" is mentioned in a will of 1653 and in 1897 "a curious stone-built pigeon house still remains behind the old mansion-house".

In medieval times an annual festival was held at Colwell. It was called the "Bridal", when one of the three village wells was decorated on St. Ulric's day.

COMBE PELE

The Combe, a farmhouse which incorporates a pele, stands on the north bank of the Tarset burn, with two other peles on the south bank, Shilla Hill and Barty's Pele. The Combe once belonged to Hodge Corbit or Corby and was known as Corbit Castle.

COMYN'S CROSS

On the lonely Haughton Common seven miles due west from Simonburn or two miles north from Sewingshields is a fragment of a wayside cross probably set up by or for one of the Comyns of Tarset, or maybe as a boundary stone or landmark. A local legend, with Arthurian colouring, tells us how a guest returning from Sewingshields Castle was slain here by his host's son who was seeking a golden chalice which had been given to the victim by his father.

CORBIE CASTLE (TARSET)

One mile north-west of Black Middings is the remains of Corbie Castle here illustrated. Nearby are the ruins of several more buildings. There is some confusion in the name of this tower. It is sometimes called Barty's Pele.

It stands on the bank of a stream and has walls fifteen feet high in places. The vaulted basement has now fallen in. Adjoining are the ruins of a three roomed seventeenth century cottage and a massively built two roomed medieval house. Nearby is Combe Pele, the home of Barty. The inhabitants of these two peles were close friends. One morning when Barty arose, he found that his sheep had been driven away during the night by Scottish thieves. He immediately summoned Corbit Jack, and they set off in pursuit, but lost the track north of the Carter Fell. Barty did not relish the idea of returning empty-handed, and the two borderers having decided, after a short council, that the Leatham wethers were the best, made a selection and drove them off. They had got as far as Chattlehope Spout when they were overtaken by two of the sturdy Scots, and a hand-to-hand conflict took place

Corbie Castle

in the long heather above the waterfall. Corbit Jack was slain, and Barty was wounded in the thigh; when making one tremendous back-handed blow, he caught the slayer of his companion in the neck, and – as he expressed it – "garred his heid spang alang the heather like an inion". His first assailant tried to make off, but was cut down ere he had run many yards. Barty took both swords, lifted his dead companion on his back, and, in spite of his own wound, drove the sheep safely over the height down to Corbie Castle, and deposited Corbit Jack's body at his own door.

CORBRIDGE

Corbridge, which is now a quiet village, once ranked as an important Northumbrian town. In Roman times it was one of the largest stations in the North of England, called in the *Antonine Itinerary* Corstopitum. But before that the Britons certainly occupied the site and many of their camps and burial mounds are to be found in the neighbourhood; remains which go back to the early Bronze Age. The Roman station occupies a gentle rising near the Cor burn, 600 yards west of the town and was approached from the south by a bridge whose foundations can be seen when the river is low. This bridge carried across the Tyne one of the great Roman military roads – the famous Watling Street, or to give it its older name, Dere Street.

Anglian Corbridge

Although some English towns sprang up on the sites occupied by the Romans the new settlements were usually in the immediate neighbourhood, possibly from superstitious motives. The parson at Corbridge informed Leland in the reign of Henry VIII:

By this broke (the Cor-burn) *as emong the ruines of the olde town is a place caullid Colecester, wher hath beene a forteres or castelle. The peple there say that ther dwellid yn it one Yoton, whom they fable to have been a gygant.*

This legend of a giant called Yoton lasted for many centuries. In 1660 we read:

Near Corbridge, not far from Northumberland, the late rains having wash'd away the earth in a place where a torrent was made by the winter rains, there was discovered the skeleton of a prodigious monster, the skull capable of holding three gallons; the hollow of the back-bone was so large that a boy of eleven years old thrust his hand up it to the elbow; the thigh bone is two yards long, lacking two inches; his whole height computed to just twelve foot or seven yards. The skeleton being found by boys, they broke it in many pieces, which my Lord Darwentwater, who hath a great part of it whole, would have given some hundreds of pounds if he had it entire. The skull hath twenty-four teeth in it. I myself have seen one of 'em in Newcastle, which is one inch and six tenths of an inch broad and three inches deep, and is now four ounces, although dryed. There is also another tooth of the same to be seen at Widow Ingram's coffee house in Prescot Street in Goodman's fields.

The first written evidence of Corbridge's existence occurs in 800 A.D. when the Anglian settlement is called *Et Corabrige*. The name is clearly derived from the Roman bridge, and is therefore one of the few places before the Norman Conquest named after a bridge. However it is not known where the first part of the word – COR – comes from. The Cor burn clearly derives its name from the village. Probably the word COR is that part of the Roman name which survived.

We are told that in 786 a bishop was consecrated at the monastery of Corbridge. This monastery is clearly the parish church whose porch was built entirely of Roman stones. The style of the building is similar to the seventh century churches of Jarrow and Monkwearmouth. It is dedicated to St. Andrew like four other Tyne valley churches, Bywell, Hexham, Heddon and Newcastle.

It has been suggested that when the kingdom of Northumbria declined and Bamburgh was no longer used as a capital the royal seat was removed to Corbridge. The town certainly prospered mainly because it was at the junction of two ancient highways, namely Dere Street (Watling Street) and the Stanegate. The Roman Stanegate (later called the Carelgate) or "ald-he-way" was the main road across the isthmus from Tynemouth to Carlisle, until General Wade built his military road. This trade led to the early establishment of a market which is first mentioned in the thirteenth century but clearly had been in existence long before. There was also an annual fair in existence in 1293, which was probably held at Stagshaw Bank a mile to the north on Dere Street. This fair survived into the twentieth century with the development of the lead and silver mines at Alston. Corbridge appears to have had a royal mint. Coins have survived of Henry I with the name of the moneyer on them EREBALD ON COLEB, the last word being Corbridge. At this time the royal tax of tallage paid by Corbridge was as high as Newcastle showing the relative importance of the two places. In 1201, when King John was in the north, he caused a search to be made at Corbridge imagining that the town had once been large and populous, and must have been ruined by an earthquake, or some sudden and terrible invasion, and that in either case the people would have been unable to remove their wealth. Tradition says the search was in vain.

Medieval Corbridge

The town was at the height of its prosperity by the end of the thirteenth century. In 1296 we have the first detailed account of taxation in Corbridge. This was a royal tax on moveables called the Subsidy Roll and a total of seventy-seven people were taxed which made this the largest town in the county after Newcastle, where 297 people paid subsidy. Alnwick had forty-nine names and Morpeth thirty-five. It has been estimated that one person in twenty paid tax, so the population of Corbridge would be 1,500, Newcastle 6,000, Alnwick 1,000, and Morpeth 700.

The names of weaver, miller, dyer, tailor, goldsmith, forester, butcher and slater attached to various inhabitants illustrate the trades carried on at that period.

In 1295 Corbridge sent two representatives to the model parliament of Edward I. Their members were Adam son of Alan and Hugh son of Hugh. Bamburgh and Newcastle also sent members, but on later occasions only Newcastle was represented.

In 1296, 1312 and 1346 the town was burnt by the Scots but 1349 was even more disastrous; it was then that the Black Death overran England. Tradition says that the only inhabitants to survive were a few who camped in an open field called the Leazes, which was north of the town in a higher and healthier situation.

Writing in 1830 Hodgson thus describes the town:-

The town (for such its antiquity demands that it be styled) is dirty, and in all the streets except that through which the Newcastle and Carlisle road passes, is filthy with middens and pigsties, with railing before them of split board, etc. The population seem half-fed; the women sallow, thin armed, and the men flabby, pot-belied, and tender-footed; but still the place bears the appearance of being ancient.

To such an extent had the town declined from its ancient estate.

Seventy years later Tomlinson describes Corbridge "as one of the most picturesque and interesting of Northumbrian villages, as it is one of the most considerable. From its high and dry situation on a gravelly hill, which is sheltered on the north and south by the steep sides of the river gorge, combined with the loveliness of the surrounding country, Corbridge has become one of the most popular health resorts in the country. Few villages, indeed, have so many natural advantages, and these are supplemented by historic associations of exceptional interest".

The Vicar's Pele (1)

There are many peles in Northumberland which have been (and still are) used as vicarages but this is the only one actually standing within the churchyard. Although there is no record of its erection the architectural features suggest a time about 1300. It is first mentioned in the list of fortalices drawn up in 1415, wherein it is described as belonging to the vicar. A survey of 1663 describes it as "a tower scituate on ye churchyard wall, to ye south-east of ye church, said to have been antiently ye lord's goale, but now is ye place where ye lord's court is usually kept, but ye roofe is in much decay".

The tower is of one date and well built of Roman-worked stones brought from Corstopitum. It is a good example of the smaller pele and shows domestic arrangements rarely seen in such perfection. It is three storeys high and has an embattled parapet carried round the corners on projecting corbels forming machicolations.

The entrance is at ground level by a heavy door of old oak planks covered with an iron grate similar to that at Bywell Castle, leading to a vaulted basement where the vicar stabled his horse and stored his provisions. A stair mounts in the thickness of the wall to the first floor which was used as a living room. On the first floor landing is a stone table with a wash basin.

Pele Tower
CORBRIDGE
on Tyne

The first floor is entered by a pointed doorway and is lighted by three windows. It has two wall cupboards, a large fireplace and window seats. The floor above, of the study bedroom, is gone. Near a small window in the north wall is a recess clearly intended as a book rest. While reading the window commanded a view of the church and its approaches. It is easy to picture life in this medieval tower.

Bridge (2)

Leland (1540) recorded that "The Stone Bridge that now is at Corbridge over Tine is larg, but it is set somewhat lower apon Tine than the old Bridge was. There be evident Tokens yet seene where the olde Bridg was and thereaboute cummith downe a praty Broke on the same side that the Town is on." He is clearly referring to the Roman bridge which carried the road to Corstopitum.

In dry summers the south abutment and two of the ten piers are still visible. The piers were 15 feet wide and 29 feet long, pointed on the

upstream and flat on the downstream face. The roadway was in wood and our reconstruction shows part of the bridge. The stones of the piers were removed in 1840 to build the water mill at Dilston.

~Roman Bridge at Corbridge~

The Roman bridge above Corbridge disappeared during the Middle Ages and the ford across the river was a quarter of a mile below the present bridge. The ford was approached from the north by a lane leading from the Newcastle road at the east end of Main Street. In 1235 a new bridge was built and this medieval structure was the predecessor of the bridge we see today. In 1674 it was replaced by a seven-arched bridge which was the only one to survive the great Tyne flood of 1771. Tradition says that a man called Johnson was the builder and that during its erection one man had a penny a day more than the other workmen, his duty consisted in filling every crevice and opening with hot running lime, so that the whole became one solid mass. In 1881 the bridge was widened by three feet, but its appearance was not spoilt. It consists of seven arches with outlets at every pillar. At the present time an ugly temporary bridge runs parallel with it.

Corbridge Market Cross.

Market Cross (3)

In the middle of the market-place used to stand a market cross. It was emplanted on a large Roman altar. The cross stood until 1807 and was replaced in 1814 by a cast-iron structure. From the cross the proclamation of Stagshaw Bank Fair used to be made. The cross for many years stood in front of the Roman Catholic Cathedral in Newcastle, but is now back in Corbridge.

Inns and Taverns

The drawing by R. Embleton shows the *True Briton* coach outside the Angel Inn early in the nineteenth century. The Directory of 1827 tells us that the *True Briton* ran every day between the Turf Hotel, Newcastle and the King's Arms, Carlisle. The coach changed horses at the "Angel". Formerly called the Head Inn it is the oldest hostelry in

114

Corbridge. It is said that the king's commissioners stayed here, when on their mission to suppress the monastery at Hexham.

From 1752 until the opening of the railway the "Angel" was the posting inn for Corbridge; once a week the mail coach halted at the inn and the landlord read to the local people who had assembled at the Coen's-foot the news from the Newcastle papers.

The central portion of the inn is the oldest. The semi-arched doorway and the mullioned Tudor window on the right of it belong to the original structure. The wings on either side have been considerably altered and re-built. In the west gable are two small and original circular openings. Above the door is a fine old sun-dial bearing the inscription E. W. A. 1726, for Edward Winship and his wife Anne. There is also a stone carved with the arms of Newcastle accompanied by a couple of masonic symbols. This is the emblem of the Incorporated Company of Masons of Newcastle. Why it has been put there is a mystery. In the view here shown of the inn in the nineteenth century can be seen a stone dog on the gable. This has been removed for safe keeping and now stands on the lounge mantelpiece. Its age and origin are shrouded in mystery. Some people even claim it is Roman!

In the interior are several ancient features, the timbered ceiling, the balustrade of the staircase, and remains of a large fireplace with a "spit". The stonework at the rear is of early date and the old stables still have their original dividing stalls. The "Angel", like other inns of the same name probably derived its sign from a religious picture of the Annunciation. As parts of the picture faded only the angel remained visible to passers-by.

The Boots and Shoes Inn, another old posting inn, used to stand in Water Road. It has now disappeared. At one time shoemaking was the principal trade of Corbridge. Large quantities of shoes were made for lead and coal miners and Shields fishermen. The inn clearly derived its name from this local industry.

At the end of Main Street is the picturesque Jacobean style house called Monksholme. It was the residence in the eighteenth century of the Gibsons of High Balk near Great Whittington.

When the Gibson family had Monksholme it was an inn and since there is a cellar with a barrel shaped ceiling the house was probably built for that purpose. In Parson and White's Directory of 1827 it is called the New Inn with George Gibson as landlord. There is a mounting block and a little window at the side of the house where drinks could be handed to horsemen without dismounting.

Although its thatched roof has gone the Wheatsheaf (5), another old hostelry, still remains. It dates from the closing years of the seventeenth century but has been modified and enlarged since then. In the stable yard can be seen two curious stones, probably of Roman workmanship.

The chief of these is a stone figure thought to represent the goddess Ceres. In one building there is a corner stone showing two heads facing in opposite directions.

The Golden Lion Inn (6), in Hill Street, was built with stones taken from Dilston Hall when it was demolished in 1768. The part of Dilston Hall taken down had been erected in 1618 by Sir Francis Radcliffe.

Corbridge Pele Tower EAST END

Low Hall (7)

Apart from the Vicar's Pele the oldest remaining house in Corbridge is the Low Hall at the east end of Main Street where the Newcastle road passes into the village.

The nucleus of the building is a medieval pele tower three storeys high. It retains many of its original features including the vaulted roof of the basement. In entering the tower from the adjoining house by the

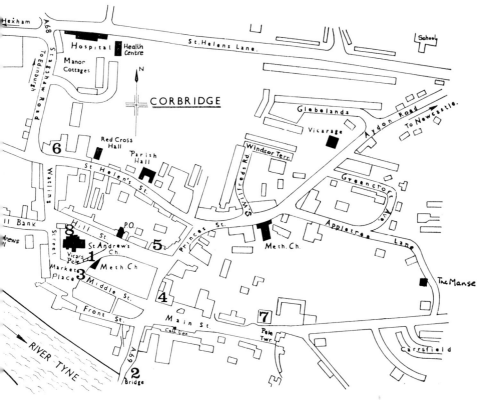

CORBRIDGE

CORBRIDGE MARKET-PLACE.

117

original entrance there is first a small lobby from which a straight stair goes up in the thickness of the wall giving access to the upper floors, and a door head admits to a vaulted basement. It is lighted by a small loophole in the north wall, and the window looking on to the road probably occupies the position of another loophole.

The tower itself was built by the Baxters, probably in the late fifteenth century and for long was known as Baxter's Tower. The Baxters were a prominent Corbridge family at that time. One of them, called Alexander Baxter, was setter and searcher of the watch at Corbridge in 1552.

The Baxter property came into the hands of Richard Gibson of Hexham in 1675. He was probably the builder of the Low Hall attached to the Baxter's tower. Over the entrance is a sun-dial dated 1700. The hall was lighted by mullioned windows and at the same time windows of a like character were inserted in the tower, and a gabled projection was built onto the rear. Later all the mullioned windows were replaced with smaller ones. The window tax of the period was probably responsible for this reduction in window size.

George Gibson, grandson of Richard Gibson took part in the Jacobite rebellion of 1715 and was attainted of high treason and died in the Fleet prison the following year. Most of his property, including the Low Hall, was forfeited to the Crown. It was bought for £360 by John Aynsley, a Hexham attorney.

Church of St. Andrew (8)

Corbridge Church, one of Northumberland's oldest, is largely built of Roman stones from the neighbouring station of Corstopitum. Its origin was monastic, although there are no traces of monastic buildings attached to it. Probably they were built of wood. The first mention of the church occurs in the Northumbrian Annals for the year 786, recording the consecration of Aldulf, Bishop of Mayo.

It is possible to recover the plan of the first church. The lower part of the western tower and the walls of the nave arcade are the original structure. High on the north side of the nave arcade two original windows are visible. In the eleventh century the porch was raised and turned into a belfry tower similar to those being built at the same time at Bywell, Ovingham and Warden. The tower is built entirely of Roman stones. The lofty round arch might have been a gateway at Corstopitum from which it has been transferred in its entirety. Instead of rising from the impost it rises from a stone built on the top of the impost, and so has the appearance of being stilted.

The nave is separated from the aisles by three arches on each side, resting on octagonal pillars. The south aisle was added in the middle of the twelfth century. It is the western part of the wall of the south aisle that remains containing a beautiful Norman door. On a window sill in the south aisle is part of a fine Saxon cross. The north aisle was added about 1200 A.D.

The thirteenth century chancel is long and spacious, with three lancet windows at the east end, and a priest's door with a finely-

Tower of St. Andrew's Church. From S. F. Dixon's "Corbridge", 1912.

proportioned trefoil head. In the middle of the chancel aisle is a fine thirteenth century gravestone, with a beautiful cross carved in relief, and a pair of shears and the words – Hic Jacet Alicia Vxor Willelmi De Tyndale Orate Pro Anima.

Under a low arch at the end of the thirteenth century north transept lies a tombstone with a foliated cross and a crook. Nearby is another monument with a Latin inscription to Hugh Fitz Aseline, a Corbridge landowner of the time of Edward I.

Two houses near Corbridge need to be mentioned.

Howden Dene

Many hundreds of years ago an old town assembly was held near Howden Dene, the land being described as "the waste place where the assembly is upon Easter Day". In 1799 when the open common fields of Corbridge were enclosed there was no house at Howden. The land was given to Bartholomew Winship. In 1890 the land and the house which had been built there were purchased by J. H. Straker. He enlarged and improved the property. However the Newcastle to Carlisle road ran very close to the house. Early in the twentieth century this disadvantage was solved. We quote from Walter Iley's *Corbridge*. Journeying from Corbridge to Newcastle shortly after leaving the village behind "the road takes a sudden swing to the left round the grounds of Howden Dene – it returns by an equally abrupt turn later. The old road followed the direct route – the present drive to Howden Dene Hall – but this is where the owner desired privacy, and had the main Newcastle-Carlisle road diverted at his own capital cost, and at a cost to the public's time, money, convenience and safety ever since. It was not only the rolling English drunkard who made the rolling English road."

Prior Manor (or Prior Mains)

The rectory house stood outside the old town's limits. Once the manor house of the Priory of Carlisle it has been considerably altered but today is mainly eighteenth century work. It is now divided into two houses. The building on the right, now called Prior Cottage, a low two storeyed building still has one mullioned window. The projecting stone porch is in the middle of the south front. The larger house on the left, now called Old Prior Manor, has a fine old doorway. The windows have been altered. The fine old fireplaces inside have recently been revealed when later plaster work was removed. It is rather confusing but the name Prior Manor is applied to other houses nearby.

Roman Station (Corstopitum)

The Roman site at Corbridge lies half a mile west of the village. It was originally a fort which flourished during the Roman occupation of Scotland and then a supply base. Later it became in the third and fourth centuries an arsenal with a large civilian settlement around it.

The original fort was probably built during the governorship of Julius Agricola (78-84 A.D.) who conquered the north of England and the southern part of Scotland. Remnants of this Roman fort, with its earth rampart, have been discovered. It was probably garrisoned by a cavalry regiment from Gaul called the *Ala Petriana*. A tombstone in Hexham Church shows a standard-bearer of this unit. It probably came from a cemetery at Corbridge.

When Hadrian built the Roman Wall in 122 A.D. the Corbridge fort seems to have been replaced by the one at Halton.

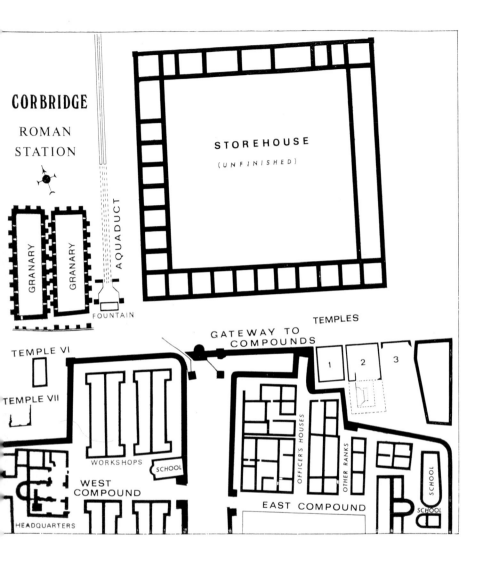

CORBRIDGE

ROMAN STATION

STOREHOUSE

(UNFINISHED)

GRANARY

GRANARY

AQUADUCT

FOUNTAIN

TEMPLES

GATEWAY TO COMPOUNDS

TEMPLE VI

TEMPLE VII

1 2 3

WORKSHOPS

SCHOOL

OFFICER'S HOUSES

OTHER RANKS

SCHOOL

WEST COMPOUND

EAST COMPOUND

SCHOOL

HEADQUARTERS

In 139 A.D. the fort at Corbridge was rebuilt in preparation for the invasion of Scotland, its position on Dere Street making it tactically important. But its period of greatest importance came after the withdrawal from Scotland, when Corstopitum became the ordnance depot for the whole eastern part of the frontier. It fulfilled this function until the Romans finally abandoned the north of England.

The civilian settlement at Corbridge was very important. Here lived many wealthy merchants, as well as craftsmen such as smiths, potters and leather workers whose tools may be seen in the Museum. Besides catering for the needs of the troops the large civilian community was also engaged in trade with the natives to the north of the wall. Corbridge

121

was also the centre of a rich agricultural area and nearby mines of coal, lead and iron were exploited.

The fort was probably occupied until a few years after 400 A.D. What became of the civilian population we do not know for certain but within a century and a half the village of Corbridge was in existence.

Excavations at the Roman site were started in 1906 and a wealth of material illustrating Roman life in north Britain has been found. The Museum exhibits many of these discoveries while the remains of numerous buildings can be seen on the site which is under the control of the Department of the Environment.

Reconstruction of Corstopitum. R. Embleton

Corbridge Lanx

This is one of the most remarkable pieces of antiquity found in the north of England. It was discovered in 1734 by a girl gathering sticks near the river. It was sold by her father to a goldsmith in Newcastle. However, the Duke of Northumberland claimed it as a treasure trove and it is now in Alnwick Castle.

The Corbridge Lanx

CORSENSIDE

One mile north of West Woodburn to the east of Watling Street (A68) stands the village of Corsenside which now consists of an old church and farmhouse. The church of St. Cuthbert is in an exposed position. The first name of the village *c.*1250 is CRESSENSET. This gave rise to the legend that St. Cuthbert's body was once here on its wandering and a preaching cross set up. However the first element of the word is the Gaelic name *Crossan,* who were probably the first family to settle here. The church is basically Norman (see especially the chancel arch) but all the original windows have been replaced by Georgian ones as in a house. The bell-cote is also an eighteenth century addition. In 1311 the income from Corsenside church was given to the nuns of Holystone who were having financial problems and they continued to receive it until the Dissolution. The records of the church are meagre. In 1663 the curate's stipend was £6.13.8. He was called John Graham and he was described as a "sordid and scandalous" person.

Close to the church is an interesting seventeenth century farmhouse.

Corsenside by Paul Brown. 1938

CRINDLEDYKES

Here are the fine remains of a corbelled lime kiln. Lime burning for agricultural purposes was common from the sixteenth century onwards. Old kilns can be found in various localities and the fine specimen near Vindolanda is well known.

CUPOLA BRIDGE

A cupola is a vertical circular furnace for smelting and the bridge receives its name from a lead smelting mill which once operated in the neighbourhood. It carries the Haltwhistle to Alston road across the river Allen at the point where the East and West Allen meet. It was built about the year 1778 and consists of three segmental arches with projecting keystones.

DALLY CASTLE

Lies four miles west of Bellingham on the Chirdon Burn, a tributary of the North Tyne. It was probably built in 1237. On Speed's map of 1611 it is called Dala and earlier in his *Britannia* Camden called it Delaley. Its history is obscure. Originally it was an oblong building of two storeys. Later two turrets were added to the north corners and a south wing constructed. The stones were used to build Dally Mill and only the foundations can be traced. Dally Castle has its tragic legend. The owner's sister fell in love with her brother's enemy, Gilbert of Tarset. One of their meetings was surprised by her brother who pursued Gilbert to the summit of Hareshaw Common. A fight took place and Gilbert of Tarset was slain. The spot where he fell is known to-day as Gib's Cross.

DEADWATER

The border between England and Scotland passes through Deadwater Railway Station. The land to the south was in the Middle Ages called Threapland or debateable land. But in 1552 the boundary was fixed. On Deadwater Fell at the foot of Peel Fell (1975) the river Tyne has its source. The land here is flat and because it was difficult to tell which way the water was flowing the rivulet was called Deadwater. It retains this name until it joins Bell's burn.

The railway here closed down in 1956 for passengers and 1958 for goods, after 100 years of service. The Border Counties Railway was built in 1856 to open up the coalmines at Plashetts and the ironstone mines at Bellingham and was completed across the Border in 1862. However almost from its commencement the railway was not a commercial success. Passenger and goods traffic failed to develop.

On the summit of Peel Fell is the Kielder Stone, 46 feet in length and estimated to weigh 1,500 tons. It is vaguely connected with the Cout of Kielder who was either a border chieftain or a supernatural creature. As with most large stones it is unlucky to go round it three times widdershins (i.e. contrary to the sun's course).

> Green vervain round its base did creep,
> A powerful seed that bore;
> And oft of yore its channels deep
> Were stained with human gore
>
> And still, when blood-drops, clotted thin,
> Hang the green moss upon,
> The spirit murmurs from within,
> And shakes the rocking-stone.

A little to the south of Deadwater are the foundations of the *Kirk of the Bells* where in peacetime the English and Scottish wardens of the March used to meet. It is first mentioned in 1326. In 1715 Warburton describes it: "Bells: a mean village near ye head of North Tyne, where are the ruins of an old chapell." In 1825 we are told "Every vestige has long been obliterated, except some graves, which may yet be perceived with a plain small stone at the head and one at the foot, as is the custom in Scotland." Outside the churchyard a group of stones marks the grave of the "Cout of Kielder".

> This is the bonny brae, the green,
> Yet sacred to the brave,
> Where still, of ancient size, is seen
> Gigantic Keilder's grave.
>
> The lonely shepherd loves to mark
> The daisy springing fair,
> Where weeps the birch of silver bark,
> With long dishevell'd hair.

The grave is green, and round is spread
  The curling lady-fern;
That fatal day the mould was red,
  No moss was on the cairn.

Where weeps the birch with branches green,
  Without the holy ground,
Between two old grey stones is seen
  The warrior's ridgy mound.

And the hunters bold of Kieldar's train,
  Within yon castle's wall,
In a deadly sleep must aye remain
  Till the ruin'd towers down fall.

Each in his hunter's garb array'd,
  Each holds his bugle horn;
Their keen hounds at their feet are laid,
  That ne'er shall wake the morn."

NORTH TYNE HEAD.

Amelia Countess and Heiress of Derwentwater 4th October 1868 Dilstone Castle

The story of the Derwentwaters, however, had a comic finale 150 years after James Radcliffe was executed, when an elderly lady turned up in the north to claim the Derwentwater inheritance stating she was a descendant of John Radcliffe who had died childless.

Let us now quote from *The Strange Story of the "Countess of Derwentwater"* by Maurice Milne.

"Early in the morning of 29th September, 1868, Amelia set out on a short but momentous journey. Attired in an Austrian military uniform, complete with sword, she mounted a pony. Her retinue included a cart loaded with various possessions, attended by two sturdy retainers: Andrew Aiston, a keelman, and Michael Carlton, a porter at Blaydon railway station. The destination of this determined band was Dilston Castle.

"In front of the crumbling tower Amelia cut a sod, which her attendants solemnly placed in her hands. In this time-honoured fashion she took seisin of the Dilston estates. She then took some furniture into the only room with four walls intact and covered a corner of it with a tarpaulin. Beneath this makeshift canopy Amelia began composing eloquent letters:

I found not a voice to cheer me; nothing but naked, plasterless walls; a hearth with no frame of iron – the little chapel, which contains the sacred tombs of the silent dead, and the dishonoured ashes of my Grandsires.

"Meanwhile, in neighbouring Corbridge, the news of this event stirred a certain Professor Softly to pen these immortal lines:-

> *Oh yes, I think the time is come*
> *When hordes of heathen race*
> *Will yield James Radcliffe's sacred tomb*
> *Up to his child's embrace.*
> *If such the care on every hand*
> *To wield the justice rod,*
> *Throughout the realms of England,*
> *Before Almighty God.*
>
> *Oh, could the human hand obtain*
> *Then all it would bestow,*
> *Again would Countess Amelia reign*
> *Where her sires did long ago.*
> *The justice, mercy and gratitude,*
> *Go hand in hand,*
> *And give to his heart its latitude*
> *And Countess Amelia her land.*

"Their Lordships of the Admiralty ordered firm action. Their men removed Amelia's furniture. When she drew her sword to defend her ancestral home they disarmed her and carried her out in her chair.

"Far from retiring from the scene, the indomitable lady pitched her tarpaulin on the roadside, over a damp and insalubrious ditch, and withdrew into this makshift tent. There, like Achilles, she remained, brooding on the ill-treatment meted out to her.

"The Northumberland climate is hardly suitable for middle-aged spinsters who choose to spend autumnal evenings in gypsy fashion. The Hexham Highway Board declared the hut an obstruction, a fine of ten shillings was imposed and the hut was dismantled. Thus ended Amelia's home-coming".

The rest of the story and there is a good deal more can be read in Maurice Milne's booklet.

Greenwich Hospital demolished the Derwentwater mansion in 1765. The present Dilston Hall was built about 1835 for John Grey, the famous Northumbrian agriculturist, who two years earlier had been put in charge of the Greenwich Hospital Estates. He established an improved system of land cultivation and cattle breeding. A charming biography of him was written by his daughter, Josephine Butler, a noted social reformer.

Today the tower of Dilston is in ruins. Two windows in the east wall of the castle are all that is left of the Radcliffe mansion. Near the castle is a narrow seventeenth century stone bridge which appears on most pictures of Dilston.

Dilston Castle and Hall have passed through many building periods. The 17th century manor house has completely gone. The tower of which parts still survive is first mentioned in 1464. It was extended and altered about 1566. Then in 1622 Sir Francis Radcliffe extended the castle in the Jacobean style to transform the old castle into a house. Nothing remains of this period of building but fortunately the architect's plans and his full written contract have survived. We here reproduce them from the *Northumberland County History* (Vol.X).

Artickles of an agreement indented, made, etc., the second day of January in the nyntenth yeare of the reigne of our soverigne lorde James, etc., 1621, betwixt Edward Radclyffe of Devilston within the countye of Northumberland esquire of th'one partie, and John Johnson of Lytle Langton of th'other partie.

First yt is covenanted . . . that he the said John Johnson, his heires &c, shall before the feaste of St. Michaell the Archangell next ensuinge the dayt hearof, at his owne proper costes and chardges, well and suffyceyntlie erecte, make, and build . . . at Devilston aforesaid a parte of the house wherin Sir Francis Radcliffe Barronet now dwelleth, of thre stories heighe, of good and suffycyent free stone and other stone of the best he can or may convenientlie gytt within one myle next to the same house, according to the plottes therof maid, bearinge dayt of these presents and subscribed with the hand of the said John Johnson, in forme in effecte followinge, viz.—

In the first and lowest storye six stone doores, whereof two of them muste stand in the porch which is to be wrought with mouldinge and the rest playne; also two chimneys in the same storye for the kytchinge and fower wyndowes, with fower leightes in every wyndowe on the foresyde, and two wyndowes with two leightes in eyther wyndowe and two wyndowes with thre leightes for either wyndowe on the backsyde, with suffycyent tables over every of the said wyndowes suffycyently and well wrought, and to be of three foote heighe of cleare leight, and fiftene inches in breadth; all the walles of the same storye to be perfectly walled according to the length and breadth of the same plott, and to conteyne in breadth three foote and about three yeardes in height to the first flower; also one payre of stone stares to the height of the hall flower, and one payre of round stares to the lowe roome at the east end of the court; and to build and bringe upp the porch with hewen stone and fower pillers to the height of the first storie.

The second story the walles thereof to be two foote and a halfe in thickness with the porch of hewen stone; and a window of nyne leightes transomd, and fower more with fower leightes wyndowes transomd, with tables over the same; also fyve windowes of thre leightes transomd, and two of two leightes untransomed, three foote in height, all of these to be likewise tabled; alsoe thre hewen stone chimnes, two hewen stone doores in the same storye. The wall of the thirde story to be two foote in thickness to the full height of the wall of the ould house whereon yt must adjoyne with the hewen porch, and a windowe of nyne leightes untransomed and

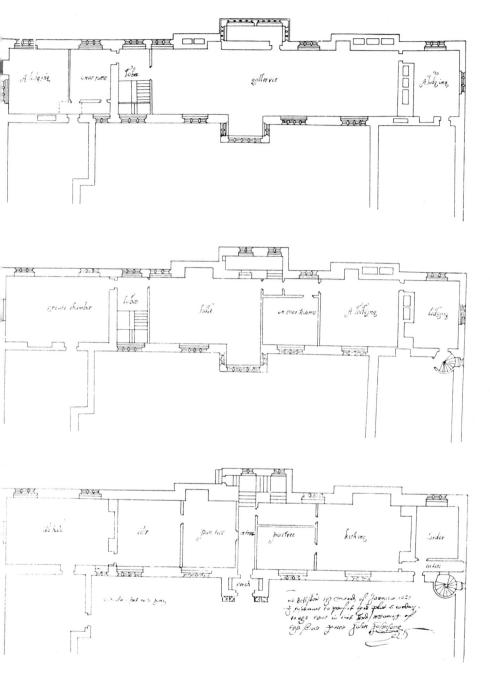

Dilston Hall

thre fote of cleare leighte; also fower leightes untransomd of the same height and on the foresyde, and fyve three leight wyndowes on the backsyde, and of the same height with all their tables, thre chimnes of hewen stone in the same storye; alsoe a batlement of stone called vent and creaste over the porch and turrett of the same story, together with sufficyent fynnells for the corners of the same house. And that all the walls of the same house be well wrought with lyme well tempered with sand, and all thinges necessary for the same.

In consideracion wherof the said Edward Racliffe doth . . . conveante . . . that he the said Edward Radcliffe . . . shall at th' end of every moneth next after the begynnynge of the said recyted worke by the said John Johnson as aforesaid until the said fesate of St. Michael th' arkangell next, well and trewlie content and pay . . unto the said John Johnson . . . twentie pounds . . . or more or lesse, at the seight of indeferent persons, ratable, as the said John Johnson . . . shall have deserved the same in forwardnes in performinge of his said bargaine . . . untill the sume of two hundred and fyve pounds be paid. And yf any parte of the said sume of two hundred and fyve pounds shalbe behinde and unpaid at the said feast of St. Michael th' arkangell next, then the said Edward or his assignes shall well and trewlie pay . . . the remainder . . . at the finishinge and final endinge of all the covenantes before specyfied on the partie of the said John Johnson to be performed. And likewise grauteth hearby full licence and authorytie for the said John Johnson . . . to digg' sincke, and wynn quarries of stone, and to hewe and dresse the same upon or in any parte or parcell of his parke at Devilstone . . . and . . . to lead and carry the same the most conveniente waye and waies . . . for the finishing and buildinge of the said newe house. And that the said Edward Radcliffe . . . shall bringe unto the said newe worke . . . sufficyent tymber and fleakes for scaffoldinge in and about the said workes, and cause such suffycyent number and quantitie of coles to be carried and conveyed unto such kills as the said John Johnson or his assignes shall build for burninge of lyme to erecte the said new house as the said John Johnson shall buy and pay for Whittingstall pittes and mynes; and shall find and allowe unto him the said John suffycyent wood for him the said John Johnson to burne in and about the said lyme kylls . . . at all tymes duringe the continuance of the buildinge of the said newe house.

We know little of John Johnston the designer of Jacobean Dilston but he may have been a northern builder of some importance. We know so little about the local builders of the seventeenth century. In 1620 or 1621 John Johnson "surveyor" headed a group of men who reported on the state of the Castle at Newcastle.

It is a great pity that we have no drawing of this Jacobean mansion and nothing of the work has survived. We have only one description that Celia Fieunes who, about 1700, merely describes it as "an old building, not very large". When, in 1710, the third Earl of Derwentwater paid his first visit to Dilston he decided to replace the Elizabethan-Jacobean house with a new building which was only partly complete when he took up residence in 1714. Wartburton, a well known antiquary, described it as "a spacious, beauteous and commodious structure, and ye additional parts, if well consider'd, ye most finish'd building in these parts". However an engraving published in 1766 ("A Perspective View of Dilston Hall and the Seat of the unfortunate James, Earl of Derwentwater." Drawn by T. Oliver, engraved by Spilsbury) shows the new Derwentwater mansion was not an architectural masterpiece but more like a large barracks. The gardens were large and beautiful.

In 1731 the Derwentwater estates came into the possession of Greenwich Hospital. They showed little interest in the house and let it fall into disrepair. It was demolished in 1765 and the stone was used for a number of buildings in Corbridge.

Dilston Hall.

Drawn on the Spot by Thos Oliver of Hexham in Northumberland & pub-d according to Act P. July 17 1766. Reduced from original, print to ½ size.

135

136

DILSTON BRIDGES

Beside Dilston Mill a narrow fourteenth century bridge crossed the Devil's Water. Hodgson says it once had ribbed arches, but the picture by Carmichael, drawn between 1820 and 1829, shows it to have then been a wooden bridge on plain piers. The engraving is shown below.

A short distance upstream is a private bridge leading to Dilston Hall and probably built in 1621. Its segmental arch is 50 feet wide with double arch-rings. An engraving of it by E. Swinburne is shown on the opposite page.

DOTLAND

The County History (Vol. 4. 1897) describes it as "a well-built, grey-slated homestead, with a house built more squarely than is usual in the district, and is sheltered on the west by a plantation of ash and sycamore. It stands between the seven and eight hundred feet contour-line, forms a prominent feature in the landscape, and from its elevation commands a view on the north as far as the Cheviot hills."

A Hexhamshire rhyme tells us:-

> *Dowly Dotland stands on the hill*
> *Hungry Yareesh (Yarridge) looks at it still:*
> *Barker's House a little below,*
> *There's mokes i' the cairn at Hamburn Ho:*

"Dowly" means lonely when applied to a country house. "It's a *dowly* pleyce i' the winter time." (Heslop).

DOTLAND PARK

Dotland Park was probably a hunting lodge of the Prior of Hexham. It appears to have been built some time after 1355 when the Archbishop gave the canons permission to enclose their land there with a high wall. All that survives are three windows in a farmhouse. They are all blocked up and one can only be seen on the inside. The latter is a two light window with the arms of Prior Smithson of Hexham (1491-1524) in the spandrels.

DUKES HOUSE

Lies one mile south east of Hexham in a well wooded park. It was built about 1873 by Edward Backhouse of Sunderland a member of the well known Quaker banking family. The name arises from the fact that the woods were once owned by the Duke of Portland. This wood was the scene of the encounter between Thomas Spence (1750-1814) the radical reformer and the Duke of Portland's gamekeeper. Here is Spence's account of the episode:-

138

"While Spence continued to reside in the pleasant valley of the Tyne, a "sylvan joke" (as he describes it) occurred, very characteristic of his peculiar vein. Being alone in the wood, gathering nuts. "the forester popped through the bushes upon him, and asked what he did there." "Gathering nuts," was his reply. And "Dare you say so?" was the rejoinder. "Yes; why not? Would you question a monkey, or a squirrel, about such a business? And am I to be treated as inferior to one of these creatures? Or have I a less right? But who are you that thus take upon you to interupt me?" The schoolmaster's questioner said he would let him know that,when he laid him fast for trespassing."Indeed!" ejaculated Spence; "but how can I trespass here, where no man ever planted or cultivated; for these nuts are the spontaneous gifts of nature ordained alike for the sustenance of man or beast that chooses to gather them; and therefore they are common". This was doctrine which the wondering woodman could not understand. The wood, he said, was *not* common: it was the Duke of Portland's. "Oh! my service to the Duke of Portland: Nature knows no more of him than of me. Therefore, as in nature's storehouse the rule is "First come, first served," so the Duke of Portland must look sharp if he wants any nuts."

DUKESFIELD HALL

At Dukesfield, three miles west of Slaley, are the remains of the Dukesfield Smelt-mills. Here at the beginning of the 19th century the lead from Mr. Beaumont's mines in Allendale was smelted. They were laid in about 1834. Nearby still stands the old mansion house called Dukesfield Hall, probably the home of the manager of the smelt mill. It is three storeys high and white-washed. An advert in the Newcastle Courant of December 5th, 1807, tells us that there were on the ground floor "two good sitting rooms in front, a back kitchen, dairy and pantry with an excellent cellar underneath, five lodging rooms on the first floor, each conveniently communicating with a roomy landing-place and staircase. The yard contains a stable for five horses . . . ."

ELISHAW BRIDGE

Two miles past Otterburn on the road to Carter Bar is the farm of Elishaw. Once there was an important village here and a hospital which provided accomodation for travellers crossing the wilds of Redesdale. It provided the same function as an inn. The name Elishaw is derived from the name of its founder one *Illa*. The expression *he'll be left on the haughs anunder 'lishaw if he dissn't hurry on* refers to the fact that the Rede usually deposits here all the floating rubbish it brings down after a flood. Another local proverb, *the lang gaunts o' Elishaw were heard 'm't coans o' Blakelaw* probably originates in some forgotten feud between the people of Elishaw and Blakelaw nearby but is used in derision of lover's sighs.

Elishaw was once a favourite resort of gypsies and Jamie Allan, the Northumbrian Piper, often played at the merry gatherings held here.

ELTRINGHAM

Eltringham (a Scandinavian word meaning the "village of Haltor's people"), lies on the south bank of the Tyne. It is famous as the birth place of Thomas Bewick who was born at the farm of Cherryburn in 1753. Writing in 1884 Austin Dobson describes the place:-

"The old cottage now only exists in part, and that part fulfils the homely office of a "byre" or cowshed, over one door of which is the inscription—'Thomas Bewick born here, August 1753.' In the vicinity of this now rises a larger dwelling, still inhabited by Bewick's grand-nieces. What remains of the older house formed the central portion of the building shown in John Bewick's sketch of 1781, printed as a frontispiece to the 'Memoir'. Beyond the fact that the 'byre' is still thatched with ling or heath, and was tenanted, when the writer visited it, by a couple of calm-eyed, comfortable-looking cows, there is nothing about it that calls for especial remark. But the little dene or orchard at the back is still filled with cherry and plum trees, and violets and primroses bloom as of yore beside the now dry bed of the once musical burn which gave the place its name. In Bewick's day there was in this orchard a spring-well under a hawthorn bush, the site of which may yet be traced; while a precipitous little garden to the north pre-sumably remains much as it used to be. From the slope on which the house stands you may look towards the Tyne, still crossed by boat-ferries at Eltringham and Ovingham. Behind you lies Mickley, and away to the left and south formerly stretched the great fell or common, comprising, until it was divided in 1812, some eighteen hundred acres of blossoming 'whins' and scented heather, and fine pasturage, watered

CHERRYBURN HOUSE.

FROM THE ENGRAVING BY JOHN BEWICK.

THOMAS BEWICK
(*From a portrait by James Ramsay*)

Thomas Bewick, Tailpieces

by trickling streams. Over the hill to the right are Prudhoe and Wylam; and across the river, also to the right, rises the square romanesque tower of Ovingham Church, where Bewick and his brother John lie buried, and in the parsonage of which – a pretty old-fashioned stone house with shelving garden terraces – they went successively to school. A railway now comes winding from Newcastle through the Prudhoe meadows, and an embankment runs along the Tyne to Eltringham. But, in spite of these drawbacks, and the smoky activity of brickworks and collieries hard by, it is not impossible, on a fresh May morning, with a blue shower-washed sky overhead, and the young green triumphing in the shaws and braes, to realise something of the landscape as it must have looked more than a hundred years ago, when Thomas Bewick first saw the light."

Thomas Bewick was the son of a small farmer and received an elementary education in the parsonage of Ovingham nearby. He early showed signs of artistic talent and so was apprenticed to a Newcastle engraver. Later, after a short period in London, he entered into partnership with his former master, Ralph Beilby.

The works on which his reputation mainly rests – his *History of Quadrupeds* (1790) and *History of British Birds* (1797) were completed in his spare time after his arduous day's work as a jobbing engraver. Bewick's success in reviving the wood engraving as a work of art led to a great increase in book illustration and an improvement in quality. His own books were perfect examples of the happy marriage between letterpress and pictures. His "tailpieces" embellished the work without being artificial.

Bewick was a realist. He depicted life as it was. His birds and animals he engraved in their natural background.

The men and women of Tyneside, whom he knew so intimately, he presents with realism and sympathy. Often critical, but in a good-humoured way, he presents a detailed picture of the daily life of the common people.

In politics Bewick was a Left Wing Whig or a Radical. His religious views were outspokenly non-sectarian. Although they seem mild enough today, they shocked his contemporaries, who tried to have them omitted from his autobiography. On most social issues he was consistently progressive.

After his death his *Memoirs* were published in 1862. Although the first edition was "censored" by his daughter, because she objected to her father's progressive political and religious views, the *Memoir* is one of the most interesting and valuable of our north country books. It gives us an insight into the character and beliefs of Tyneside's greatest artist and presents a vivid picture of the times in which he lived.

Although Bewick has suffered grievously from the "bibliophiles" and "collectors" his work is becoming more and more appreciated by ordinary folk for whom his books were created.

The mansion house here contained some panelling brought from Dilston Hall. Fallowfield however is famous today because of the *Written Rock*.

On the moors above the hamlet is a large ridge of sandstone on which is the celebrated "written rock" carrying in deeply chiselled letters the inscription PETRA FLAVI (I) CARANTINI. It is thought that Flavius Carantinus may have been the foreman of the gang who were quarrying stones here for the Roman Wall.

FALSTONE

FALSTONE

The name of this small village is derived from *Fallaw-stone* meaning dull-coloured yellow. Here was discovered a fragment of a Runic cross bearing an Anglo-Saxon inscription, the oldest post-Roman inscribed stone found in Northumberland. The words are

usually translated as "Eomaer set this up for his uncle Hroethberht. Pray for his soul". It has been suggested that Hroethberht is the Robert of our day and that his descendants would be called Robertsons or Robsons which is the chief name around Falstone. A romantic suggestion which cannot be taken seriously. The Robsons of Tynedale were a famous border clan who were often at feud with the Grahams or Graemes and Armstrongs of Liddesdale. There is a North Tynedale tradition that the Robsons once made a foray into Liddesdale, to harry the Grahams, and drove off a flock of their sheep down into the North Tyne. Unfortunately the sheep proved to be scabbed, and communicated the disease to the other sheep of the Robsons. Upon this the latter made a second raid into Liddesdale, and took seven of the most substantial of the Graemes they could lay their hands upon, and hanged them forthwith, with the warning that "the neist tyme gentlemen cam to tak their schepe they war not to be scabbit". Scotchmen are proverbially slow to see a joke, and it is scarcely likely they would appreciate, under the circumstances, the grim humour of a remark like this.

Tombstone, Falstone.

147

The tower of Falstone has now disappeared and of the three peles in the neighbourhood only a fragment of one has been incorporated into Falstone Farm south of the church. The lintel of the entrance bears the date 1604 and the letters of the alphabet, and the ground floor is vaulted.

Falstone Farm   Inscription on doorhead.

FEATHERSTONE CASTLE

Three miles south-west of Haltwhistle, in a secluded vale near the confluence of the Hartley burn and the South Tyne, stands Featherstone Castle, a handsome castellated mansion, which has for its nucleus an old square pele tower. It has been described by C. J. Bates as "perhaps the loveliest tower in the county with its corner bartisans and carved corbels".

The first recorded owner of the manor of Featherstone was Helias de Featherstonehaugh who was residing here before 1212. The manor was at that time part of the barony of Langley which was then under Scottish rule. We do not know when the original castle was built but the

Featherstone Castle   Print 1778

Featherstone Castle

Old Print c 1860

pointed doorway, here illustrated, and dated not later than 1200, is clearly part of the original building. It is in the main building north of the tower. Nearby is a thirteenth century buttress. About 1330 Thomas de Featherstonehaugh, a man of great power, who was guardian of Hexham, Wark and the barony of Tindale, erected a strong tower at the south-west corner of the range of buildings already existing. The tower is "L" shaped and of three stages marked by sloping set-offs surmounted by a five battlement with four corbelled bartisans. The battlement is very high with an embrasure over each angle. The merlons on two sides are decorated with a pierced quatrefoil. The basement is vaulted in two spans.

Featherstone Castle

13th Century Doorway

17th Century Doorway

Probably in the reign of James I the south and east faces of the tower were constructed again as well as the range of thirteenth century buildings to the north, in the Jacobean style. The west doorway with its flat ogee and square hood moulding is from this period. The last period of building was carried out by the Hon. Thomas Wallace (circa 1828) who added three more towers, an office wing and a long garden wall. The dining room, known as the Blue Room, was reconstructed. It has a fine timbered roof with heraldry and some beautiful fifteenth century woodwork taken from the choir of Carlisle Cathedral. The new buildings were carefully blended with the old in an harmonious combination.

There is a famous poem associated with Featherstone. The ballad, by R. S. Surtees, commemorates the death of Sir Albany Featherstone-haugh in a border feud in 1530. Here are the words:-

"Hoot awa', lads, hoot awa',
Ha' ye heard how the Ridleys, and Thirlwalls, and a'
Ha' set upon Albany Featherstonhaugh,
And taken his life at the Deadmanshaw?
    There was Willemoteswick,
    And Hardriding Dick,
And Hughie of Hawden, and Will of the Wa',
I canno' tell a', I canno' tell a',
And mony a mair that the de'il may knaw.

The auld men went down, but Nicol his son
Ran away afore the fight was begun;
    And he run, and he run,

Featherstone Castle, Tower from South-east

151

top, which was called the Fairy-trough, and traditionally said to have had a pillar fixed in it." The tradition that the *Fairy-stone* was used as a secret post office by the Earl of Derwentwater, when planning the Revolt of 1715, is called "silly" by Hodgson. Countless "silly" stories of a similar kind are told about the unfortunate Earl who, in spite of the legends built around his name, was a rather foolish creature.

Hodgson (1840) has the following interesting description: "Fourstones, a grey village, fronting the south, under the brow of a whinny hill, scarred with a long sandstone quarry, seems to sit darkling in the sun under a load of grey slate, sad and dour as an incubus, but is really a cheerful spot, and enjoys a delightful prospect over the rich and beautiful valley of the South Tyne."

GATEHOUSE

This lonely hamlet possesses two ancient Castle-houses, one on each side of the road and at right angles to one another. Nothing is known of their history but they are probably late sixteenth century buildings. They are both oblong with entrances on the ground floor and one on the upper floor entered by an outer staircase.

Our illustration shows the north house which is the best preserved.

Gatehouse

GREATCHESTERS (AESICA)

The fort of Greatchesters is six miles west of Housesteads. The first printed account was by Robert Smith, in 1708, who wrote:

"At a place called the *Chesters,* two miles East of *Caer-Vorran,* are the ruins of another square City, much about the compass of the above-mentioned *Caer-*

154

vorran; where are likewise abundance of old Housesteads, and tracks of houses, to be discerned, as there are likewise on the south side Vallum of it".

The fort lies south of the wall and is small of only three acres. Its purpose was to guard the Caw Gap (The Caw burn being the name given to Haltwhistle burn at this spot.) It is approached by the farm road which leaves the Newcastle-Carlisle road just west of Haltwhistle Burn. The fort is completely behind the wall and longer from east to west. Farm buildings occupy the east corner of the fort but the farmhouse is outside. The third century garrison was the Second Cohort of Astures with a detachment of Raeti Gaesati. Today the fort is in a state of extreme neglect.

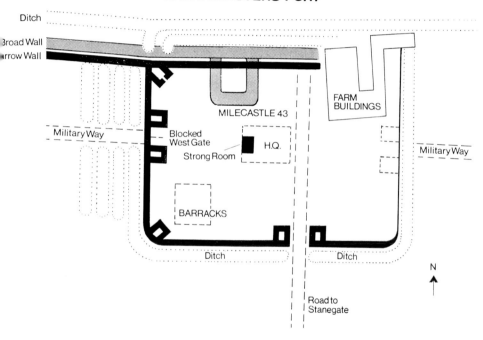

GREATCHESTERS FORT

In 1724 a visitor reported the fort-wall as still standing to a height of nearly 13 feet. All the west wall can still be traced, including the gateway. Originally a double portal it was altered several times, narrowed and finally closed. The south wall and ditch are almost complete. The west tower of the south gate provided a hoard of jewellery including the famous *Aesica Fibula*. It is a Celtic-Romano gilt bronze brooch of the late second century. It has been described: "Of its kind it is probably the most fantastically beautiful creation that has come down to us from antiquity."

155

Our illustration is the size of the original.

PRAETORIUS

The north west angle of the fort is of great interest. Here the north wall broad foundation can be traced and on it was milecastle 43 with its gateway through the Wall. This was all planned before the fort was built. Then a decision was taken to bring the fort on to the line of the Wall. First four ditches were built on the west side. When the time came to complete the Wall which was to be narrow it couldn't be built on the broad wall foundations because the milecastle obstructed this work. So the narrow wall was built a little south of the broad wall foundations slightly covering the north side of the four ditches. The milecastle would then be demolished later.

The headquarters building was excavated in 1893 and its vaulted underground strong room can still be seen. A barrack block was also uncovered. The east gateway – the main entrance to the fort – cannot now be traced, neither can the east wall. A building inscription of Hadrian was found at this gateway.

The military way entered the fort by the east gate and left by the west. A branch road from the Stanegate (now the farm road) comes in by the south gate.

The vicus lay to the south and east of the fort and 100 yards south of the fort and east of the farm road was the bath house.

Dr. John Lingard (1771-1851) writing in 1807 was the first to notice the remarkable aqueduct to be found here. He mentioned that the "water for the station was brought by a winding aqueduct still visible from the head of Haltwhistle burn. It winds five miles". The aqueduct is actually six miles long but because it was necessary to

IMP. CÆS. M. AVR. SEVE
RVS ALEXANDER PI[VS] F[ELIX]
AVG. HORREVM VETV-
STATE CONLABSVM M[ILITES]
COH. II. ASTVRVM S[EVERIANÆ]
A[LEXANDRIANÆ][1]
A SOLO RESTITVERVNT

. . . . .

The Emperor Cæsar Marcus Aurelius Severus Alexander pious happy[2] august. This granary through age dilapidated the soldiers of the second cohort of Asturians styled the [Severian Alexandrian from the ground restored

. . . . .

Size, 4 feet 1 inch by 3 feet 4 inches.

Inscription found in 1767 *at Aesica*

157

wind in order to keep the water flow the direct line is just a little over two miles. Only one bridge was necessary and although it has now gone its site is called *Banks Bridge* today. The aqueduct is marked on the Ordnance Survey.

A short distance to the west of Greatchesters is a fine stretch of the Wall on Cockmount Hill, here shown.

Lithograph from Bruce's Roman Wall, 1867

GREENHEAD

It lies by the Tipalt Burn on the main Newcastle Carlisle road. The church is by Dobson (1826-8) with a chancel added in 1900. Across the bridge is the village of GLENWHELT. The fine farmhouse was formerly an inn of considerable importance in the old coaching days. The fine classical doorway bears a dial with the face of a flaming sun, and above is the date 1757. Close to Greenhead is the water shed of northern England. The Tipalt which flows east and the Irthing which belongs to the western water-shed approach within two miles of each other.

GREYSTEAD

Here is another one of Seward's churches built in 1818 for the Commissioners of Greenwich Hospital. We quote Archdeacon Singleton's account of the parish (1832).

"This is the poorest and most secluded of all the new rectories. The house and church are on the same plan with those of Thornyburn and Wark, but the smartness of the place is gone, as the Rev. Mr. Rennell the rector is in confinement as a lunatic at Newcastle and Mr. Stubbs the curate, a respectable non-graduate, has no means of keeping up the neatness of the walks and fences and shrubberies. Mr. Rennell as far as I can learn was an orderly and temperate man, which Mr. Burdon a fellow sufferer from the neighbouring living certainly was not, but still I almost suspect that the contrast from the din and bustle of the ward-room and cock-pit school of a man of war to the stillness and solitude of these moorland benefices is too great for those who do not seek refuge in literature of some sort or another.

The value of the living is £130 from tithe, the house and garden, 1½ acres of land near the house, including the churchyard, and

face the south-east, so as to catch the early morning sun. In most of these huts a portion of the space has been partitioned off, to form an inner chamber or recess. That the tastes of these rude oborigines was being influenced by the proximity of their Roman conquerors is shown in the relics which have been found in the huts, such as an iron armlet, iron ring, harp-shaped brooch of bronze, iron nails, and fragments of Roman pottery. Traces of terrace culture may be seen about two-thirds of the way down the south-fronting declivity of the crag. Fifteen yards from the entrance gateway an interesting discovery was made of an earth-oven. This was a stone-lined circular pit, having charcoal and ashes at the bottom, and bearing marks of the long-continued action of fire. This was the cooking and feasting place of the camp, and a mound close to had evidently been the kitchen-midden, as bones of animals in great number and variety were found in it. In the case of a successful attack of the camp by an enemy, on the only assailable side, the vanquished would be driven over the tremendous precipice, and to judge from the number of human remains found amongst the crag-talus, such a disastrous occurrence has indeed taken place. Quarrying operations have made great changes here.

One mile north of Gunnarton Nick is the hamlet with the curious name of *Pity Me*, derived, it is suggested, from the British Beddau Maes, "field of graves". Here is an entrenched fort below the "Camp-hill".

HALLINGTON

The small village of Hallington may once have been of some importance. Leland tells us "there is a fame that Oswald won the batelle at Halydene a two myles est from St. Oswald's Asche, and that Haliden is it that Bede caulith Havenfeld". Hallington Hall is first mentioned in 1769 by Wallis the historian. He describes Ralph Soulsby's house as "a neat modern structure of white freestone . . . . before it is a grass area extending to the brink of a deep gill, wherein is a small stream which falls a little below into Erring burn". Nearby is Cheviot farm where a cluster of prehistoric barrows can be seen. A mile and a half to the east is a hill called Moot Law which has a square entrenchment on the top with a hearthstone in the centre. This is often described as a signal station, but it is more likely to have prehistoric origins. The outstanding feature however is Hallington reservoir belonging to the Newcastle and Gateshead Water Company, covering 142 acres with an average depth of 18 feet (Act of Parliament for its construction obtained in 1868). This reservoir is connected by a tunnel and open aqueduct of about $2\frac{1}{2}$ miles length with two smaller reservoirs to the north east called Colt Crag and Little Swinburn. A great variety of birds frequent the reservoirs and a number breed here especially on the island in the middle of East Hallington reservoir.

Halton Tower

HALTON TOWER

The quiet hamlet of Halton has a castle, an old church and a Roman fort. Halton Tower is of fourteenth century date. It is four storeys in height (including the basement). In the fifteenth century a manor house was erected on the north side of the tower, and in the seventeenth century a Jacobean house was built on the east side.

Halton Tower is built of Roman stones and measures 31 by 24 feet on the exterior. The battlements are first class and genuine. There are circular bartizans on the corner like those of Chipchase. Entrance is in the south west corner, through the manor house, by the original door, set in a pointed arch bearing on its jambs the marks of strong bolts and bars. Three feet inside a second door leads into the great vault with its cylindrical stone roof. Crossing this chamber we ascend by a newel staircase to the Tower Room. It is well lighted and has two curious trefoil-headed walled recesses. The second and third floors are now one.

A curious inventory of the goods of Lancelot Carnaby of Halton who died in 1624 has been preserved. In Mr. Carnaby's bedroom were "one low bed with a cannibye, one mattresse and a feather bed, a paire of blanketts, one coverlett, one greene rug and a Courting belonging to the cannibye, two boulsters, one cubbert and a long sattle bed".

163

HALTON CASTLE

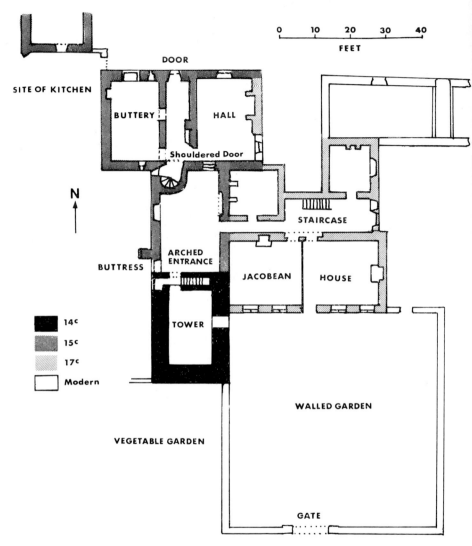

In the Great Chamber were "one long table with a frame; thre leverye cubberts with a pare of virginalls; a dozen and a halfe of buffet stooles; halfe a score of cushins with thre long cushins for the windowes: a long carpet cloath with two cubbert cloaths: a cubbert cloath of wrought nedle worke with two low stooles: one blacke chayer: one turkye cubbert cloath".

Halton Castle is surrounded by beautiful gardens and the three buildings stand in a very pleasant situation unlike so many border holds.

164

Halton Castle by F. C. Lewis, 1835

The fifteenth century manor house was built on the north side of the tower the whole building forming the letter T. Entrance was on the north giving access to a wide passage from which the buttery and kitchen was entered on the right. On the left a "shouldered" door led to the hall which was reduced in size in the seventeenth century. This hall today still has fine ceiling beams. An arch opposite the entrance leads to a newel staircase which allowed entrance to the second floor. When the Jacobean house was built the fifteenth century manor house was allowed to become a ruin and later was reduced in size and slightly altered.

The seventeenth century house had a southern frontage and was of two storeys and five bays. A central doorway with a curly open pediment gives access to one of the two main rooms which have cross-windows. Behind these two rooms is a staircase and several other apartments. The walled garden in front has two large rusticated gate-posts with moulded capitals crowned by elaborate vases. In the garden is a fine sundial with the initials J.D.—A.D. and the arms of Douglas impaling those of Hutchinson. Since John Douglas bought the Halton estate in 1695 it is safe to assume that he built the Jacobean house and made other alterations. The drive to Halton Castle from the Military road is entered through interesting gate posts.

John Douglas bought Halton for £4,000 when John Carnaby was in financial distress. His granddaughter Anne carried the estate by marriage to Mr. (afterwards Sir) Edward Blackett in 1751 and the estate today belongs to the same family. Early in the nineteenth century

TO SIR WILLIAM BLACKETT BART:
THIS SPECIMEN of an IMPROVED BREED of CATTLE is RESPECTFULLY INSCRIBED by HIS HUMBLE SERVANT Thomas Bates

Thomas Bates (born 1775) a famous shorthorn breeder lived at Halton Castle. Our illustration shows one of his cattle with Halton Castle and church in the background. The print is dated Feb. 20th 1808 artist S. Wilson of Newcastle. Thomas Bates resided from 1821 to 1830 at Ridley Hall and died in 1849 at Kirklevington in Yorkshire.

HALTONCHESTERS FORT

The Roman fort near Halton is called Haltonchesters (in Roman times ONNO). It covers five acres and is divided in two by the modern road. It was garrisoned by a cavalry regiment called the Ala Sabiniana. From Corstopitum it is distant about two and a half miles. It guards Watling Street which traverses the valley immediately beneath it. A portion of a monumental slab, now at Trinity College, Cambridge refers to the fort. It was built between 122 A.D. and 126 A.D. At a later date an extension was built on to the south west side giving the fort an unusual L plan.

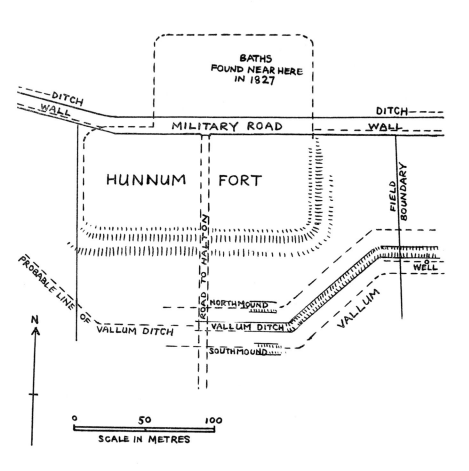

BATHS
FOUND NEAR HERE
IN 1827

---DITCH---
---WALL---

DITCH----
WALL----

MILITARY ROAD

HUNNUM FORT

FIELD BOUNDARY

WELL

PROBABLE LINE OF VALLUM DITCH

ROAD TO HALTON

NORTHMOUND

VALLUM DITCH

VALLUM DITCH

VALLUM

SOUTHMOUND

N

0   50   100
SCALE IN METRES

Size, 1 foot 9 inches by 1 foot 3 inches.

. . . . .

S NORICI AN. XXX.
[M] ESSORIVS MAGNVS
FRATER EIVS DVPL. ALAE
SABINIANAE.

[To the Divine Manes]
of Noricus, 30 years of age,
Messorius Magnus
his brother a duplarius of the
Sabinian wing [placed this].

167

When in 1827 the field north of the road (called the "Brunt-ha-penny" field) was first ploughed a fine bath house was discovered belonging to the late fourth century. Large internal bath-houses are rare in the Wall forts. In the south part of Hunnum (called Silverhill, probably from the discovery of Roman silver coins) an elaborate slab in Antonine style was discovered. It is here reproduced.

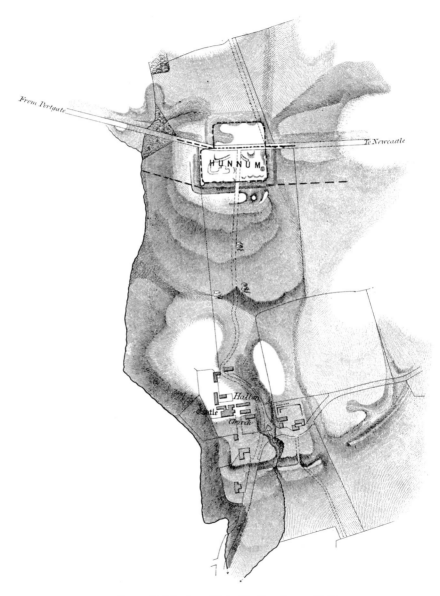

From H. MacLauchlin's Watling Street, 1857.

LEG[IO]
SECVNDA
AVG[VSTA]
F[ECIT]

Legion
the second
the august
executed
this work.

HALTWHISTLE

Haltwhistle is a pleasant market town whose centre is almost untouched by ugly modern development. Although there are no secular buildings of outstanding merit the main street is an harmonious grouping of simple northern buildings. The town has had a turbulant though unimportant history of which few records have survived. In 1311 when Robert Brus, the King of Scotland invaded Northumberland his followers carried off the vicar of Haltwhistle, called Robert de Pykwell. A letter from the bishop of Durham gave him permission to farm out "the fruits, rents, offerings and profits" of his vicarage for one year in order to raise the necessary ransom. In the following year when King Edward asked the bishop to collect the £10 10s. 6d for which the vicar was assessed he was told "the goods of the vicar of Haltwhistle are not to be found, because they are destroyed by the Scots."

The church of the Holy Cross is one of the best in Northumberland and is noteworthy because it has no tower. It is an early English parish church erected about 1250. It consists of a nave with two aisles and a chancel. All the windows in the church are lancets, the finest being the eastern triplet in the chancel. Here also are three sedilia-priest's seats – each with a trefoil head, and three black oak armchairs of the seventeenth century, two of them with panelled backs showing bearded smiling men.

In the church are three fine medieval gravestones of about the year 1350. Two belong to the Thirlwall family but the best is of a Blenkinsop. It has a floreated cross and sword and the family arms together with a staff and a bag indicating that he had once gone on a pilgrimage.

Fixed to the south wall of the chancel is a stone slab which bears a long rhyming inscription. It commemorates John Ridley, "lord of

169

Above:
Part of the pele tower built into Red Lion Hotel Haltwhistle.

Left:
Some carved stone worked into the pele tower.

172

For he cam riding o'er the brae,
As gin he could na steal a cow;
And when we'd got our gear awa'
Says – "Wha this day's work will avow?"
I wot he got reply enow.
As ken the Armstrongs to their grief.
For to tine the gear and Simmy too,
The ane to the tither's nae relief.

Then cam Wat Armstong to the town,
Wi' some three hundred chiels or mair,
An' swore that they wad burn it down;
A' clad in jack, wi' bow and spear,
Harnessed right weel, I trow they were;
But we were aye prepared at need,
And dropt ere lang upon the rear
Amangst them, like an angry gleed.†

Then Alec Ridley he let flee
A clothyard shaft, ahint the wa';
It struck Wat Armstrong in the ee'
Went through his steel cap, heid and a'.
I wot it made him quickly fa',
He could na rise, though he essayed;
The best at thief-craft or the ba'‡
He ne'er again shall ride a raid.

Gin should the Armstrongs promise keep
And seek our gear to do us wrang;
Or rob us of our kye or sheep,
I trow but some o' them will hang;
Sharp is the sturdy sleuth dog's fang,
At Craweragge watchers will be set,
At Lingthaugh ford too, a' neet lang,
Wow! but the meeting will be het.

*Belly   †Kite   ‡Football

Haltwhistle Bridge

"We proceed towards Haltwezell, in hopes to pass the river by
the ferry-boat; but the boatman, who thinks himself a competent
judge of the necessity there is for his attendance, was not to be found;
and we were obliged to pass the ford, which is broad and deep, with
a bottom of very large stones, over which a horse, breast deep in the
water, unaccustomed to the passage, incessantly faulters or stumbles.
These circumstances would have been greatly aggravated by our
ignorance of the place, had we not met with a person to conduct us.
Instances of well applied charity characterize this age: it would not be
one of the least, to give a stipend to an attendant at such fords as these,
by which many valuable lives would be saved, Is it not shocking, that
a traveller should be exposed to infinite perils, by the stupidity or folly
of a boatman, who presumes to determine on a matter of such moment,
as the fate of his fellow creature! A wretch whose character, perhaps,
is one of those humiliating subjects, which serve to reduce self-estimation
and human vanity, by showing how near man in the lowest class is to
the brute creation."

With these strong remarks W. Hutchinson describes his difficulty about the year 1776 to cross the Tyne. A wooden bridge replaced the ferry in 1826, at a cost of £700, with five spans of 60 feet each.

A concrete bridge now crosses the Haltwhistle Burn at the eastern end of the village.

Not many people have written about Haltwhistle but Celia Fiennes stayed here one night in 1698. She wrote:-

This Hartwhistle is a little town; there was one Inn but they had noe hay nor would get none, and when my servants had got some elsewhere they were angry and would not entertaine me, so I was forced to take up in a poor cottage which was open to the thatch and no partitions but hurdles plaister'd; indeed the loft as they called it, which was over the other roome was shelter'd but with a hurdle; here I was forced to take up my abode and the Landlady brought me out her best sheetes which serv'd to secure my own sheetes from her dirty blankets, and indeed I had her fine sheete with hook seams to spread over the top of the clothes, but noe sleepe could I get, they burning turff and their chimneys are sort of flews or open tunnills that the smoake does annoy the roomes. This is but 12 miles from another part of Scotland, the houses are but a little better built – its true the inside of them are kept a little better.

An anonymous writer in 1769 writes:-

"Haltwesel: a manufacture of coarse bays has been lately established here, to the great advantage of the labouring poor".

The Manor House Hotel, opposite the Red Lion, was originally the Griffin Inn and before that the home of the lord of the manor.

Railways of the Haltwhistle area

The area around Haltwhistle was rich in minerals, particularly coal and lead. Their successful exploitation needed transport on a big scale which only the railways could supply. The earliest railway in the area was Lord Carlisle's early-nineteenth century waggonway which conveyed coals from the coalmines on Denton Fell (locally known as "Coal Fell") and Hartleyburn Common. It linked up the collieries of Lambley, Midgeholme and Roachburn with Brampton. It was a remarkable work for its time and sections were still in use during this century. It can still be traced.

The lead mining districts of Allendale and Alston needed an outlet and in 1846 an Act was passed to build a railway from Haltwhistle to Alston. The first section from Haltwhistle to Shafthill (4½ miles) was opened for passengers on 19th July 1851. The next 8½ mile section (Alston to Lambley) was opened six months later. The magnificent Lambley Viaduct shortly afterwards joined the two sections together. The original plan envisaged continuing the line from Alston to Nenthead but this section was abandoned. The lead mines in the

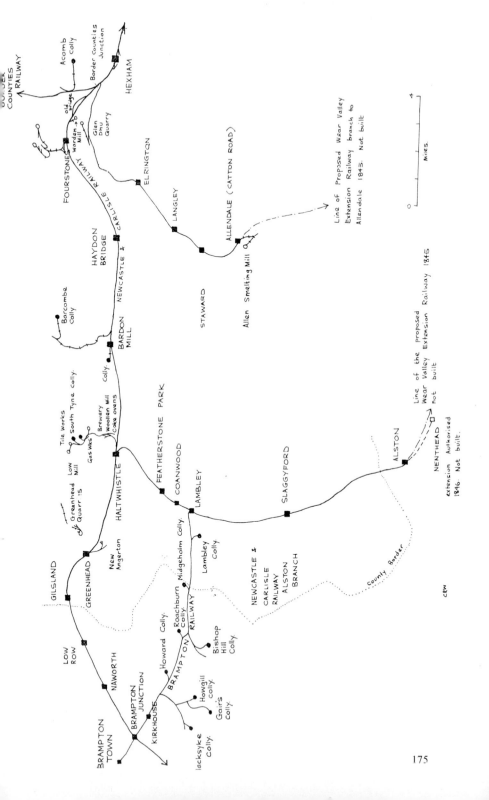

BORDER COUNTIES RAILWAY

Acomb Colly

Border Counties Junction

HEXHAM

old bridge

Warden Mill

Glen Dhu Quarry

FOURSTONES

HAYDON BRIDGE

ELRINGTON

LANGLEY

ALLENDALE (CATTON ROAD)

STAWARD

Allen Smelting Mill

Line of Proposed Wear Valley Extension Railway branch to Allendale 1845. Not built.

Miles.

Barcombe Colly

BARDON MILL

Colly.

Tile Works

South Tyne Colly.

Gas Wks

Brewary

Woollen Mill

Coke ovens

Greenhead Quarr.s

Low Mill

HALTWHISTLE

FEATHERSTONE PARK

COANWOOD

LAMBLEY

SLAGGYFORD

ALSTON

NENTHEAD

Line of the proposed Wear Valley Extension Railway 1845 not built

extension Authorised 1846. Not built.

GILSLAND

GREENHEAD

New Angerton

Midgeholm Colly.

Lambley Colly.

NEWCASTLE & CARLISLE RAILWAY ALSTON BRANCH

County Border

CRW

LOW ROW

NAWORTH

BRAMPTON JUNCTION

KIRKHOUSE

Howard Colly.

Roachburn Colly.

Bishop Hill Colly.

BRAMPTON RAILWAY

BRAMPTON TOWN

Howgill colly.

Gair's Colly

Jacksyke Colly.

NEWCASTLE & CARLISLE RAILWAY

175

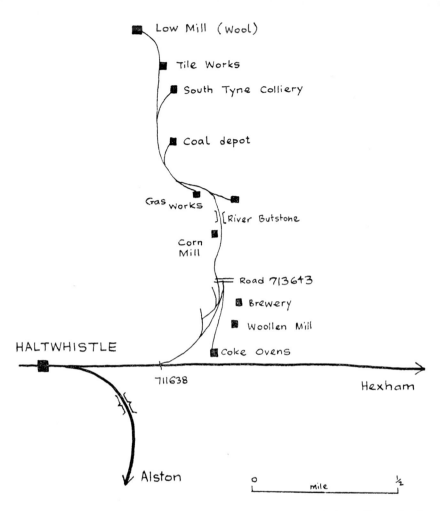

Low Mill (Wool)

Tile Works

South Tyne Colliery

Coal depot

Gas Works

River Butstone

Corn Mill

Road 7|36+3

Brewery

Woollen Mill

Coke Ovens

HALTWHISTLE

711638

Hexham

Alston

0   mile   ½

Alston area, however, were beginning to decline and the railway had to depend on lime, coal and agriculture, augmented by foundry products from Alston

The line was 13 miles long and stops were made at Featherstone Park, Coanwood, Lambley and Slaggyford. The passenger trains took 35 minutes to do the journey in 1911 and after sixty years of progress, using modern diesel trains, the time was cut to 34 minutes. The line was never a commercial success and by the 1960's began to lose money. Subsidies had to be introduced to keep the line open. The railway is one of the most picturesque in Britain and could be a great tourist attraction. A local railway society tried to raise the money to purchase the line and use it for such purposes but received insufficient support and the line has now closed down. The railway society is trying to salvage something and based on Alston railway station hopes to rebuild some of the track.

HALTWHISTLE
From *Parson and White's Directory*, 1827

DIRECTORY.

POST-OFFICE, Market-Place ; MISS ELIZABETH CICELY LAMB, Postmistress.

Letters from HEXHAM, arr. 10 min. bf. 12 at noon ; and are despatched at 10 morning.
Letters from BRAMPTON, arr. at 10 mng. ; and are despatched at 10 min. bf. 12 noon.

MISCELLANY—Consisting of the Names of the Inhabitants not arranged in the List of Professions and Trades, with the Names of the Gentry and Clergy.

Armstrong James, yeoman.
Bell Thos. & Co. flannel, &c. manufacturers
Benson Rev. Francis, A.M. curate of Haltwhistle
Carr John, yeoman
Coulson John Blenkinsopp, Esq., Lieut.-Colonel of the Northumberland militia, and Deputy-lieutenant of the county, *Blenkinsopp Hall*
Crew William, butcher
Cuthbertson Miss Elizabeth

Dawson Mrs. Barbara
Fox Rev. James, A.B. curate of Haltwhistle
French John & Co. brewers and maltsters
Hollingsworth Rev. Nathaniel John, A.M. Vicar of Haltwhistle, *Vicarage house*
Jackson Mrs. Margaret
Lowes John, Esq., *Alland's green*
Lowes John, saddler
Maughan Mrs. Elizabeth

Nanney Lewis, gentleman
Ritson Joseph, parish clerk
Saint Wm. dyer & bleacher
Scaife William, gentleman
Scott Henry, wine & spirit merchant
Snaith Christopher, gent.
Stephenson Rev. Jas. Presbyterian minister
Walton John, sen. hay-rake maker
Walton John, jun. hay-rake maker
Wood Thos. wheelwright

ACADEMIES.
Lee John
Scott William
Skelton Robert, (free school)
BLACKSMITHS.
Jackson Francis

Jacksor Henry
Thirlwell John
BOOT & SHOEMKRS.
Brown John
Carr George
Hunter Robert
Musgrave Simon

CLOGGERS.
Dobinson Robert
Robson Edward
Scott Thomas
Whitfield Joseph
COOPERS.
Pearson George

Walker Michael
CORN MILLERS.
Snowdon Thomas, Manor mill
Wilkinson John, Wall mill

FARMERS.
Armstrong James, East Calf fields
Armstrong Geo. Fell end
Bell Isabella, Harding hill
Heslop Thomas, High Cross bank
Kettlewell John, Ditchfield gate
Makepeace John, Lees hall
Pattison John, Spittle
Pratt Wm. Comb hill
Robson Matt. Oakey know
Robson Thomas, West Calf fields
Robson Wm. Comb hill

Telford Thomas, Fell house
Thirlwell Joseph, Comb hill
Wallace Matthew, Comb hill
GROCERS & DRAPERS.
Marked • are Grocers only ; and thus † Linen & Woollen Drapers.
Bell Robert, (& druggist and tallow chandler)
*Birkett John
*Blenkinsop Eleanor
Brown John
Liddle Ann
†Madgen William
Patterson Jas. (& gardener)

Patterson Ann
Ritson Joseph
*Robinson Elizabeth
†Smith John, (and iron-monger)
Storey Edward
Tweddell Edward
Walker Michael
HOTELS & PUBLIC HOUSES.
Board, Ann Armstrong
Board, William Cowen
Griffin, Ann Bell
Red Lion Inn, (posting-house & excise-office) Jas. Smith
Sun Inn, (& posting-house) Robert Bousfield

JOINERS & CABINET MAKERS.
Glenwright John
Liddle George
Snowdon Thomas
Winter John
MILLINERS, &c.
Ainsley Ann

Bell Elizabeth
Brown Jane & Margt
French Ann
Saint Mary
STONE MASONS.
Brown Joseph
Graham John
Saint John

SURGEONS.
Elliot Robert
Smith William
TAILORS.
Birkett Joseph
Birkett Miles
Ridley Edward
Ridley John

Storey Edward
Tallentire George
Welton Mark
WEAVERS & LINEN MANUFACTURERS.
Ritson John
Ritson Joseph
Storey William

COACHES, &c.

The ROYAL MAIL, from the Red Lion Inn, to *Carlisle*, arrive 10 mg. ; dep. 10 min. bef. 12 noon.—*Hexham*, dep. 10 mng. ; ret. 10 min. bef. 12 noon.
The TRUE BRITON, from the Sun Inn, to *Carlisle*, dep. 9 mng. ; ret. 11 mng.—*Hexham*, arr. 9 mng.; dep. 11 mng.

CARRIERS.
Carlisle, Edward Tweddell, Mon. & Fri. dep. 12 night ; ret. Tues. & Sat. night.
Newcastle, Edward Tweddell, Mon. & Wed. dep. 6 mng. ; ret. Wed. & Fri. 6 evng.
Newcastle, Wm. Cowen, Wed. dep. 4 mng. ; ret. Fri. 10 evng.

177

There were several minor railways and waggonways in the area serving quarries such as those at Barcombe, Fourstones and Greenhead and an interesting railway from Haltwhistle ran for 1½ miles up the valley of the Butstone serving ten different industrial enterprises. Our plan of this line is from C. R. Warn's *Rural Branch Lines of Northumberland.*

The most important railway in the district is the Newcastle/Carlisle Railway which was built in the 1830's. For long there had been a need to improve on the communications between Newcastle and Carlisle. The road was completely inadequate. The first idea was for a canal but this proved abortive. On 28th March 1825 a meeting in Newcastle decided to build a railway to connect the two cities. The line was commenced in 1830 and completed in 1839. Alone of all our north country lines the building was recorded in a superb series of engravings by the local artist J .W. Carmichael.

Between Haydon Bridge and Haltwhistle the line followed the valley of the Tyne, usually on the north bank but crossing the river twice. At Whitchester near Haltwhistle the railway passes through a tunnel. West of Haltwhistle it follows the Tipalt valley and crosses the watershed of the Irthing and Tipalt in deep cuttings at Longbyre and Burnt Walls.

HAUGHTON CASTLE.

HAUGHTON CASTLE

HUMSHAUGH (pronounced Humshaff) stands in beautiful surroundings on the west side of the North Tyne. The rope-and-pulley ferry which crosses the river from Barrasford was discontinued some

Haughton Ferry

years ago but attempts are being made to get it going again. It was started in 1788 when William Smith made the dam to provide water for his new paper mill. But before that time, as early as the reign of Henry II, Ranulf of Haughton and William de Swinburne agreed at their joint expense to provide a ferry here. This is one of the many places which claim to be the origin of the famous Northumbrian folk song – *The Water of Tyne*. The church dates from 1818 and was one of the early works of John Dobson.

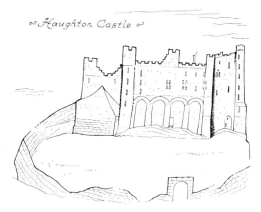

Haughton Castle in 1538. From a sketch at the Record Office

179

lying upon the steps descending from the floor of the vault, starved to death. In the agonies of hunger he had gnawed the flesh from one of his arms. In the dead of night shrieks of the most agonising kind were heard issuing from the dungeon, piercing and resounding through every room in the castle, which was henceforth haunted until the spirit of the famished moss-trooper was exorcised by means of a black-lettered Bible."

Beside the river, close to Haughton Castle, is a disused paper mill, of four vats, which was built in 1788 and ceased working a century later. The builder was William Smith (1751-1825) the most remarkable of the owners of Haughton Castle. He had been a sea-captain and was nicknamed the Buccaneer. In the garden of the castle "there is a sundial with the inscription 'Haughton Castle 1796'; there was formerly cut on it a number of small dials each with the name of a foreign port, and it is believed that it was Captain William Smith's hobby to arrange them so that they showed the time at the different ports he had visited, but they have now become illegible owing to weathering of the stone". (N.C.H.).

Soon after being built the mill was used to make paper for forged notes called *assignats*, a currency which had been issued by the revolutionary government in France. They were sent with the English Army, under the Duke of York, in his unsuccessful expedition to the Austrian Netherlands in 1793 and were intended to depreciate the value of the enemy's currency. One of the moulds for making the paper is in the Black Gate Museum at Newcastle.

The mill is a Georgian building and the upper part of the west wing, with its large openings, was used as a drying room. Remains of water channels can still be seen near the disused building.

Paper making is still carried on at Warden.

HAYDON BRIDGE

The village of Haydon Bridge is built round a bridge on both sides of the South Tyne. The early bridge was destroyed in the Tyne flood of 1773 but was rebuilt. The traffic is now carried on a modern structure a short distance downstream.

In his Historical Notes of Haydon Bridge (published at the Herald Office, Black Bull Yard, Hexham, in 1876) W. Lee describes the village in his day:-

"In Haydon Bridge itself there is little of interest for the antiquarian or pleasure-seeker. It is a quiet agricultural village, with little to vary the monotonous details of daily life. There are no stirring fairs, no weekly activity, and it has none of these elements of outward life to disturb the normal quietude that broods over it".

A market was once held at Old Haydon but was broken up in 1835.

It was however the centre of a mining and industrial area. The

HAYDON BRIDGE.

Ralph Heslop, Deputy Post-mastmaster.—Letters arrive from Hexham 20 min. past 10 mng.—From Carlisle 15 min. past 11 mng.

* Letters for Allendale and Whitfield are left at this Office.

Bell John, yeoman
Coats William, maltster
Cook Mrs. Margaret
Cowing John, farmer
Dodd Humphrey, spirit merchant
Fairlamb John, clogger
Ferguson Rev. Wm. Inde-

pendent minister
Maughan Michael, gent.
Pearson Thomas, cooper
Surtees John, chapelry clerk

ACADEMIES.

Birkett Rev. James, A.M. head master, *Free school*

Morris Henry, 1st usher
Pickering Thos. 2d usher

Ewbank Ann, Girls' free school
Ford Rachel, (ladies) school

BLACKSMITHS.	GROCERS AND DRAPERS.	Black Bull, Joseph Oliver	MILLWRIGHTS.
Corbett Thomas			Bell Joseph
Robson John	Davison Joseph	Scotch Arms, Wm.	Shiel James
Rowell William	Kirsop Edward	Pearson	SADDLERS.
	Makepeace Gabriel	JOINERS.	Carrick Robert
BOOT AND SHOE MAKERS.	Pattison Matthew	Muse John, (and	Lee George
	Shiel James	cartwright)	STONEMASONS.
Elliott John	Siddell Thomas	Reed Ralph, (and	Bell William
Mitchell Nicholas	Temperley Matthew	builder)	Davison Joseph
Potts John	Turnbull Robert	MILLINERS AND	Davison William
Urwin John	Wright John	DRESS-MAKERS.	Howden Edward
Wood George	HOTELS & PUBLIC HOUSES.	Dickinson Jane	Howden John, (and
		Foster Ann	builder)
BUTCHER.	Anchor, John John-	Mews Ann	Howden William
Clowing Robert	son	Wright Elizabeth	Kirsop Edward
STRAW HAT MKRS.	Routledge George	Spark Thomas	Fairlamb John, (and
Dodd Miss		Turnbull Robert	linen mfr.)
Ridley Miss	TAILORS AND	Urwin Henderson	Nicholson Robert
SURGEONS.	DRAPERS.	WEAVERS.	Topping John
Barwick Michael	Howey William	Armstrong John	

COACHES.—The *Royal Mail* and *True Briton* Coaches, to Carlisle and Newcastle, call at the Anchor Inn, Haydon Bridge, every day before noon.

CARRIER *from Haydon Bridge to Newcastle*, John Dickinson, Mon. dep. 9 mng. arr. Wed. 2 afternoon.

From Directory of 1828.

Haydon Bridge Iron Works were established in 1843 and belonged to William Benson of Allerwash House. He employed many men here and at his works at Fourstones and Prudham. Three miles north east of Haydon Bridge were two noted lead mines at Settlingstones and Stonecroft which employed many men and boys. Three miles south west were the Langley Smelt Mills.

The Old Church stands half a mile to the north where the medieval village of Haydon Bridge once lay. Its nave was pulled down in 1795 and the stone used to build a new church in the middle of the village. The chancel became a ruin but was restored in 1882. It was first built about 1190 with a chantry chapel added to the south in the 14th century. Many of the stones in the building are of Roman origin taken from one of the camps nearby. At the end of the chancel is a triplet of small lancet windows separated by round pillars. At the east end of

183

John Martin, the thirteenth child of Fenwick Martin, was born at East Landends, Haydon Bridge, on July 9th, 1789. "By birth", he later wrote, "my station could scarcely have been humbler than it was, My father's disposition kept the family exceedingly poor."

At a very early age Martin's mind was directed to the art of painting, and many stories are told of his juvenile skill. Unable to obtain materials for his art he often went down to the river bank to sketch with a stick on the smooth sand.

"One day," we are told, "while the three masters of the school were standing together he took a burnt stick and sketched the group on the wall near the fireplace." Both teachers and scholars were amazed at the accuracy of his attempt. In other charcoal sketches he depicted two of the boys fighting and one of the ushers thrashing a boy over his knees.

His first oil painting was one of his grandmother's cat. It was executed on top of an old picture which he found in what were then the ruins of Langley Castle. Some of the pigments he made himself, some he obtained from a local house painter.

Young Martin also painted a number of pictures on cheap calico, and on the occasion of some village fete he adorned his father's cottage with a display of his own paintings, hung on short poles.

"A celebrity of Haydon Bridge", writes Tomlinson, "very different from Martin, was Ned Coulson, an eccentric character, remarkable for his swiftness of foot, born April 28th, 1754. Various feats of his are recorded. On one stormy winter's night, when the roads were very bad, he went 50 miles with a message, and returned the next morning. On being asked by his master his reason for not going he replied, 'I have been there and back again, and here's an answer to the message I took'. Another time, after walking 65 miles and performing a piece of work, he reached home in time to take a successful part in some athletic sports which were held on the green by the side of the river. At Brampton races, Ned having said that he could run as fast as the horses, a wager was made, and he tried his speed against a certain horse, the distance being from Brampton to Glen Whelt. They kept pretty even until reaching Denton toll-bar, and, the gate being closed, the rider was obliged to draw his horse up. Ned, however, never halted but leapt over the toll-bar, astonishing the rider, who inquired of the toll-keeper who the man was. 'Ned Coulson,' he was told. 'No, no,' replied the rider, 'it must be the devil, as no man can keep pace with this horse!' The rider went no further, but Ned finished the distance; and as proof that he had done so, got the landlord of the public-house in Glen Whelt to write a few lines to that effect. Ned returned, and arrived at Brampton before the rider, the latter having been completely pumped out. A curious habit of his was to go to the old church near midnight, clothe himself in the minister's surplice, ascend the pulpit, and quietly read aloud a chapter of the Bible by the light of two candles. Among his many other accomplishments was the power to perform on his violin whilst he ran along the road, with the instrument behind his back".

The most famous person associated with Haydon Bridge was undoubtedly Thomas Spence. He was born on the Newcastle Quayside on June 21st 1750 and died in London in 1814. He was a pioneer of socialist ideas, the first man to suggest land nationalisation and the supporter of many radical causes. He was brought up in extreme poverty but managed to educate himself. He became a schoolmaster at St. Anne's School on the Quayside but was dismissed for his radical views. In 1776 he found a new post at the school at Haydon Bridge. He went to London where he became a radical publisher and bookseller. His writings are now acknowledged as being of great social significance.

One and a half miles down the river is Haydon Spa, approached by a path from the Hexham road. All that can be seen today is a small basin in which water trickles. The spa was never able to develop.

The main inn of Haydon Bridge is the Anchor Hotel a large white building on the south bank of the Tyne near the old bridge. Its history is difficult to trace. It is first mentioned in 1828 when it was called *The Anchor*. Writing in 1840 Hodgson tells us "The Court-Houses of the leet and court baron of the barony of Langley are on the south side of the river, and have appended to them a commodious inn, built by the Commissioners of Greenwich Hospital." Bulmer's Directory of 1888 describe it as a "posting establishment". In 1865 the Greenwood Hospital Estates were transferred to the Admiralty and they built a house "for the accomodation of the receivers of its revenues when here on business". The "Admiral's House" is now incorporated into the hotel.

An interesting trial took place at the Anchor Inn in 1837. Here is an extract from W. Lee's *Historical Notes of Haydon Bridge* (1876).

"On the 15th December, 1837, a writ of enquiry of damages from the Queen's Bench, in the action of 'The Duke of Northumberland V. Thomas Pattinson', was executed at the Anchor Inn, Haydon Bridge, before Mr. Gibson, the Under-Sheriff of Northumberland, and a jury. Mr. John Fenwick, as steward of the Barony of Wark, appeared on behalf of his Grace, and read an extract from the third institute of Lord Coke. Witnesses having been called, included the late Mr. Joseph Fairless, and Mr. John Trotter Brockett, F.S.A., who estimated the value of the coins at £18, the jury returned a verdict for the Duke of Northumberland for £18 damages." For the story of these coins see "Thorngrafton".

The famous athlete, Edward Coulson (1754-1807) often drank at the Anchor. We are told "he could run with the greatest of ease before a post-chaise, and he has often alarmed travellers by passing them, then hiding himself, re-passing, and at length bidding them good night. He had a method of putting his finger in his mouth and producing a sound somewhat resembling the report of a pistol, and this he mischievously employed to intimidate travellers. He has often been sitting in the Anchor Inn, Haydon Bridge, when travellers have arrived wet with perspiration, caused by the fright he had given them."

Haydon Bridge

The *Pontem de Haydon* is first mentioned in 1309, and in 1336 Anthony de Lucy was given a grant of pontage for four years for its repair.

Haiden-brigg is mentioned once again in 1381 and 1426. It was rebuilt, after the Great Flood, in 1773. In 1806 one arch collapsed and this necessitated the rebuilding of three of the six arches. It is now by-passed by a modern bridge.

East Land Ends

In this house John Martin the famous painter was born on July 19th, 1789. It is situated on the south side of the river half a mile to the west of the village. On the gable end a plaque records this event. The small cottage has been extended by taking in the farm building at the end the stone arches of which can still be seen.

Drawing by David Westle

HEAVENFIELD CROSS

In the fourth decade of the seventh century the Christian kingdom of Northumbria was engaged in a life and death struggle with the Welsh under their king Cadwallon. The first great battle took place in 633 at Heathfield (Hatfield) near Doncaster which ended in the death of King Edwin and the destruction of his army. A great part of Northumbria was then laid waste and pillaged. The task of saving the kingdom fell upon Oswald, the second son of Ethelfrith, who had been trained by the Celtic monks of Scotland.

Collecting a small army he met the victorious Cadwallon near Hexham. He chose as the site for the battle a plateau, protected to the north and west by rocky banks and to the south by the Roman Wall. Bede – who wrote when the battle was still vividly remembered – tells us that Oswald erected a cross of wood as a standard for his army. Then he led his men in prayer; kneeling at the foot of the cross he said: "Let us all bow the knee, and together pray the Almighty God, living and true, that He will in His mercy save us from the proud and savage enemy, as He knows that we have undertaken a just war for the salvation of our nation". They then awaited the onslaught of the foe. In the bitter conflict the Welsh were utterly routed and their king slain. "Never was day more lamentable for the Britons, or more joyful for the Angles", as the chronicler said.

The Britons fled down Watling Street and it was at the Denise-burn identified as the Rowley Burn, seven miles south of the battle-field, that Cadwallon was killed.

The battle became known as Heavenfield and on the site a memorial church was built. The Chapel of St. Oswald, rebuilt in 1737, is thought to be in the same place and nearby were the fields in which the battle was fought. Opposite the Chapel, on the south side of the road, is a field called Mould's Close where the greatest slaughter took place and here many skulls and sword fragments have been dug up. According to Camden, when the Chapel of St. Oswald was being repaired in the time of Elizabeth, a silver coin of Oswald was found with his head on one side and a cross on the reverse.

The battle of Heavenfield was one of the decisive battles of English history. It finally decided the struggle between the Celts and the Anglo-Saxons and led to the complete conversion of Northumbria to Christianity, but to the Celtic not Roman version.

After a brief but brilliant reign Oswald was slain at the battle of Maserfield (said to be at Oswestry – Oswald's tree – Shropshire) in 642, his victor being the pagan king of the Mercians, Penda.

HEDLEY

Hedley lies on the south of the Tyne and is a southern portion of the county of Northumberland. The village stands on a range of hills which form the southern bank of the Tyne and the village on the south crest overlooks the valley of the Derwent in Durham. The name is common in Northumberland and means "a clearing overgrown with heather".

The village is famous because a legendary goblin called the Hedley Kow frequented the neighbourhood. In 1729 one Thomas Stevenson of Framwellgate in Durham swore before a magistrate called Burdus that "on 7th August, 1729, between eight and nine at night returning from Hedley in Northumberland, he saw an apparition that looked sometimes in the shape of a foal, sometimes of a man, which took the bridle off his horse, beat him till he was sore, and misled him on foot three miles to Coalburne; and that a guide he had with him was beat in the same manner, and that it vanished not till daybreak, and then, though he touched not the bridle, after it was taken from the horse, but as he felt the stripes of it he felt it bound about his waist. His horse he found where he first saw the apparition, by Greenbank top, and saith it was commonly reported by the neighbourhood that a spirit called HEDLEY KOW did haunt the place.

Several stories of the Hedley Kow are told, all similar in style. Stephen Oliver in his *Rambles in Northumberland and the Scottish Border* relates many of these tales and ends his account with the following:,-

A farmer riding homeward late one night, observed, as he approached a lonely part of the road where the Kow used to play many of his tricks, a person also on horseback at a short distance before him. Wishing to have company in a part of the road where he did not like to be alone at night, he quickened the pace of his horse. The person whom he wished to overtake, hearing the tramp of a horse rapidly advancing, and fearing that he was followed by some one with an evil intention, put spurs to his steed, and set off at a gallop; an example which was immediately followed

was finally enlarged in 1864. The grounds were laid out by Capability Brown in 1776. His original plans are at the house.

At Hesleyside is still preserved a spur, shown here, of the date 1580-1600. About this spur there is the well known tradition that when the larder was empty it was served up at dinner in a covered dish by the lady of the house as a sign that another foray must be made. This incident is represented in one of William Scott's historical paintings at Wallington.

A work of art associated with Hesleyside is the famous *Standard of Hesleyside* which is a goblet of Newcastle glass, eleven inches in height, decorated by William Beilby of Newcastle and his sister Mary. It is dated 1763 and is a beautiful specimen of the glass for which Newcastle was famous in the eighteenth century.

Hesleyside was held by a local family called Charlton. An infamous member of this clan, called William, was a notorious Jacobite who lived at the Bower, five miles away. Of William Charlton the steward of Hesleyside wrote: "Bowrry Charlton wass all wayes vearry a-Bousiffe and scornful man to my master – and would a made him foudelled and sould him deare Bargains, and abused him when he had done".

CHARLTON

HEXHAM

The district of which Hexham is the centre abounds in remains of our early history. Roman stations, Saxon churches, medieval castles, and Georgian country houses are found in profusion. Hexham itself is a picturesque old town which has to a large extent escaped the concrete-plastic invasion of the last two decades. It stands on a shelf or terrace overlooking the Tyne Valley with low hills in the background. The site is very suitable for a large country town with all the important local roads meeting at or near the place. Although not in a strong position for defence it is protected on the most vulnerable side by the

river Tyne which is only fordable when the river is low and even then is dangerous because of the quicksands in its bed.

Few prehistoric remains have been found within the vicinity of Hexham and although numerous Roman stones can be seen here they probably all came from Corbridge. So the Romans appear to have had no settlement here.

However in Saxon times it became a flourishing town. The early names given to the locality are all of Saxon origin. The earliest name of the place we know is *Hagustald* which is used in the *Anglo-Saxon Chronicle* (681). In the thirteenth century the word Hextildesham came into use. The origin of these two names is obscure. They could have arisen from the Anglicizing of a Celtic river name (the modern Cockshaw Burn) or might mean "Batchelor's river" which signifies the home beside the water where the younger son dwelt. Be that as it may it must have been a place of some importance for Wilfrid to select it as the site of his church.

St. Andrew's Church

Following the victory of Latin over Celtic Christianity at the synod of Whitby in 664 Wilfrid was supreme in the northern church. In 674 Queen Etheldrid of Northumbria granted him an extensive stretch of land in Hexhamshire and Wilfrid decided to build there a great Roman church. Eddius thus described it: "In Hexham he founded and built a house of the Lord in honour of St. Andrew the apostle. My feeble tongue will not permit me to enlarge here upon the depths of the foundations in the earth, and its crypts of wonderfully dressed stones, and the manifold buildings above the ground, supported by various columns and many side aisles and adorned with walls of notable length and height, surrounded by various winding passages and spiral stairs leading up and down . . . Nor have we heard of any other house on this side of the Alps built on such a scale". This vague description only shows us how impressed was the writer.

The church was built in the Roman fashion and inspired by the basilican churches of the continent. On Wilfrids death in 709 he was succeeded as bishop of Hexham by his friend Acca who, according to Bede "enriched the structure of the church with manifold adornments and marvellous workmanship". Acca raised the church at Hexham to a height of importance it never before or afterwards attained.

In the year 875 Halfdene the Dane ravaged the whole of Tyneside and Hexham church was plundered and burnt to the ground. For the next two centuries the history of Hexham is obscure. The priests of Hexham began to marry and have children and the church property was handed down from father to son. About 1050 one Eilaf was put in charge of Hexham, although as treasurer of Durham, he probably never came there. After a quarrel with the Bishop of Durham over

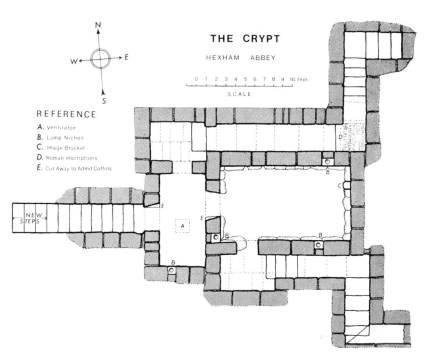

THE CRYPT

HEXHAM ABBEY

0 1 2 3 4 5 6 7 8 9 10 feet

SCALE

REFERENCE

A. Ventilator
B. Lamp Niches
C. Image Bracket
D. Roman Inscriptions
E. Cut Away to Admit Coffins

NEW STEPS

FRAGMENT OF SAXON CARVING AT
HEXHAM. The centre is repeated large above

Cross of Acca, Hexham.

THE HEXHAM HOGBACK.
Late 11th century.

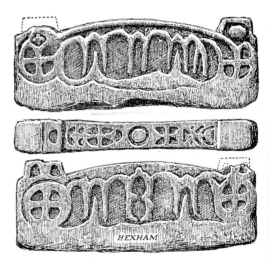

the question of married priests he handed over the lands of Hexham to the Archbishop of York and for many years afterwards Hexhamshire belonged to York and not to Durham.

Eilaf was instructed to rebuild Hexham Church which then lay in utter ruin. His son Eilaf II completed the work probably building in the Norman style.

There has been much controversy as to the shape and size of the Saxon church at Hexham. However here we need only discuss what has survived, namely the famous crypt and the Apse of Wilfrid's church which was discovered under the present choir.

The crypt is a plain structure of four chambers. Here were exhibited the relics which were a feature of Wilfrid's church. It consists of a chapel with an ante-chapel at the west end, two side passages with enlarged vestibules at the west and three stairways. The chapel and ante-chapel are barrel-vaulted. In the chapel are three lamp niches, in the ante-chapel one. The passages are roofed with large flat stones and the vestibules with two sets of flat slabs forming a triangular arch. All the stones used are of Roman workmanship and many are carved or with inscriptions. Some of the original roof plaster remains. Two of the stairways were for the use of worshippers the other was used by the priests.

The Saxon apse was discovered during investigations in 1908-10. It can be seen under a trap door in the present choir.

Of the furniture of St. Wilfrid's church only the frith-stool remains. Originally the bishop's seat it was later used as the seat of sanctuary. There are also the remains of a number of crosses of which the finest once stood at the head of Acca's grave. It is now in the Cathedral Library at Durham (Replica at Hexham). It is carved in the Italian

The Frithstool.

199

style. A number of other remains associated with the saxon church are described below.

Size, 3 ft. 1 in. by 2 ft. 10 in.

IMP · CAES · L · SEP . . .	Imperator Cæsar Lucius Septimius [Severus]
PERTINAX · ET · IMP C . .	Pertinax et Imperator Cæsar [Marcus]
AVR ANTONINV	Aurelius Antoninus [pius felix Augusti]
VS	. . [et Publius Septimius Geta]
. . . . HORTE . . .	[Cæsar per co]horte[m et]
VEXILLATION	vexillationem . . . .
FECERVNT SVB	fecerunt sub . . . .

This inscription is on a slab which forms the headway in one of the passages o, the crypt.

Translated it means "The Emperor Lucius Septimus Severus Pius Pertinax and his sons the Emperor Marcus Aurelius Antoninus Pius Augustus and Publius Septimus Geta Caesar the cohorts and detachments made this under the command of . . ."

The words erased are of great interest. After the Emperor Geta was murdered by his brother an edict was made at Rome ordering that whenever the two names appeared in combination that of Geta was to be erased. This was done in the present case but so poorly that the name can still be read.

The reason why so many inscriptions are found in the crypt is that the Saxon builders always put the lettering outside to serve as a key to the plaster they used.

```
. . . APO . . .

. . . APO . . .

. . P · AE . . .

. . . VS . . .

. . . . . . . . .


[Deo] Apo[lli-] (?)

[ni M]apo[no] (?)

P[ublius] Æ[lius] (?)

. . . . . . . . .
```

Size, 3 ft. 2 in. by 9 in.

This inscription is in the crypt of the Priory Church. It has been cut away to form the circular headway of one of the passages. It was an important inscription, probably dedicated to Apollo Maponus.

The Middle Ages

In the twelfth and thirteenth centuries Hexham suffered grievously from Scottish raids. In 1296 the town was burnt to the ground. "Its beautiful church was fired, its priceless relics wantonly thrown into the

201

Saxon Font, Hexham.

flames, and the gold and gems that adorned its shrines were torn off and carried away by the triumphant invaders. With a barbarous cruelty. distinguished even among their other excesses, the Scots blocked up the doors of the Hexham school, and set fire to the building, which was full of young scholars. Even their patron saint could not command their respect, and they cut off the head of the image of St. Andrew, observing, amid loud laughter, that he might return and plough his own country"N.C.H.

During the fourteenth century the town was repeatedly ravaged but in the following century the church was restored and considerably embellished.

In 1536 the rising known as the "Pilgrimage of Grace" can be said to have started at Hexham which was the only monastery which offered determined resistance to the Act for the Dissolution of the Smaller Monasteries. Although the Priory of Augustinian Canons at Hexham did not really come within the scope of the Act since their

202

yearly value was more than £200 per year, it had for some reason been included. The priory appears to have been morally and financially in a bad state but it was important as one of the few centres of hospitality in the barren regions of the North. When the Royal Commissioners came to the town in 1536 the canons under the leadership of the Master of Ovingham resisted them by force of arms. The rebellion was however suppressed by the Duke of Norfolk and many of the monks were "tyed uppe, without further delaye or ceremony, to the

W. Armstrong's map, 1769

203

terrible example of others". The lands of the priory were granted in 1538 to Sir Reginald Carnaby, then to Sir Christopher Hatton and later to the Fenwicks, the Blacketts and the Beaumonts.

Hexham Market in nineteenth century

Hexham Riot

During the Civil War Hexham suffered little, likewise during the rebellions of 1715 and 1745. But in 1761 an event of great importance took place known as the "Hexham Riot".

It was the practice at this time to choose members of the militia by a ballot of those liable for service. Previously the landowners had hired men to serve. There was a strong feeling in Durham and Northumberland that the system was unjust. The balloting for 1761 began at Durham where there was a disturbance. At Morpeth and Whittingham large crowds stopped the balloting taking place. Trouble was expected at Hexham and two battalions of the North York Militia were sent there. On the day appointed a huge crowd of 5,000 assembled in the Market Place. The troops, numbering 240, were drawn up in front of the Town Hall. The magistrates refused to postpone the balloting, the crowd heaped insults on the soldiers. The Riot Act was read and the crowd refusing to disperse the soldiers opened fire. 51 people lost their lives and 300 were wounded. The soldiers lost two men. Warrants for arrest of those who had participated were issued and the soldiers scoured the countryside looking for them. One man Patterson, who had not been at Hexham, was arrested, tried and hanged, the only judicial victim of the Riot. When he was on the scaffold the rope gave way, and he called out, "Innocent blood is ill to shed".

For many years afterwards the North York Militia were known in the area as "the Hexham Butchers". Three sermons were preached and published following the massacre. The sermon at Hexham was "On the important duty of subjection to the civil powers".

In 1766 the shambles, still standing in the market place, were erected at the expense of Sir Walter Blackett, the lord of the manor; and in 1771 the market cross was removed to Haydon Bridge and was later destroyed.

In 1806 Mary Russell Mitford, the author of Our "Village" visited Hexham and in a letter has some interesting remarks about the town. She was received by Colonel Beaumont at his home in the old Abbey house. "It was a fine specimen," she writes, "of the Saxon-Gothic (!) architecture; but he has built upon the same foundation, retaining all the inconveniences of the ancient style, and lost all its grandeur. It has on the outside an appearance of a manufactory, and the inside conveys the exact idea of an inn. I should have thought it absolutely impossible to construct so bad a house with so many rooms. There is but one good one, which is the ball room, and this is made the passage to the bed chambers.

"In order to render the bad taste of this abominable modern house still more conspicuous, it is contrasted with the singular beauty of the adjoining cathedral, whose gloomy magnificence and fine pointed arches delighted me extremely. The Colonel is the patron, I may almost say the proprietor, of this fine church (for he is what they call a lay bishop, and still receives the tributary pence from the communicants), yet that part of the edifice where the pews are placed is in a most shocking state. The bottom of one of the pews, situated exactly under his own, is covered with straw like a London hackney coach; and even his own pew seems quietly resigned to the moths and other depredators. Everything, in short seemed to testify it was a place he seldom visited.

"We dined at a very wretched inn, for I must confess that Hexham is a shocking gloomy place. After dinner I had the pleasure of visiting the house where my darling was born. It has been an extremely good one, and still retains a very respectable appearance; but it is now divided, and on one side of the street door is a collar maker's shop and on the other a milliner's. We entered the latter, and purchased three pair of Hexham gloves, both as a memorial of the town and of the house".

Miss Mitford would probably be pleased to know that 12 years after her visit the Abbey house was almost destroyed by fire. The part that remains is now occupied by the police.

Hexham Abbey Church.   L. Clennell, 1815.

Hexham Abbey

Hexham Abbey was re-founded as a Medieval Augustinian Priory in 1113 but the part of present building dates from 1180 to 1250. It has suffered much from "destructive restoration". The east end was restored in a barbarous manner and the beautiful fourteenth century chapels under the great east window demolished. The church was intended to be cruciform but the nave was never completed until 1908.

The choir has been described as a very text-book of the early English period of pointed church architecture. Its elegant arcade has pointed arches. The triforium above has round arches each framing two pointed ones and above is an almost unique clerestory. The lofty roof is supported by huge blocks of oak with carved floral bosses.

Choir of Hexham Church, looking eastward.   Engraved 1809.

Hexham Abbey.   North Transept, 1810.

The transepts at Hexham are extremely long and imposing. The north transept was built between 1230 and 1240. Its eastern wall aisle is vaulted in stone and its western wall is elaborately pierced and arcaded. The south transept, built in 1220, has richly arcaded upper walls and against the west side is one of the most famous features of the Abbey, the stone staircase which formerly led to the dormitory of the canons, and now called the Night-stair; it was used by the canons when they came into the church for Matins. At the top of the staircase is a door leading to a small room, in former times "most probably

Hexham Abbey Staircase (to the Dormitory) in the South Transept.

Shield with the initials of Prior R. Leschman.

used by the man who watched during stated hours for any one fleeing to the church for sanctuary, as its position would command the town and the Market Place, across which anyone must have gone when running to the church from any of the four sanctuary crosses, and seeking to enter the precincts of the Priory by the east gate".

Prior Leschman's Chantry

Hexham Priory has many rare monuments and carved woodwork. In the north aisle of the choir is the beautiful chantry chapel of Prior Rowland Leschman who died in 1491. This Chapel has been moved about the Church but in 1908 it was put back into its original position. Within is a stone effigy of the Prior with long coat, tunic and cloak with a hood which is pulled over his eyes. The basement of the shrine

The Leschman Chantry before its removal from the choir in 1858.

From W. B Scott's "Antiquarian Gleanings in the North of England," 1851.

Hexham Abbey
by Hugh Thomson, 192(

is of rudely carved stone depicting St. George, the fox in the garb of a monk preaching to the geese, men playing musical instruments, a lady curling her hair and a monkey eating a pile of buns. The oak screen work is noted for its delicate flamboyant tracery, the roof ornamented with carved bosses, the centre one showing the figure of an angel holding a shield with Prior Leschman's monogram upon it. At the east end is a stone altar bearing the five consecration crosses. The contrast between the rudely carved stonework and the delicate woodwork is striking.

Choir Screen

In the north of the chancel is a wonderful painted screen of oak. Beneath carved canopies are medieval paintings of the seven Hexham bishops who became Saints. Beneath these larger panels are four smaller ones representing the Dance of Death; from left to right, a Cardinal, King, Emperor and Pope. In front of this screen is a lower one thought to have been used in the refectory. It projects in the middle to form a pulpit. In the traceried panels are faded paintings of Our Lord, The Blessed Virgin and the Twelve Apostles. None of the panels in the choir screen are in their original positions.

The Rood Screen

The Rood Screen, a magnificent piece of woodwork, is one of the finest in England. It was the work of Thomas Smithson, Prior from 1491 to 1524. The paintings depict The Annunciation and The Visitation, 16 portraits of the Bishops of Hexham and Lindisfarne, and other prelates.

The Font

The bowl, made from the base of a Roman pillar, belonged to St. Wilfrid's church. The stem is Early English and the cover Jacobean.

The Ogle Chantry

It was erected by Robert Ogle who died in 1410. It was practically demolished in the nineteenth century, but much of the woodwork survived and has been assembled once again and restored.

The Saxon Chalice

This small Saxon chalice was found in a stone coffin in the north transept. Only two other Anglo-Saxon chalices are known, the Trewhiddle chalice in the British Museum and one found at Hazleton which has now disappeared. It was probably a small chalice used with portable altars like the one of St. Cuthbert in the Library of Durham Cathedral. (*There are now doubts whether this chalice is of the Saxon period*).

Trade

Hexham was an important market town from very early times. The weekly market and the two fairs were fixed in 1239. Being the centre of a large and fertile agricultural district it was an important centre for the sale of grain and its cattle markets were famous in the eighteenth century.

Hexham was also once the centre of some important local industries. The chief was the leather trade in all its branches. The basis was tanning which flourished as early as the seventeenth century. The bulk of its output went to the manufacture of gloves which made Hexham "Tans" famous. In 1823 111 men and 1,000 women were employed in the production of more than a quarter of a million pairs of gloves which were sold all over the country. The industry now only survives in the names of places. The farm of *Okerland* derives its name from the clay there dug up to make ochre which was used in the glove trade. Mallows for dyeing were grown at the farm of *Mollersteads* (Maller Steedes, 1608) while next door is the *Dye House*.

Another local industry was the manufacture of stuff hats and in 1823 there were 16 master hatters in the town.

These trades gave rise to a number of guilds. There were four of them as follows: 1. Weavers. 2. Tanners and Shoemakers. 3. Skinners and Glovers. 4. Hatters.

*West Side of Market
Place in 19th century
after J. W. Carmichael.*

*East Side of Market
Place in 19th century
after J. W. Carmichael.*

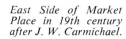

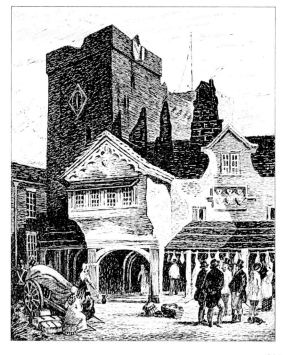

213

Hexham Market Place in 1832, by T. Allom, showing White Horse Inn.

We see the inn to the right of the tall gatehouse in Thomas Allom's view of Hexham Market sketched in 1832. A few years later it was visited by artist William Bell Scott, who painted the murals at Wallington Hall depicting scenes from Northumbrian history. In his Memoirs he describes his stay in this interesting old house.

"Midway between the eastern and western shores of our hard-working island I found myself in the old-fashioned, sleepy town of Hexham, and settled down in a small apartment in the half-timbered hostelry called the White Horse. This apartment was over the porch, and the front of it was one continuous narrow casement with a long bunker seat under it, looking out on the quiet market-place and great church, once a Cathedral, partly destroyed by the Scotch, but still large enough for all the inhabitants of the town. This long window, with the casements opened, and this market-place seen without, was my subject, and the landlady's daughter posed to me at full length on the window-seat knitting. I entered into the homely daily life of the narrow circle, and soon began to know the bellman and the beadle, the apothecary and the mercer, and to recognize the domestic damsels, each one at her regular moment coming for the daily water to the fountain. Then the sun was always shining, my casement was always open, the pigeons and the jackdaw, the "familiar" – a quite innocent one – of the market-place, sat on the sill looking at me in their sidelong bird fashion. Every quarter of an hour the great clock of the cathedral chimed soberly – one for the quarter, two for the half, and so on till it struck the hour. I begun to think it said this, accenting the first word of each line:

Now must I show my power –
Here it surely comes once more –
Now must I declare the hour –
Day and night, and o'er and o'er.

At noon, before the last stroke of the bell had ceased to vibrate, the clatter of wooden shoes and the hubbub of children's voices showed that the school had been opened. Into the wide paved space they tumbled, Esaus and Ishmaels starting to fight over the horse-trough, splashing the water about, and pairs of good Davids and Jonathans keeping their arms round each other's necks. The tall maiden Isabell, my model, by and by disappeared to cook my dinner and to eat her own, and when my hour came I very often found a roasted duckling before my solitary plate.

This hostelry was scarcely ever disturbed by traveller, except on one day, the market-day of the week, yet the landlady, who had her cares, having lost everything sixteen years before, when her son was banished for forgery, cheerfully said the world had been very good to her; she had now something in the bank of her own again, her son was now a prosperous man, and she was looking for his return".

Towards the end of the nineteenth century a speculative builder demolished this fine building, replacing it with a row of shops.

Gibson's chemist shop (c. 1880) in Fore Street is a fine example of ornate Victorian design.

There are many small buildings in Hexham of great interest. Gibson's chemist shop (*c.* 1880) in Fore Street is a fine example of ornate Victorian design. The doorway is illustrated above. Unfortunately, as we write, the interior – an unspoilt Victorian pharmacy – has been gutted, as far as we know without local protest, and the fittings taken to a London Museum. If it had been preserved it would have eventually become one of the treasures of Hexham as public (and official) awareness of such historic buildings grows. *St. Mary's Chare* or *Back Street* preserves the spirit of old Hexham and has been the least affected by modern "improvements". Our illustration shows a bow-fronted shop.

The Grammar School

In 1578 there were only 21 schoolmasters in Northumberland of which eleven were at Newcastle. Hexham had none but in 1599 a school was founded called the Free Grammar School of Queen Elizabeth. The school was poorly endowed and never "free" and appears to have played only a slight role in the development of the town. Its original home is uncertain but in 1684 a school house, which still stands, was erected on the Hall Stile Bank at a cost of £150.

Streets and Houses

Besides the Priory and the two Towers a number of old houses still survive in Hexham while the street names recall many aspects of early life.

Hencotes – Place where poultry of convent kept.

Gilesgate – Road to hospital of St. Giles.

Priestpopple – Where recipients of alms lived.

Sele – Corruption of Champs du Ciel.

Battle Hill – Derived from some old conflict.

The Sele

The Sele is a grassy hill near the town centre laid out as a park, the summit being called the Priest's Seat. In the survey of 1547 it is listed as belonging to the Carnabys. It was opened to the public as early as 1753. About 1820 it was proposed to carry the Newcastle to Carlisle road through it, but fortunately the plan fell through. The original name Champs du Ciel suggests it was once the property of the Priory.

Hexham House

The eighteenth century Georgian Hexham House stands in its own grounds. It is built of stone, with five bays and three storeys, parapeted. There are large quoins to the angles as well as the centre bay which also has a large porch built on square pillars. The two storeyed wing is a nineteenth century addition.

Hexham Castle

In Hexham today are two towers which at one time were probably joined together by a curtain wall to form a castle. They are the gate

tower or Moot Hall and the prison or Manor Office. The date of the erection of the prison is known. In 1330 Archbishop Melton of York ordered that a gaol be built and nineteen months later one John de Cawode, a barber, was appointed the gaoler at a salary of two pence a day. The date for the foundation of the Moot Hall is not so clear but it was built in the second half of the fourteenth or first half of the fifteenth century. The gaol was intended not only for the border mosstroopers but mainly for the archbishop's tenants. When Lord Dacre administered the regality the prison was always full. In 1515 the townspeople revolted and tried to release the prisoners. On this occasion they did not succeed but a few years later the prisoners were freed. In the great survey of the Borders by Sir Robert Bowes in 1552 both the towers at Hexham are said to be "muche in decaye, because there is no yerly reparacons allowed to be doone upon them".

The Manor Office is an oblong with triple corbels meant to carry machicolations. It has two vaulted chambers on the ground floor and one room on each of the two upper floors. The original spiral staircase has been removed and there have been considerable internal alterations. It is built almost entirely of Roman stones taken from the station at Corbridge. It is now a tourist information centre.

Hexham Bridge

Whether there was a bridge at Hexham in medieval times is unclear but if there was it only lasted for a short period. The Tyne was crossed by two ferries called the east and the west boats which of course were useless when most needed, that is when the river was in flood. The want of a bridge was long and severely felt and as a result of persistent agitation a bridge was started in 1767 and completed in 1770. It stood nearly opposite to the gate of the Spital Cemetery, was built by a Mr. Galt and consisted of seven arches. Less than a year later it was swept away in the great Tyne flood of 1771. In that flood eight bridges shared the fate of Hexham. A contemporary letter tells us "whole acres of ground, houses and families, are swept away and lie buried in the mighty ruins. The river rose 7 or 8 feet on the main floor of a new and beautiful house at Bywell; at Hexham it was highest, rising six feet above the flood of 1763, and was swelled to a degree of violence far exceeding anything before experienced, handed down by tradition, or even imagined".

In 1774 a new attempt was made fifty yards to the west by Mr. John Wooler, an engineer who had been working on the new Newcastle bridge. Piles were sunk to carry the piers but work was abandoned on discovering that the "soil beneath the gravel was a quicksand with no more resistance than chaff".

Prophetically he remarked that "whoever meddled with a bridge there, would burn their fingers. Assisting him was Jonathan Pickernell (*c.* 1738-1812) who subsequently supervised the building of the bridge designed by John Smeaton. In 1766 Pickernell was appointed Surveyor of Bridges in the County of Northumberland, a post he held for five years.

The authorities next approached Smeaton whose name as an engineer was famous. John Errington of Beaufront was given the contract for the sum of £5,700 and work started in 1777. Although the half completed piers were washed away the following year work continued and the new bridge was opened to traffic in 1780. It was highly commended and "even the Gilligate people ceased their visits, who had come constantly to inspect the bridge after every flood, in hopes of witnessing its downfall". However on March 10th, 1782 there was a heavy fall of snow, followed by a violent hurricane. The valleys of the north and south Tyne were inundated. The baliff of John Errington (the contractor for the bridge) went down to see the effect of the floods. He sent back a report that *all was safe* but immediately afterwards the collapse started and the nine arches were completely overturned. They are still visible and act as a sort of weir. Legal proceedings against Errington were constituted and eventually he had to pay £4,000 damages.

In the meantime Robert Mylne, a famous architect and engineer, was called in to report on the feasibility of rebuilding Smeaton's bridge. He was eventually given the contract to build a fourth bridge. This he did and the work was completed in 1793. Today this handsome bridge still stands as a monument to his genius.

Mylne designed many north country bridges. Except for Newcastle which was removed in 1873 all stand today. C. Gotch in *Archaeologia Aeliana* thus sums up his work.

"Mylne holds a particularly significant position within his epoch for his genius brought him to the forefront of two professions at a time when they had parted irrevocably on the threshold of the mechanical era. Through his journal he is revealed as a titan of his age. Although Telford makes a strong bid, there seems to be no other truly bi-professional artist of this period to compete with Robert Mylne".

Medieval Bridge

Near the Abbey is a remarkable medieval bridge which is unknown to the thousands of people who cross it every year. It carries the path between the public gardens and Hexham House over the Halgut or Cockshaw Burn. It has no parapet and the burn passes through the park by a tunnel so it is not noticeable. It has a single pointed arch with a span of 15 feet, and four strong ribs. The photograph on the following page shows the underneath of the bridge. It was taken by Hylton Edgar under difficult circumstances.

The South Gate at Housesteads

Building, the granary and the last building whose use was uncertain but probably used as a workshop. The *via principalis* terminated in the massive north gate. Visitors often think this must have never been used because of the sharp drop to the north. But originally there was an inclined road here which was removed during excavations.

The *via quintana* ran parallel to the main *via principalis*. It was a minor road giving access to the barracks and also to the granaries. It is joined in the middle by the *via decumana*. Both these roads are named after divisions in the larger legionary camps. The *via quintara* (*quintus-fifth*) divided the fifth maniple from the sixth. The *via decumana* (*decimus-tenth*) was the area occupied by the 10th cohort.

Headquarters (Principia)

The *principia* or headquarters building was, as is normal, in the centre of the fort. It was the finest building at Housesteads and was the administrative and spiritual centre of the fort. It was entered from the main street by a large arched and projecting gate.

On entering the soldier came into a paved courtyard surrounded originally on four sides by a colonnaded veranda (later on the north, east and south only). From this forecourt another arched doorway led to the great hall which could also originally be entered from the two side streets but later only the north entrance was available. This mighty basilica was roofed in, the roof being supported by a row of columns which ran the length of the hall. In the north west corner is a large block of masonry called the *tribunal* where the fort commandant took his seat on ceremonial or public occasions. In the opposite corner was another raised platform probably occupied by a statue. The hall was the highest building in the fort and would be lit by upper clerestory windows as in a church.

Farthest from the entrance lay a range of rooms, five in all. The central one was the *aedes* or shrine where were kept the standards of the regiment, the statue of the emperor, and possibly other altars. It was guarded day and night. This central shrine could be seen as soon as one entered the main entrance. In the *aedes* was usually an underground strongroom where the regiment treasures and money were kept but because of the hard whinstone it does not feature at Housesteads. The two rooms to the north of the shrine were occupied by the adjutant (*corricularius*) and his clerks who were responsible for the administration of the unit. The two rooms on the south were used by the standard bearers (signiferi) who were responsible for the pay and savings of the troops. Originally the three central rooms had wide arched entrances. The cross hall was the place where the commandant issued his orders, heard complaints, dealt out punishments and received visitors. It would also be used for a variety of meetings specially of the centurions.

In later years drastic changes were made to the *Principia*. The forecourt was changed into living accomodation, the hall became a kitchen and mess room, and the adjutant's office became an armoury. As danger threatened the Wall only the barest of administration was maintained.

Plan of Hospital

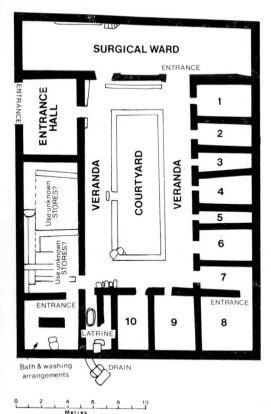

SURGICAL WARD

ENTRANCE

ENTRANCE HALL

ENTRANCE

Use unknown STORES?

Use unknown STORES?

VERANDA

COURTYARD

VERANDA

ENTRANCE

ENTRANCE

10 9 8

LATRINE

Bath & washing arrangements

DRAIN

1
2
3
4
5
6
7

N

0 2 4 6 8 10
Metres

The Hospital

Behind the headquarters building stands a courtyard type of building. Although little of medical significance was found during the two excavations (1898 & 1972) the building was undoubtedly the fort's hospital. Analogy from other Roman forts make this supposition almost certain. It has four ranges of rooms including an operating theatre, rooms for patients, latrines, baths and medical stores. It was a stone building with tiled roof; and no heating arrangements, and unless the rooms marked *use uncertain* were used for that purpose it had no kitchen. Food would be brought in from the main kitchens. The building was altered many times and in the third and fourth centuries was probably used for workshops. Our plan tries to show the building in its original form.

Commandant's House

The house was built on sloping ground with a stone slated roof. The main entrance was from the *via principalis*. On the left was the reception room with the kitchens on the right. The dining room was in the North wing. There were 19 rooms but their uses are difficult to interprete. It is a typical courtyard house of Mediterranean type, probably unsuitable for the climatic conditions at Housesteads.

The Temple to Mithras

Outside the fort the most important building as yet discovered is the Temple to Mithras.

Many altars have been discovered at Housesteads showing that several deities were worshipped but the most important was the Persian sun-god Mithras whose temple stood in the valley below the farmhouse. Nothing can now be seen but when excavated valuable sculptures and inscriptions were found. Mithraic temples were all very similar and were dark to suggest the cave where Mithras slew the bull. The altars found at Housesteads were all dedicated by fort commandants of the third century when the worship of Mithras flourished.

Civilian Settlement

The *vicus* or civilian settlement was on the south and probably also on the east and west of the fort. One of the houses uncovered is known as the Murder House. Here a man and a woman were murdered some time in the fourth century and their bodies hidden under the floor. Burial within a settlement was forbidden under Roman law. South of the village are numerous terraces formed for the purpose of cultivation. Many prehistoric hill forts in Northumberland have them. Those at Housesteads were almost certainly built by local people who lived in the *vicus*. Food production was one of their most important tasks.

The water supply at Housesteads was a problem. Many visitors who have been drenched in the heavy rains which occur here may think this a strange remark. However unlike Chesters and Vindolanda there was no well at Housesteads since the fort is built upon whinstone, one of the hardest rocks to be found. Because of its height Housesteads could not be supplied by an aqueduct so elaborate arrangements had to be made to collect water from the roofs. Since rainfall at Housesteads was probably as high in the times of the Romans as today there would be a plentiful supply available. When necessary, perhaps in the summer, the supply could be supplemented by water from the Knag Burn although it is very unlikely that the water was pumped to the fort (the Romans had the technical knowledge to do this if they wanted). When needed the water would have been transported in containers on the backs of mules.

The water tank which collected rain water from the roof of the north gateway can still be seen. The sides are worn, but not by Romans sharpening their swords as is often suggested but probably by farmers many centuries later who sharpened their agricultural instruments here. As can be expected there was a large tank near the latrines which collected water from the angle tower.

The well near the south gate of the fort is fairly modern.

Knag Burn Gateway

This gateway, along with another which once stood at Portgate is one of the rare gateways through the wall used for civilian purposes. It was closed by double gates with a guard room on each side entered from the gate passage. The gateway is not original and was probably built after 300 A.D. when the civilian settlement was flourishing and trade was expanding. Lying on a drove road it was clearly intended to regulate traffic and levy necessary tolls. Custom tolls were collected by a Roman official called a *beneficiarius* and we know there was one stationed at Housesteads. The existence of this gateway probably led to the establishment of an important market here.

Milecastle 37

450 yards west of Housesteads we come to milecastle 37. It measures internally 57 feet 6 inches from east to west and 49 feet 6 inches from north to east with side walls nine feet thick. A building inscription informs us it was built by the second legion in the governorship of Aulus

Sketch of the interior of Milecastle 37, as excavated by John Clayton in 1852.

Platorius Nepos who came to Britain in 122 A.D. The milecastle is of the normal type with the wall acting as north side. The southern corners are rounded externally but squared on the inside. It was approached by a branch road leading from the military way and entered by a gateway in the centre of the south side. A road led north to a similar gateway through the wall. Inside on the east side was a store building probably used as barracks by the garrison of perhaps 20 men. Between it and the north wall were ovens. On the west side stood timber buildings used for stores and equipment and probably horses as well. The stone steps leading up to the rampart of the wall were probably in the north west corner.

Housesteads Bastle

Hodgson tells us that "Housesteads was once celebrated as the seat of a daring clan of thieves of the name of Armstrong". In the seventeenth century Housesteads bastle was probably the home of Hugh Nixon who was known as a cattle thief and receiver of stolen goods. The bastle is built against the southern wall of the Roman fort east of the south gateway. The walls are four feet thick and naturally built of Roman stones. The wall of the Roman fort has been pierced with an entrance to the guard room which was probably used as extra accommodation for the bastle. Later a kiln was built in it. The upper floor has completely gone but a turf bank against the east wall shows evidence of an outer staircase.

244

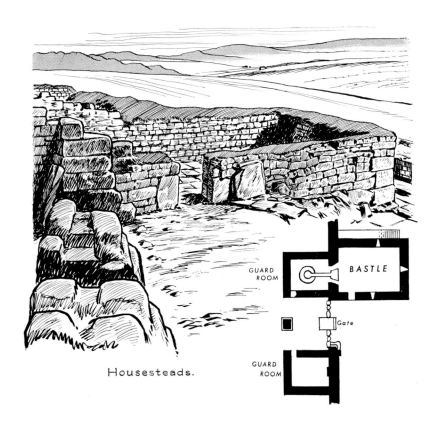

GUARD ROOM

BASTLE

Gate

GUARD ROOM

Housesteads.

HUMSHAUGH

Humshaugh is half a mile north of Chollerford on the west bank of the North Tyne. It is a picturesque village in a beautiful rural setting. The houses are stone built, many of them very old. The finest however is a red brick Georgian mansion called Humshaugh House. It is of five bays and two storeys with stone quoins and stone lintels above the windows. The doorway is pedimented. The church of St. Peter was erected in 1818. The architect is unknown although Persner mentions Seward. John Dobson's daughter claims her father was responsible. The old inn is called the Crown. The village name means the "haugh of a man called Hun". The rope-and-pulley ferry which crosses the river from Barrasford is not now in use. It was started in 1788 when William Smith made the dam to provide water for his new paper mill. Before that time, as early as the reign of Henry II, Ranulf of Haughton and William de Swinburne agreed at their joint expense to provide a ferry here. A path through the fields leads to Haughton Castle.

KIELDER

On Kielder side, the wind blows wide,
There sounds nae hunting horn,
That rings sae sweet, as the winds that bleat
Round banks where Tyne is born.

A. C. Swinburne.

Two miles further up stream from the Lewisburn comes the Kielder Burn. Near where it enters the North Tyne is Kielder Castle. The story of the "Cowt of Keilder" has been told in a well-known border ballad.

"The young Cowt of Kielder being near the castle of his deadly foe, Lord Soulis of Hermitage, is decoyed, with his train, into the hall, to partake of some refreshment. He escapes the horrible death prepared for him by the treacherous Lord Soulis, and hews his way through the glittering lances of his foe's retainers. The brown man of the moors – a malignant fairy – rises up and tells Lord Soulis the secret of the Cowt's invulnerability. He wears charmed mail, and carries in his helmet the mystic 'holly green and rowan leaves', which avail nothing against running water. Crossing the burn the Cowt stumbled, and the talisman was washed away, and his enemies coming up, held his head under the water until he was dead. The name 'Cout, or Colt', was given to him on account of his strength and activity".

There are several ancient sites in the neighbourhood of Kielder. Traces of camps, may be seen at Bell's Hunkin, Raven's Hill, Hitchill Wood, Camp Rigg, Lowery Knowe and Hobb's Knowe, all within a radius of little more than a mile. To the north-east of Kielder lies Peel Fell (1,975 feet). At the top of the watershed from which streams flow into England and Scotland is the farm of Deadwater. The source of the Tyne is near the former railway line between Kielder Station in England and Saughtree in Scotland, about two miles north of Kielder just across the Scottish border, at which point is a sulphur well once reputed to be able to cure scrofulous complaints.

The engraving of Kielder Castle here reproduced was by William Beilby, the famous Newcastle glass engraver. The view is described as follows:-

"It was built by Earl Percy, in the castellated style; but its resemblance to a genuine remain of antiquity is, like most modern attempts in that way, but slight. It is but a moderate-sized building, and is chiefly used as a hunting seat.

"Scarcely anything can be conceived more dreary than the scenery surrounding this castle. On all sides the country is wild and uncultivated and the road to the house, which is over moors and bogs, is for horsemen only. Nature seems here arrayed in her rudest garb, and the spot could only be chosen, as is the case, by a nobleman or gentleman, from its conveniency for field-sports, and as affording a retreat for the exercise of hospitality, where no other could be found. It should be observed, however, that from the hills behind, which rise with un-

Keelder Castle in Northumberland, the Seat of Earl Percy.

W. Delly del.

W. Warner Sculp

Published as the Act directs Nov.r 1.st 1783 by W.r White, Fleet Street.

247

common grandeur, the prospects are very extensive, commanding in clear weather the sea, both to the east and west, and compensate in some measure."

Kielder Castle is picturesquely situated on Humphrey's knowe at the junction of the North Tyne and Kielder burn. It was built as a house for moorgame shooting between 1772 and 1775. It is quad-rangular in plain with an arched entrance designed in the Gothic style then popular. In the nineteenth century the south front was rebuilt in a plain severe baronial style. It is now occupied by the Forestry Commission.

When Macaulay published his famous *History of England* he quoted Sir Walter Scott about the state of the Border and asserted the area around Kielder was peopled by a race scarcely less savage than the Indians of California. He then quoted from the *Journal* of Scott's visit to Alnwick in 1827 when he referred to a conversation with the Duke. "He tells me his people in Kielder were all quite wild the first time his father went up to shoot there. The women had no other dress than a bed-gown and petticoat. The men were savage, and could hardly be brought to rise from the heath, either through sullenness or fear. They sang a wild tune, the burden of which was 'orcina, orcina, orcina'. The females sang, the men danced round, and at a certain part of the tune they drew their dirks which they always wore'. The remarks of Macaulay and Sir Walter Scott roused a storm of protest. Sir J. Swinburne wrote in 1856 :- "I have been landed proprietor at the head of North Tyne for seventy years and more; my acquaintance commenced some twelve years before. I remember old people who inhabited that country before the rising under Lord Derwentwater (1715); but I never witnessed myself, nor ever heard a word from any person of such customs as Macaulay alludes to. The Borders were as quiet in my earliest youth as they are at the present day."

Disparaging remarks were not however confined to foreigners. In his *View of Northumberland* published in 1776 W. Hutchinson describes the shepherds of the Border :-

I muft not quit this country without remarking, that as we advanced towards the boundary of the kingdoms, the hills were cloathed with a fingular verdure, affording fine fheep walks; and the flocks and herds were numerous. The cottages of the lower clafs of people are deplorable, compofed of upright timbers fixed in the ground, the interftices wattled and plaiftered with mud: the roofs, fome thatched, and others covered with turf; one little piece of glafs to admit the beams of day; and a hearth ftone on the ground, for the peat and turf fire. Within, there was ex-hibited a fcene, to touch the feelings of the heart: defcription fickens on the fubject, and a tear of pity blots out the moving line, which ftrives to depict. I wifhed for fome of the difcontented great ones, who, palled with luxury, defpife their palaces, to change the fcene for a little, juft time fufficient to gain conviction, that the cottager and crowned head are both of one fpecie of animals, and of one race. The damp earth, the naked rafters, the breeze-difturbed embers, and diftracted fmoke that iffues from the hearth, moved by contrary blafts, breaking through a thousand crannies; the mid-day gloom, the wretched couch, the wooden utensils that scarce retain the name of convenience, the domestic beast that stalls with its master, the disconsolate poultry that mourn of the rafters, form a group of objects for a great man's contemplation.

The inhabitants are of abject countenance, and miserably cloathed, seeming to confess the lowest degree of poverty. The employment of the men is in the field; most of them are shepherds or herdsmen. The corn land, which is very little in quantity compared with the meadows and grazing grounds, lays mingled with the other over the open faces of the vales, without any fences; to protect which, many an indolent herdsman stands for hours wrapped up in his plaid, hanging over a staff, half animated; or otherwise laying prostrate upon the ground. During the time he is engaged in this duty, if he had a spade put in his hand, and was broke into the rules of industry, he might be most usefully employed: he could fence the ground which he tends, in the time he spends in herding it: but evil customs, when they correspond with habitual indolence, are as hard to be eradicated, as to move a mountain – a long series of applications and labour, and the redoubled effects of example and experience, must effect it. In consequence of this stupid custom, the farmer is necessarily obliged to keep a multitude of servants. Their wages are paid in the products of the land – grain, wool, maintenance of sheep and cattle; very few money payments being used.

Four miles south west of Kielder on the Border is a piece of land called Bloody Bush, recording some forgotten Border fray. Here the drove road from Scotland entered Northumberland. At this spot is a large monument which records no battle but tells us that the road is private and tolls are collected at a gate near Oakenshaw Bridge. The toll for sheep, calves and swine is $\frac{1}{2}$d, for cattle 1d, for horses 3d, unless they were leading coals when the charge was 2d.

"BLOODYBUSH" ON THE OLD DROVE ROAD FROM SCOTLAND.

KIRKHARLE

A few scattered houses and a small church are all that is left of Kirkharle. The word is derived from the personal name *Herela* and *kirk* meaning church. The village is five miles north west of Capheaton. The tower here is first mentioned in 1722. Kirkharle was a manor included in the barony of Bolbeck and was held in 1365 by Sir Robert de Harle and later by the Loraines. The tower was demolished at the end of the nineteenth century with the exception of the east end which was converted into a farmhouse. The tiny church of Kirkharle was rebuilt about 1336 and the mason work of the old parts is of a high standard. The bell-cote, built in the eighteenth century has a bell dated 1732 and when being cast it had three silver coins of George I inserted into it. This is a relic of an old superstition that a current silver coin must be inserted into a newly cast bell. The church was thoroughly restored in 1885. Kirkharle is chiefly notable as the birthplace of Lancelot Brown who was born here in August 30th, 1716 and educated at Cambo. He began his career as a gardener to Sir William Loraine and then worked for Mr. Shaftoe of Benwell. But he left Northumberland in 1739 for Stowe where his abilities were noticed and he became head gardener at Windsor and Hampton Court. He was known as "Capability Brown" because he was always using the word *capability* to describe the potentialities for improvement in the scenery of the places where he worked. He not only became famous as a landscape gardener but was an architect with a high reputation. He died in 1783 after a life's work which had a considerable influence on the development of the English landscape. Near Kirkharle is Little Harle tower overlooking a wooded park. The remains of the tower are incorporated in a large Victorian mansion. It has been elaborately modernised. In the survey of 1541 it is described as "in good reparations". It formerly belonged to the De Harles, passing successively into the hands of the Fenwicks and the Aynsleys. In the mansion is an interesting fireplace which came from Anderson House, Newcastle.

In a field near the remains of Kirkharle Tower is a stone pillar which was set up by Capability Brown's employer. It replaced an old stone which commemorated his ancestor Robert Loraine, "who was barborously murdered in this place by the Scots in 1483 for his good services to his country against their thefts and robbery, as he was returning home from the church alone, where he had been at his private devotions".

KIRKHAUGH

Two miles south of Slaggyford lies the small village of Kirkhaugh. Our illustration shows the church in 1840 before restoration. Here on December 3rd, 1714, John Wallis the historian of Northumberland was christened. He was born at Castle Nook Farm near Whitley Castle. He tells us:-

Northumberland being Roman ground, and receiving my first breath in Whitley Castle one of their castra I was led by a sort of enthusiasm

Kirkhaugh Church

to an enquiry and search after their towns, their cities, and temples, their baths, their altars, their tumuli, their military ways, and other remains of splendour and magnificence.

A little to the north is Barhaugh Hall a modest old country house. Also nearby, just across the border in Cumbria is Randalholm Hall an ancient pele tower with an ancient armorial stone escutcheon on the north front of the whitewashed house.

KIRKHEATON

The pleasant village of Kirkheaton contains the seventeenth-century manor house of the Herons. It is two storeys high with hood-moulded windows and door. The walled garden is entered by rusticated gate piers. At the end is a square addition with Georgian windows which was built on the walls of a medieval pele tower. There is a tradition that Oliver Cromwell once stayed here.

The house was restored in 1931. The plan shows the layout of the ground floor at this time. There were five main rooms in the Tudor section, one for each window, but the height of the ceiling was only $6\frac{1}{2}$ feet. All the fireplaces, especially the plain arched one in the kitchen were of interest. There was also a secret recess as shown on the plan, probably a priest's hiding place.

We do not know when the ancient chapel at Kirkheaton was built. The first reference to it is in an inventory of 1553: "Churche Hetton; one challes of tenne, one vestment, one albe, ij alterclothes, one bell". In 1753 a new building was erected on the site. Four grotesque heads

KIRK HEATON CHURCH
Co^y of North^t

Published Feby 1828 by W Davison Alnwick

Rev Humprey Brown Chaplain   *Drawn by T.Sopwith*
J.Kerr Sculp

at the angles of the nave, under the water table, are perhaps relics of the medieval chapel. Our illustration was published by W. Davison of Alnwick in 1828.

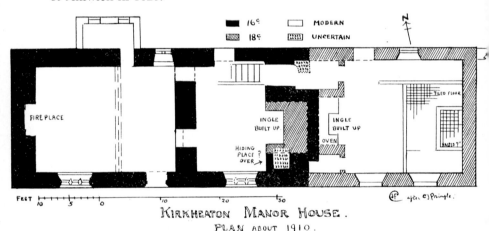

KIRKHEATON MANOR HOUSE.
PLAN ABOUT 1910.

KIRKWHELPINGTON

This quiet stone-built village lies just off the main Newcastle-Otterburn road, situated on rising ground above the river Wansbeck which is crossed here by a stone bridge built in 1818. It is first mentioned in the Pipe Rolls of 1182 where it is called *Welpinton*. Two well-known antiquaries lived here. Anthony Hedley was curate from 1814 to 1819 and John Hodgson, the great Northumbrian historian was vicar from 1823 to 1832.

The church, dedicated to St. Bartholomew, was originally a cross church but its transepts have been removed and it now consists of a tower, nave and chancel. The tower is low and broad, with massive square buttresses. The church is entered by a stone-roofed porch with a sundial of 1764. The entrance to the nave is through a thirteenth century pointed doorway decorated with two round pillars.

The tower arch and chancel arch are thirteenth century work. The tower arch has zigzag decoration and is supported on two round shafts with two orders of scalloped capitals. The wide chancel arch has low octagonal responds with a tall double-chamfered arch. In the church is a wall inscription to Sir Charles Algernon Parsons who was buried here in 1931. Sir Charles was a great local engineer and industrialist. He is best known as the builder of the steam turbine *Turbinia*. He was greatly interested in optics and founded works in Walker for making telescopes.

The vicarage dates back to the 18th century but contains one wall from a medieval vicar's pele. By the door leading from the vicarage to the churchyard is a bronze inscription to John Hodgson's wife and two children who were all buried on the same day having died of a fever.

Beside the pele tower incorporated into the vicarage there was in Hodgson's day (1827) at Kirkwhelpington another pele called Bolt House which has now gone.

THE CHURCH OF WHELPINGTON,

KNARESDALE

The village of Knaresdale lies seven miles south-west of Haltwhistle on the South Tyne. The name is derived from the Knar stream, "a rough mountain torrent which intersects the western portion from west to east." The first earls of Knaresdale were called Prat. They were probably of Norman origin and had their lands from William the Lion, King of Scotland, as early as 1177. But the Prats offended Edward I who sent them "home" to Scotland and handed the manor over to the Swinburnes.

The church is first mentioned in 1680 when an injunction was made for repairing the church and bell. It was pulled down and rebuilt in 1838. In the churchyard is the strange epitaph of Robert Baxter, who died October 4th, 1796.

KNARESDALE CHURCH.

All you that please these lines to read,
It will cause a tender heart to bleed;
I murdered was upon the fell,
And by the man I knew full well;
By bread and butter which he'd laid,
I, being harmless, was betrayed.
I hope he will rewarded be,
That laid that poison there for me."

Knaresdale Hall was built in the seventeenth century on a knoll between the Milburn and the Tyne. It still retains some mullioned windows.

John Hodgson (1840) describes the hall as a "gentleman's place of the seventeenth century, now, and for a long time since, occupied by the farmer of the adjoining grounds, and consequently despoiled of many appendages to the dignity it was wont to assume while it was the seat of the lord of the fee of Knaresdale and its contiguous demesnes. The garden walls have lost their trimness, the malt-kiln and the brew-house are gone, and little now remains but the usual extensive suite of stables, which, in gone-by times, were at once the joy and ruin of the old race of country squires. Its site, however, is still the same, on a proud, natural knoll, between the Milburn and the Tyne, and defended on every side, but on the line of approach, by steep banks; and overlooking, upwards and downwards, the green haughs and woody braes of the Tyne".

Since Hodgson's day the hall has been restored. A story connected with it is summarised by Tomlinson:-

The laird marries a young wife, who falls in love with her husband's nephew, and proves unfaithful to her marriage vows. The young man's sister learns the secret, but keeps silence for her brother's sake. The guilty pair, however, grow suspicious of her, and resolve upon a dark deed. One terribly stormy night the girl is sent to close an outer door in the rear of the house, where she is siezed by her brother, who was on the watch, and plunged into an old pond much swollen by the rain. The old man, unsuspicious of foul play, falls asleep, but is awakened by the hideous howling of one of his dogs, and starting up in an agony, beholds his niece standing by the kitchen fire wringing the water from her long hair. At the sound of his voice the apparition vanishes. The guilty brother disappears, and is no more seen, and the lady dies from a brain fever, after having revealed in her unconscious ravings the dreadful secret.

LAMBLEY

A short distance south of the point where the Blackburn enters the South Tyne is the village of Lambley which is first mentioned in 1201. Here was the site of a small convent of Benedictine Nuns. In 1296 the house of the holy nuns of Lambley' was burnt by the Scots. The convent was restored. When it was dissolved by Henry it had six inmates and the yearly revenue was £5 15s. 8d. Now not a trace remains since most of the ruins have been swept away by the river.

Nearby is the famous Lambley Viaduct spanning the South Tyne at a height of 110 feet. It is one of the great monuments of the Railway Age. The Haltwhistle to Alston line was completed in 1852 but in spite of opposition was closed down in 1977.

The church at Lambley was built in 1885 replacing an earlier edifice.

LANGLEY CASTLE

Langley Castle was the head of the barony of Tynedale in feudal times. It is one and a half miles south of Haydon Bridge and is a fine example of a tower house of the fourteenth century. It is first mentioned in 1365 and was probably built a few years earlier by Sir Thomas de Lucy. It was destroyed in 1405 by Henry IV as he advanced into Northumberland to put down Archbishop Scrope's rebellion which had been joined by the Earl of Northumberland. In the well known book *The Beauties of England and Wales* (1801-15) is the following description:

"It is well situated on the south bank of the Tyne and though it has of late years been barborously handled, it is by far the most perfect ruin of the kind in the county. It is in the form of the letter 'H', its walls near seven feet thick, its inside twenty-four feet by eighty feet. and the towers, one at each corner, about sixty-six feet high. The rooms remaining are all arched with stone; those in the towers are fourteen feet square, and the four small fire rooms on the east each eleven feet by thirteen feet. The ground rooms, on the east and west, four on each side, have been much injured by being used as farm offices. The windows which have lighted the great hall, kitchens etc. are large; those in the chambers mostly small, and built at an angle that would

A steam train, on the Alston to Haltwhistle railway, crossing Lambley viaduct

LANGLEY CASTLE, NORTHUMBERLAND, 1884.

prevent the entrance of an enemy's arrow. The stones of which this fabric is built are yet so remarkably fresh as to exhibit in their primitive sharpness the characters of the masons. The whole of the inside is red with marks of fire". In the 1890's the castle was restored by Cadwallader Bates.

The castle, like Haughton, is an oblong house with four symmetrical towers at the angles. Originally each tower had a room on each floor, with a single room in the centre. Very soon after building an entrance tower was added on the east face containing the main staircase and a vaulted guard-room on each floor. The doorway on the ground floor had a portcullis the slot of which can still be seen as well as a boss in the vaulting with a face through the mouth of which the rope for the portcullis passed. The main entrance is on the first floor through a double doorway, in the original east wall. The doorway is flanked with fine ornamental shafting. The south-west tower contains only latrines which are so numerous that the castle must have had a large number of inhabitants. The battlements are the work of C. Bates but the corbelled out bartizans are probably similar to those on the original building. Very few of the original windows remain. Those in the central portion change as they ascend from Decorated to Perpendicular style.

257

LEE HALL

Lee Hall is a charming English country house in a beautiful rural setting. In 1715 it was described as a "neat house" so it must have been built some time before then. It is built of stone with five bays and two-and-a-half storeys. "Its high pitched gables, instead of the pavilion roof proper to this kind of front, show the strength of the local Jacobean building tradition." The entrance is an arched doorway in the middle with heavy keystones and an arched window above. The staircase on the left is of interest. It is for the servants. Many halls had special entrances for retainers.

Lee Hall was the ancient seat of a branch of the Charlton family. The misdeeds of William Charlton of Lee Hall who was county keeper at the end of the seventeenth century were long remembered in the district. "He is said to have been closely connected with an organised gang of horse-stealers, who made their raids on both sides of the Border. His feuds with Lowes of Willimoteswick, the county-keeper of South Tynedale, were long remembered in the district. After several narrow escapes from his bold and implacable enemy, Lowes was at length taken prisoner in a fight near Sewingshields, and conveyed to Lee Hall, where he suffered, it is said, the greatest indignities, having been actually fastened to the grate of the kitchen fire, with just enough length of chain to enable him to get his food at the table with the servants. He was subsequently rescued by Frank Stokoe, of Chesterwood".

On one occasion they fought together and Charlton killed his opponent's horse, on which the local people made a rhyme:-

> Oh had Lee Hall but been a man,
>   As he was never nane,
> He wad have stricken the rider
> And letten the horse alane.

A writer in 1715 tells us that "at ye Lee Hall a excellent spring, ye vertue is such yt if ye lady of ye Hall dip aney children yt have ye rickets or any other over groone destemper, it is either a speedy cure or death. The manner and form is as followeth:- The days of dipping are on Whitsunday Even, on Midsumer Even, on Saint Peter's Even. They must bee dipt in ye well before the sun rise, and in ye River Tine after ye sun bee sett: then ye shift taken from ye child and thrown into ye river and if it swim, child liveth, but if it sink dyeth".

LEWISBURN

Higher up the stream than Plashetts the Lewisburn enters the North Tyne from the south. Writing to Cardinal Wolsey in 1536 Sir William Eure writes as follows: "The rebels of Tynedale make some besyness in Tynedale, wher ther dwellings was, and in no place els they melle or dois hurt, ther abydings is a place called Lushburn Howles (Lewis Burn), a marvellous stronge grounde of woodes and waters".

The next tributary is the Gowanburn which is mentioned in the old ballad:-

> "There's walth o' kye i' bonny Braidlees,
> Ther's walth o' youses i' Tine;
> There's walth o' gear i' Gowanburn,
> And they shall all be thine".

LINNELS BRIDGE

Linnels Bridge on the line of the road from Hexham to Slaley, two miles south, spans the Devil's Water in a single picturesque arch. The present bridge was probably built in 1698 when the owners of the Linnels were presented by the grand jury of Hexham for having suffered the Linnels bridge to go out of repair.

In the parapet of the bridge is a stone slab which belonged to the earlier structure. This tablet once had an inscription on both sides but only the outside one is now legible and reads:

GOD PRESARVE

WMFOIRA

ERENGTON,

BELLDETE THIS

BREGE OF LYME

AND STONE,

1581

It is rare to find such an early inscription in the local tongue.

Stone Slab, on the parapet of Linnels Bridge.

LITTLE BAVINGTON

Little Bavington hardly exists today as a village having only two or three houses. It is named after its Anglian founder – *Babba*. Little Bavington as well as Great Bavington belonged after the Norman Conquest to the Umfravill barony of Prudhoe. In 1300 the Shafto family had property here and their name was associated with Bavington until the Rebellion of 1715, when they supported the Jacobites and forfeited their estates.

The present house at Little Bavington was begun c.1730 by Admiral Delaval. It is three storeys in height with seven bays and a hipped roof. It has entrance doors in the centre of both north and south elevations. The door in the north front is heavy arched with Gibbs surround, on the south side the slenderer pedimented doorway also has a Gibbs surround. The south front is covered with stucco. The main structure is oblong but at the north east is a lower two storeyed wing which appears to be of an earlier period and beyond it is the kitchen wing with two big arched windows.

The house contains some fine carved chimney pieces. In one room there is a fireplace and overmantel flanked by two fine Corinthian plasters right to the ceiling. Another room contains original panelling with a remarkable fireplace with termini caryatids on left and right and a curly broken pediment above the overmantel.

A short distance to the south west is a miniature castle, now ruined, with a raised centre, which was built as a dove-cote.

LITTLE SWINBURN TOWER

This tower is now a ruin which still shows the doorway and part of the spiral staircase. Not mentioned in 1415 but in 1541 it is said that "at lytle Swyneburne is a little towre of the inheritance of Thomas Mydleton of Belso, esqui' decayed in the roofes." Our illustration shows the tower as it was 150 years ago. Standing near Little Swinburn Reservoir little is to be seen today.

From a drawing by

the late Mr. Edward Swinburne.

MELKRIDGE BASTLE

Once stood on the Newcastle to Carlisle road two miles east of Haltwhistle. It was pulled down in 1955. It was an oblong tower-house measuring 38ft. by 24ft. with walls four feet thick. It was two storeys high with an attic and watch turret. The two original doorways the loopholes in the first floor and the small windows in the two upper floors can be seen in our drawing.

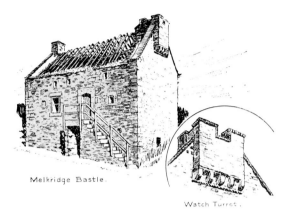

Melkridge Bastle.

Watch Turret.

MICKLEY

The old village is on high land below Mickley Moor. The nineteenth century village of Mickley Square is on the Newcastle-Hexham road. The name means "the mickle or large clearing". It was of some importance in the Middle Ages. There are no early records of coal mining in the area but about 1700 the colliery of Mickley Bank was worked by Thomas Bewick the grandfather of the famous wood engraver.

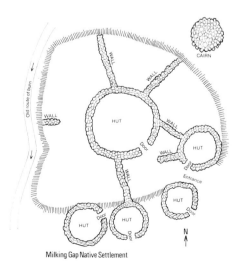

Milking Gap Native Settlement

MILKING GAP

The break in the basaltic ridge opposite the farm-house of Hot Bank is called Milking Gap. This gap affords easy access to the area north of the Wall. Through it runs the Bradley Burn which drains Crag Lough to the north of the ridge. Here the remains of a native settlement can be traced. It consists of five round houses enclosed by a turf wall, on a stone foundation but not really fortified. The central house is the most important. All the houses were built of uncut stone and rubble to the height of about five feet and the roof was supported on internal wooden posts placed near the outer wall. The entrance was closed by a plaited wattle door. The roof would be thatched, probably with reeds from the lough.

The few dated remains found on the site suggest it was occupied between 120 A.D. and 180 A.D. This is difficult to explain since, lying between the Wall and the Vallum, the native settlement would be in a military zone.

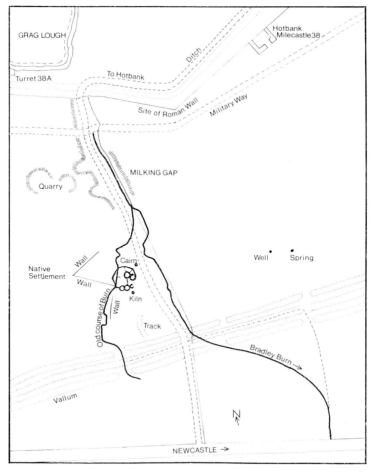

MINSTERACRES

Minsteracres is a large house, six miles south of Corbridge, now belonging to the Passionists. It stands in the midst of an extensive park with fine trees and gardens. It was built by the Silvertop family whose fortunes were laid in the eighteenth century from the control they had of several coalmines in the Ryton and Chopwell area. Nothing remains of their early home and the present mansion was apparently built on a new site by John Silvertop in the late eighteenth century. It was enlarged in 1867. Only the stables and lodges seem to belong to the first building. The Silvertops were Roman Catholics and a chapel in the Gothic style was built in 1852-4 to replace an oratory. It is connected with the hall by a cloister.

MINSTER ACRES,

MUMPS HA'

On the border of Northumberland near to Gilsland railway station once stood *Mumps Ha'* or *Beggar's Hall* the house where Dandie Dinmont (in Guy Mannering) tells the news of Ellangowan's death to Meg Merrilies. Meg Merrilies herself, although features have been borrowed from real persons, is a character from fiction.

"Mumps' Hall", says Hodgson, "according to tradition, was once a public-house, kept by a notorious person of the name of Meg Teasdale, who drugged to death such of her guests as had money. In *Guy Mannering* she glares in the horrid character of Meg Merrilies. But certainly all this tradition is deeply coloured with unpardonable slander against the ancient and respectable family of the Teasdale's of Mumps' Hall".

Writing in 1851, Dr. Bruce tells us that Mumps' Ha' was on the road leading to the railway station round which it bent at a right angle. He gives us a woodcut which shows the back of the house which

Mumps Hall, 1885

still retained the character of a Border fortress. Although Meg was not as black as the character of fiction, Bruce tells us that the tradition of the country lay one murder to her charge. "A pedlar having called upon Meg's brother, who kept a school at Long Byers (midway between Rose Hill and Greenhead) accidently presented to him a box filled with guineas instead of his snuff box. The traveller was requested to convey a note to Mumps' Hall which he did, but was not seen alive afterwards. Suspicion arising, the house was searched, and the body found concealed among hay in the barn; but the parties who made the discovery durst not reveal it, for fear of injury to themselves and families. About six weeks later, the body was found lying upon the moors." My informant added to his narrative – "probably the laws were not so active in those days as at the present, for these things could not escape now".

"When Meg was upon her death-bed, the curiosity of the neighbourhood was excited, and many of her cronies visited her, in hopes of hearing her disburden her conscience respecting the death of the pedlar. They were, however, disappointed for whenever she attempted to speak upon the subject, some one of the family, who always took care to be present, placed a hand upon her mouth."

Near Mumps' Ha' there was a deep pond where the victims were supposed to have been thrown. Local superstition said that the surface of the pond was covered with a blue phosphorescent light which was visible to passers-by after night.

Near Monks Hall is Upper Denton Church, a small ancient building. In the churchyard is buried Meg and several of her family, their four tombstones ranged in a row. Margaret Carrick died in 1717 at the age of one hundred and her daughter Margaret Teasdale in 1777, aged ninety eight. On her tombstone is the following inscription:-

What I was once fame may relate,
What I am now is each one's fate,
What I shal be none can explain,
Till he that called me call again.

NAFFERTON

Nafferton township now consists of only two farms. The greater part lies to the north of the Newcastle-Corbridge road which crosses the Whittle Dene near the remains of Nafferton Tower. The bridge was built in 1809, the stones being taken from the ruins nearby. Lonkins Hall or Whittle Tower is the name which Nafferton Castle was later given.

The remains are interesting because it was an adulterine castle, that is a castle built without licence, and as a result dismantled. In 1217 Philip de Ulecotes who had been a favourite of King John began to build a castle at Nafferton. The following year Richard de Umfraville complained that the castle was an injury to the castle and lands of Prudhoe nearby and a writ was issued in the name of Henry III ordering him to proceed no further with the building. In 1221 the Constable of Newcastle and the Sheriff of Northumberland were instructed to remove to Bamburgh the large building timber and the *bretesche* at Nafferton. But shortly afterwards they were told to take the *bretesche* to Newcastle where it was erected in place of a turret which had fallen down on account of its bad foundation. The ruins of Nafferton were used in 1809 as a source of stone to build the bridge crossing Whittle Dene.

The fame of Nafferton Castle, however, rests on the legends that grew up around it. It was said to be the castle which Lang Lonkin built for Lord Wearie, "but payment got he none". Lonkin took dreadful vengeance for the non-payment and the castle was left deserted. The ballad is known all over the British Isles and travelled to America. More than twenty versions are known. Two are from Northumberland. The version from Ovington describes how a giant freebooter called Lonkin got into nearby Welton Hall with the aid of a maidservant.

'Where's the Ladies of the Hall?'
Says the Lonkin;
'They're up in their chambers',
Says Orange to him.

'How shall we get them down?'
Says the Lonkin;
'Prick the baby in the cradle',
Says Orange to him'.

So the poor lady came down to find her child dead and the murderer there. They order her daughter Betsy to hold a gold basin to catch her mother's blood:

'To hold the gold basin,
It grieves me full sore
Oh, kill me, dear Lonkin,
And let my Mother go'.

Betsy was not murdered and tells her father on his return from London what has happened. Lonkin is hanged and the nurse burnt at the stake. There are still marks on the spiral staircase at Welton Hall which are said to be blood-stains and the lady's ghost haunts the upper room. Other versions say Lonkin hanged himself or was killed by falling from the branch of an oak into a well which turns into blood one day every year. In Whittle Dene a small cascade falls into a deep pool called the "Whirl Dub" which is said to be enormously deep. When Lang Lonkin was being chased he wrapped his booty in an ox-hide and cast it in the pool where it remains to-day. One country-man nearly recovered the treasure but lost it through profanity. He was dragging the treasure out by a rope attached to horses when he suddenly saw the oxhide appear. He shouted. "Pull, horses, pull, whether God will or not". The rope immediately broke. The ingredients of this tale are told of many places in Northumberland.

Later in the eighteenth century the ruins of the tower were said to be the haunt of highwaymen but there is no proof of this assertion.

The castle was built as a keep with two baileys but the remains are now difficult to trace.

The name Nafferton has a strange derivation. It is the home of *Nattfari*, or *Traveller by Night*, a word of Scandinavian origin. Since

PHILIP DE ULECOTE'S CASTLE, NAFFERTON.

Old Print, 1853

the nearby Welton has an equally mysterious origin, meaning *the home of the Unsteady One*, it is possible that there is some connection between the names of these places and the strange legends associated with them.

Re.^d J. Thompson Vicar. Revd G. Richmond Curate ,

NEWBROUGH CHURCH
Northumberland .
Published July, 1827, by W. Davison Alnwick.

NEWBROUGH

"Newbrough was founded and formed into a borough by the Cumin family in 1221 when they obtained a charter for a market at Thornton, which was the name of the estate upon which this *new burgh* was situated." Its position on the old Stanegate and the fertile lands around were important in its development. Edward I stayed here several weeks in 1306. The present church of St. Peter Stonecroft (built 1865) stands on the site of an ancient chapel, built in 1242. St. Mary's well nearby was reputed in days gone by to have miraculous powers to cure people. In the centre of the village is the Town Hall built in 1876.

At the church of St. Peter a Roman fort was revealed in 1930. From Newbrough the modern road follows the Stanegate for three miles to Grindon Hill on the south side of which three temporary camps are to be found.

Newbrough Hall

Newbrough Hall is a two storeyed building with central pediment built in 1821 by John Dobson for Rev. Henry Wastell. Hodgson seems to make a mistake with the date. He wrote – "In the year following (1812) Mr. Wastell built the mansion-house here, in which he at present resides, and which is very delightfully situated, and embellished with gardens, lawn, rich surrounding scenery, and a wide and cheerful prospect over the banks of the Tyne to the south."

To the north of Newbrough Hall in the farmyard are the remains of the tower first mentioned in 1542 as belonging to Lord Burrawe. It was then in good repair. Hodgson says that in his day it measured 42 feet by 33 feet and although the ashlar was gone the walls were still six feet thick. The walls today are 8 to 20 feet high but no architectural details can be made out.

Newbrough Lodge

William Ord of Sturton Grange, who married the daughter of Thomas Gibson of Stonecroft bought in 1796 from William Errington twp farmholds in Newbrough called Blackbull and Foulpool and here he built Newbrough Lodge which stands between Stonecroft and Thornton. The Directory of 1828 describes it as a "neat mansion belonging to J. N. Maughan". The stone Georgian house is of three bays and two storeys. A colonnaded extension was added later at both ends and large wings were also built in the nineteenth century. There is a fine walled garden.

Stonecroft House

In 1693 Lord Widdrington sold the Stonecroft estate to Thomas Gibson for £150. The Gibson family held it until 1822. The present house was built in 1840 using many of the old oak beams from the earlier house which was demolished.

LANGLEY.

Commissioners & Governors of Greenwich Hospital Lead Smelt Works, *Langley mill;* James Mulcaster, agent

Dickinson Jno. bookkeeper, *Langley*

Hudgill-Burn Mining Co.'s Lead Smelt Works, *Blagill mill;* Geo. Lee, Esq. actuary

Mulcaster James, lead agent

Woodman Robert, farmer, *Langley Castle*

LIPWOOD.

Coats Thomas, Esq. *Lipwood house*

Coulson John, blacksmith, *Waterhouse*

Maughan Nicholas, vict. Board, *Waterhouse*

Parker Mrs. Margaret, *Hill house*

Farmers.

*Marked * are yeomen.*

Bell John, *Whinetley*

Benson Margaret, *Grindon hill*

*Coats Thomas, *Lipwood*

*Dryden John, *Kennell*

Errington Thomas, *Simon shield*

Errington Thomas, *Lipwood well*

Kent ——, *Fleckgate*

Lambert William, *Peel well*

M'Knee Charlton, *Linstons*

Maughan Joseph, *Ratten row*

Woodman John, *Whitechapel*

NEWBROUGH.

Bambrough Sarah, grocer

Boyd Thomas, schoolmaster and grocer

Charlton George, shoemaker

Charlton Thomas, cartwright

Corbett Joseph, blacksmith

Dinning Gibson, vict. Red Lion, and joiner

Hetherington John, shoemaker

Hindmarsh Thomas, grocer

Huddlestone Thos. tailor

Lambert Richard, Esq.

Maughan Nicholas, Esq. *Newbrough lodge*

Pigg Joseph, vict. Highland Piper, *Carrow*

Wastel Rev. Henry, *Newbrough hall*

Farmers.

Barron William

Dinning Joseph

Dodd Edward, *Carredge*

Forster John, yeoman

Heslop Thomas

Heslop William, *Whorters*

Magnay Charlton, *Settling Stones*

Pigh Ralph Colleson, *Lane house*

Scott John, *Prudham Stone*

Woodman John, *Cowsike*

CARRIER *to Newcastle* Thos. Hindmarsh, Wed. dep. 12 noon, ar. Fri. 12 noon.

WALWICK.

Bell John, vict. Royal Oak

Bell Michael, corn miller, *Warden mill*

Bulman Matilda, gentwmn. *Walwick hall*

Clayton Nathaniel, Esq. *Walwick Chesters*

Kirsop George, stonemason, *Homer's house*

Short Joseph, blacksmith

Farmers.

Colbeck Christopher, *Walwick Grange*

Dixon Matthew, *Rye hill*

Downes Thomas, *Walwick*

Gregorson Rt. *Park shield*

WARDEN.

Crawford Peter Rumney, paper manufacturer

Cutter Isabella, farmer

Hedley Thos. schoolmaster, *Hindhaugh*

Leadbitter Nicholas, Esq.

Ramshaw John, farmer, *Baddocks*

Temperley Ann, farmer

Walton Rev. George, curate of Warden

WARDEN, (HIGH.)

Bell Matthew, farmer

Errington Frederick, Esq.

Heslop William, farmer, *Frankham*

WHARNLEY.

Snowball Cuthbert, yeoman

Snowball John, yeoman

Directory of 1828

Newbrough Park

This fine house stands in the village of Newbrough. Hodgson (1840) tells us something of its history.

"From the old stock of the Lamberts of Newbrough was descended Mr. Richard Lambert, an eminent surgeon in Newcastle, who in 1751, at the last meeting of a convivial society in that town, to which he belonged, suggested the establishment of an Infirmary there, as a permanent memorial of their former associations . . . When Capt. Armstrong was making surveys of Northumberland, he was hospitably entertained at Mr. Lambert's country residence in Newbrough, and therefore very properly designated it on his Map. It was a very old and curious house – of three centuries at least – with a broad meadow and fine trees before it; but times convulsions had 'tugged it to and fro', and rendered considerable repairs in it necessary, which the founder of the Infirmary's son, by re-building it in a handsome style, and embellishing with a lawn and ornamental gardens, which are all kept in good order and taste by his sister, Miss Lambert, their present excellent and respected proprietor."

The Directory of 1828 describes it as a "neat house" which Richard Lambert of Newcastle has recently erected.

Another house in Newbrough is Stonecroft. In 1693 Lord Widdrington sold the Stonecroft estate to Thomas Gibson for £150. The Gibson family held it until 1822. The present house was built in 1840 using many of the old oak beams from the earlier house which was demolished.

It is difficult to realize today but right into the twentieth century Newborough was important for the quarrying of lime and stone.

NEWTON HALL

The township of Newton-hall lies north of Bywell. The house was rebuilt in 1811 and in the grounds is an observatory or gazebo. The tower of Newton appears to have been built in the fourteenth century. It is massively built with walls in places of ten feet thickness and huge diagonal buttresses. In parts they stand to-day six feet high. The basement contains a draw well said to be thirty feet deep. It is now the Mowden Hall School. (See our book on the Old Halls of Northumberland for more information.)

NINEBANKS TOWER

The tower is part of one of the few houses in the hamlet. It is a small but picturesque building obviously the forebuilding of a larger tower or house. It has four storeys but the ground has been raised so much that the original slit of the basement is now nearly level with the road. A Jacobean newel staircase was added at the same time as the fourth storey. The sketch shows the tower in 1826.

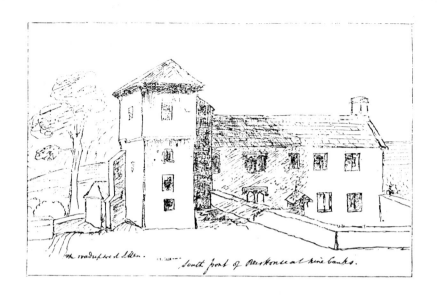

The reduced Hall. "South front of Residence at Nine banks."

NUNWICK HALL

The name of Nunwick suggests some connection with a nunnery, not one on the site but one that owned the township. A family called Nunwick lived here early in the thirteenth century. In 1379 Sir William Heron became the owner of the village. The Herons held Nunwick until in 1724 Robert Allgood purchased it. It was then a picturesque place with houses built around a green and an old manor house. It is interesting to record that in 1681 Margaret Heron participated in horse racing here on the Sabbath and entertained the gentry who attended with music at her manor house who thus failed to attend church at Simonburn. The rector, the Reverend Major Allgood, brought them before an ecclesiastical court.

About 1740 the Allgoods removed the village and on the site of the old manor house built a modern mansion. Tradition says the designer of the new house was William Adam the father of the celebrated Adam brothers. The original building was a rectangular block of brown sandstone, two and a half storeys high with five bays on the south-west and south-east fronts. In 1769 Wallis describes the house of Sir Lancelot Allgood:-

"His seat is of his own erection, after a genteel design; of white (sic) free-stone and hewn work. It stands on a rising plain, which to the east has the appearance of a park. The offices are to be the north, a grove to the west, a grass-lawn to the south, and a terraced gravel-walk to the east, which commands a view of Chipchase at one end, and a variety of prospects on the other. Two brooks unite their loquacious streams to give beauty and ornament to a neat garden, and render it an entertaining, as well as useful recess; and thence take their course by another grove on a declining hill, to the south front of the house, and fall two or three fields below into the river of North Tyne. In an adjoining field,called Nunwick-east-field, were five upright stone-pillars, in a circular order; four of them perfect and entire in 1714, the other broken; the perfect ones eight feet high, and nine feet and a half over; the circumference of the area in which they stood, ninety feet. Sir Lancelot has given a new face, as it were, to the country about Nunwick, within the space of a very few years, by making plantations, enclosures, and good roads, one of which leads to the village of Simonburn."

In 1816 and 1829 alterations were carried out by Bonomi of Durham. A four column Tuscan porch was added to the entrance on the south east and a canted bay window on the south west front. Trims were also added to the windows. A north west wing was attached of one storey (another storey added at a later date) but with two storey angle pavilions with one fine "Venetian" window, then very popular, inserted in each of the pavilions similar to the tripartite door in the centre. The service wing joined to the north corner of the main building also contains two storeyed angle-pavilions, as well as a clock-tower, forming with the stables and the wing just mentioned a courtyard.

Inside are some magnificent rooms with attractive plaster work, fine joinery and original fireplaces. Truly an outstanding house, a perfect example of its time.

When the Gothic revival became popular in Northumberland the house at Nunwick was fortunately untouched. In 1776 they restored Simonburn Castle as an "eye-catcher" and in 1768 built Gothic kennels, visible from the house (but now hidden by fine trees) but across the river. They are a low square building with battlements and lancet windows with typical Y-tracery and broad flat moulding.

"With the dogs in their low-walled courtyards on either side and the keeper in his little house nearby the kennels at Nunwick must have been one of the most charming of follies constructed really for no other purpose than to strike delight in the beholder."

(J. Macaulay – *The Gothic Revival*)

Otterburn Hall in the 18th century from a painting

Although now an hotel the house has many ancient features and interesting decorations. In the dining room is sixteenth century panelling, and above the library fireplace is a painted frieze of the Battle of Otterburn.

Otterburn Hall

This building is often confused with Otterburn Tower, partly because when Reginald Hall carried out his additions to the Tower he called it a Hall. The name Tower was restored when Thomas James erected his castellated mansion. The present Otterburn Hall was built in 1869 of red brick. The clay was excavated at the back of the house and the site is now a pond. Neo-Elizabethan in style it was added to and altered in 1901 and 1930. Now a holiday centre.

Otterburn Dene

The little valley in which it stands was known in the thirteenth century as Davy Sheles. The farm-house in the valley was bought early in the nineteenth century by Thomas Burdon of Shield Field, Newcastle, a prominent coal owner, to use it for grouse shooting. The house was known as Dene Head and was changed to Otterburn Dene.

Prehistoric Camps

There are a number of prehistoric camps near Otterburn. One and a half miles north west near *Greenchesters* is a tribal encampment which was occupied by the Scots before the famous battle of Otterburn. At Colwellhill (one mile north east of Otterburn) is an extensive camp with two earthen ramparts about eight feet high, and two ditches as deep. The fort is almost circular. Four slight depressions probably mark the position of huts.

Otterburn Hall

Half a mile west at a lower level is Fawdon camp which is an irregular circle of eighty yards with a rampart varying from six to eight feet in height. Although an univallate fort a second line of defence was probably started but never completed.

Just below Fawdon camp is the farm-house of Girsonfield in which are fragments of the house of "fause-hearted Ha's (Halls) who betrayed Percy Reed of Troughend, a keeper of Redesdale. The famous ballad describes how he was slain by a band of moss-troopers called Crozier at Batinghope near the source of the Rede.

Battle of Otterburn

The battle which has made Otterburn so famous was fought August 19th, 1388. The battle itself was of no importance, a useless carnage which had no military or political results. However the ballad singers have made the fight memorable with the romance they have created around it in their magnificent poetry.

James, Earl of Douglas, had ravaged Northumberland and Durham with an army of 4,000 men. On his return he had challenged Sir Henry Percy (Hotspur) before the gates of Newcastle and then marched to Ponteland where he had burnt the castle. Proceeding north he reached Otterburn and bivouaked one and a half miles further up the valley in an old British camp. Meanwhile Sir Henry Percy had followed him from Newcastle with a superior force of 600 spearmen and 8,000 infantry. He reached Otterburn at night. Although his men were weary after their long march he decided to attack the Scots by moonlight. Mistake followed mistake. Instead of attacking the main Scottish troops the English, due to the darkness, made their main onslaught on the area occupied by the camp folllowers. A fierce battle developed as the Scots seized their chance and attacked the English flanks with their main forces. Douglas was killed, Percy was captured and the English forces routed. They lost almost 3,000 dead and 1,000 wounded, while the Scots had only 100 killed.

Meanwhile the Bishop of Durham with 7,000 men was advancing from Newcastle to assist Sir Henry Percy but meeting fugitives from the battle his army fled back to Newcastle panic stricken. Obtaining reinforcements he once again marched north with 10,000 men. The Scots were still encamped in the same place and as the English approached they blew on the horns which each man carried "that it seemed as if all the devils in Hell had come thither to join in the noise, so that those of the English who had never before heard such were very much frightened." The bishop observed the enemy were in a well chosen and fortified encampment and declined battle returning to Newcastle. The Scots then crossed the border, taking with them their booty and prisoners.

It would be superfluous to write at length on the famous ballads which commemorate the battle of Otterburn. So much has already been written concerning the historical facts of the poems and their artistic merits. Ballad poetry is one of the glories of Northumberland. The earliest version called the *Hunting a' the Cheviat* is undoubtedly scotch in origin and the best. It was of this ballad that Sir Philip Sidney wrote in his "Discourse of Poetry" in the following words: *"I never heard the old song of Piercy and Douglas, that I found not my heart more moved than with a trumpet; and yet it is sung by some blind crowder with no rougher voice than rude stile; which being so evil apparelled in the dust and cobweb of that uncivil age, what would it work trimmed in the gorgeous eloquence of Pindar".*

The English ballad of *Chevy Chase* is a more polished version and is better known. Here are extracts from both versions:-

It fell about the Lammas tide,
    When the mui-men win their hay,
The doughty Douglas bound him ride
    Into England to drive a prey.

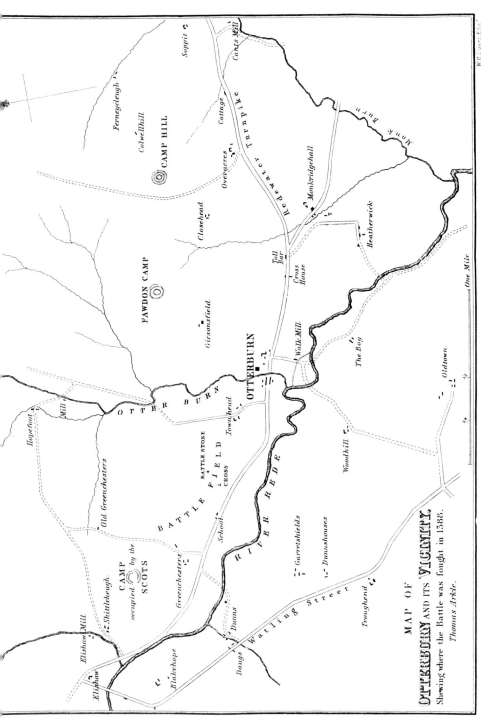

MAP OF
OTTERBURN AND ITS VICINITY.
Shewing where the Battle was fought in 1388.
Thomas Arkle.

W. H. Lizars, Edin.

Soppit

Carts Mill

Monk Burn

Fernegeleugh

Cottage

Colwellhill

CAMP HILL

Overacres

Redewater Turnpike

Mombridgehall

Closehead

Heatherwick

FAWDON CAMP

Toll Bar

Cross House

Girsonsfield

Walk Mill

OTTERBURN

The Boy

One Mile

Mill

OTTER BURN

Townhead

Hopefoot

BATTLE STONE
FIELD
CROSS

Woodhill

Oldtown

Old Greenchesters

BATTLE

School

RIVER REDE

Garretshields

Dunnshouses

CAMP
occupied by the
SCOTS

Greenchesters

Elishaw Mill

Shittleheugh

Troughend

Elishaw

Daugs

Dunns

Watling Street

Blakehope

277

He chose the Gordons and the Graemes,
    With them the Lindsays, light and gay;
But the Jardines waid not with them ride,
    And they rue it to this day.

And he has burned the dales of Tyne,
    And part of Bambroughshire,
And three good towers on Reidswire fells
    He left them all on fire.

And he marched up to Necastle,
    And rode it round about;
"O wha's the lord of this castle?
    Or wha's the lady o't?"

But up spake proud Lord Percy then,
    And O but spake hie!
"I am the lord of this castle,
    My wife's the lady gay."

"If thou art the lord of this castle,
    Sae weel it pleases me!
For ere I cross the Border fells
    The tane of us sall die."

He took a lang spear in his hand,
    Shod with the metal free,
And for to meet the Douglas there
    He rode right furiouslie.

But O how pale his lady looked,
    Frae off the castle wa',
When down before the Scottish spear
    She saw proud Percy fa'!

"Had we twa been upon the green,
    And never an eye to see,
I wad ha' had you, flesh and fell,
    But your sword shall gae wi' me.

"But gae ye up to Otterbourne
    And wait there dayis three;
And if I come not ere three dayis end,
    A fause knight ca' ye me."

"The Otterbourne's a bonnie burn,
    'Tis pleasant there to be;
But there is naught at Otterbourne
    To feed my men and me.

"The deer rins wild on hill and dale,
    The birds fly wild from tree to tree;

But there is neither bread nor kale
  To fend my men and me.

"Yet I will stay at Otterbourne,
  Where you shall welcome be;
  And if ye come not at three dayis end,
  A fause lord I'll call thee."

"Thither will I come," proud percy said,
  "By the might of Our Ladye!"
"There will I bide thee" said the Douglas,
  "My troth I plight to thee."

Scottish Version

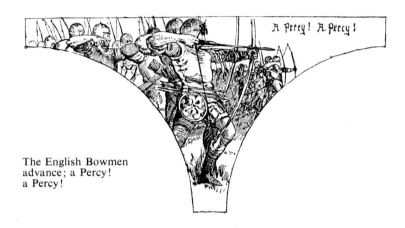

The English Bowmen
advance; a Percy!
a Percy!

The Scottish Spearmen
closing in;
a Douglas!
a Douglas!

Our English archers bent their bowes,
  Their hearts were good and trew;
Att the first flight of arrowes sent,
  Full four-score Scots they slew.

Yet bides Erle Douglas on the bent,
　As Chieftain stout and good.
As valaint Captain, all unmov'd
　The shock he firmly stood.

His host he parted had in three,
　As Leader ware and try'd
And soon his spearmen on their foes
　Bare down on every side.

Throughout the English archery
　They dealt full many a wound:
But still our valiant Englishmen
　All firmly kept their ground:

And throwing strait their bows away,
　They grasp'd their swords so bright:
And now sharp blows, a heavy shower,
　On shields and helmets light.

English version

    At Wallington Hall in Northumberland William Bell Scott painted a series of murals depicting the story of Chevy Chase. They are reproduced in full in the booklet *Scenes from Northumbrian History*.

Cross on the Battle Field near Otterburn.

BATTLE STONE REMOVED IN 1777.

Percy's Cross

    On the battlefield at Otterburn stands Percy's Cross, a pointed pillar about 10 feet high which stands among a plantation of firs, north of the main road. The story of this cross is rather confused.

About 150 yards east of the present cross once stood a monument called the *Battle Stone*. It is marked on Armstrong's map of 1769 and an engraving of it is here reproduced. It was only three feet in length resting in a socket. In 1777 the turnpike road from Otterburn to Redesdale was built and the Duke of Northumberland offered to build a memorial to the battle near the road. However Mr. Henry Ellison of Otterburn who owned the land thought the Duke might use this as an excuse to claim the ground and said he would build one himself. He chose a spot within view of the highway. A circular pedestal of rough masonary was built to the height of five feet in the centre of which the socket of the old Battle Stone was placed. Instead of a new shaft an old architrave from the kitchen fireplace at Otterburn Hall was used. Two bits of iron near the bottom of the shaft were probably used as hooks when it formed part of the fireplace. The erection was completed by placing on its top another stone tapering to a point. The old shaft from the old Battle Stone may be the stone in the porch of Otterburn Church.

Otterburn Mill

There was a mill at Otterburn in 1245 and then, in 1522, we read that it was guarded nightly against marauding Scots. The present mill was started in 1821 when William Woddell came to Otterburn from Jedburgh. Otterburn Tweed is still famous today although the bulk of it is made at the Cumberland Mills near Carlisle which is owned by the same family.

Drawing showing Otterburn in 1890

Blakehope Camp

Since Dere Street ran close by Otterburn there are a number of Roman remains in the vicinity. Near Elishaw Bridge is the camp of Blakehope. It is a cohort-fort with single ditch, massive rampart, at least two gates and an annexe to the south.

Half a mile to the south is *Dargues Camp*. It was much larger but only a temporary camp. It covers 15 acres and would hold a detachment of about seven cohorts. Four gates are still visible although one corner is obliterated by Dargues Farm.

OVERACRES

Lies two miles east of Otterburn. Here are two very fine gate posts sumptuously decorated with shields and knotwork. They were erected by one of the last of the Howards, lords of Redesdale, in advance of the building of his manor house. The Howards however were soon impoverished, the house was never built, and their manorial rights in Redesdale as well as the land at Overacres were sold to the Earl of Northumberland. The date on the pillars is 1720.

OVINGHAM

The name of Ovingham is Saxon and probably means "homestead of the sons of Offa". The name is first mentioned about the year 1200 and in 1245 is recorded as belonging to Gilbert de Umfraville of the barony of Prudhoe. However the village was already very ancient since the church tower was probably built three centuries earlier.

Although Ovingham had a weekly market in the thirteenth century and a yearly fair on St. Andrews day it never seems to have been wealthy in medieval times. In the year 1312 the Bishop of Durham was unable to obtain any taxes from the parson "because the church and villages in his parish are burnt by the Scots". A report often repeated in the following years. In 1471 the village came into the hands of the Earl of Northumberland and has been held by the Percies ever since.

In the Middle Ages the mill and fishery (first mentioned c.1200) were of great importance. In the regular reeve's accounts, which have survived, the fishery is the main item reported on. At times the rental was as high as £20 per annum, a large sum of money in those days. In the Survey of 1586 we find the following interesting account of the inspection that was carried out each year.

"The lorde of the said manor (Prudhoe) hathe the authority and libertie every yeare to view and searche all the fishers' nettes betwene the dame of Ovingham and the sea, on both sydes of the ryver of Tyne; and such nettes as are thought to be without due assyse and proportion are to be caryed to the next markett towne, which is Newcastell, and there before the maior and his brethren the nettes are to be measured, and such as are found unlawfull they are to be burned. The nettes aught to be of eight sheetes, every sheete of tenne yeardes lengthe. The bosoms or hawse of the nette ought to be of that wydenes in maste that a man standing from yt the dystance of fyve foote and do caste into yt an ould ryall, not clypped nor rounded, yf yt fall not throughe the maste is not lawfull."

The Goose Fair

In 1294 Gilbert de Umfraville claimed as his immemorial rights, a market at Ovingham every week on Sunday and a fair each year on St. Andrew's Day. With many breaks the fair survived into the nineteenth century. In Hone's *Every-Day Book,* 30th December, 1826, appears the following account probably written and illustrated by John Jackson, an apprentice of Thomas Bewick.

"The fair is principally for the sale of cattle and the show is not greater than that of Smithfield on market-day. In the morning a procession moves from the principle alehouse for the purpose of *riding the fair,* as they call it, headed by the two Northumbrian pipers, called *the Duke of Northumberland's Pipers,* in a light blue dress, a large cloak of the same colour with white cape, a silver half-moon on one arm as a *cognizance,* and white band and binding to the hat. Each is mounted on a rosinante, borrowed, without consent, by the busy hostler from some whisky smuggler or cadger, reconciled to the liberty by long custom.

"The pipers, followed by the duke's agent, bailiff, constable, and a numerous body of farmers, principally the duke's tenantry, proceed first through the fair, where the proclamation is read, that the fair shall last nine days (it never continues longer than one day), and then, the duke being lord of the manor, they walk the boundary of all that is or has been common or waste land. That task completed, they return to the alehouse with the pipers playing before them, where they partake freely of store of punch at the duke's expense. The farmers are so proud of being able to express their attachment to his grace "*in public*", as they term it, that they mount their sons on cuddies (asses), rather than they

should not join the procession, to drink with them "the health o' his grace and lang may he leeve to pratect and study the interests o' his tanentry." Then there's "Here's to ye Tam, thanks to ye goke." and so they separate for the fair there to "ettle how mickle per heed they con git for their nowte an swine."

"Ovingham fair, like others, is attended by many a "gaberlunzie," with different kinds of amusement for children, such as the "E and O, black-cock and gray" and, above all, for the amusement of the pig drivers and 'gadsmen', Punch and Toby (so called by them), and a number of those gentlemen who vomit fire, as if they swallowed the wicks of all the candles they had snuffed for Richardson".

Shortly after this description was published the fair ceased but its memory was kept up by a cross which is believed to be standing on the site of the old toll-booth. It is not the original cross but a fair copy of it. The sale of geese was a prominent feature of the fair and there is probably some connection between it and the industry of making quill pens which existed in Ovingham until quill pens ceased to be used. The goose fair has recently been revived and it is hoped it will continue yearly in the future.

Ovingham – Pack Horse Bridge

There is still standing at Ovingham a seventeenth century packhorse bridge with two fine round arches spanning the Whittle Burn. The width between the parapets is less than five feet. It was once a busy spot when the Newcastle-Carlisle turnpike road passed through the village. There is now a concrete bridge nearby to cross the burn.

Pack Horse Bridge, Ovingham.

Ovingham Church

The Church of St. Mary the Virgin has a pre-Conquest tower with the rest of the church mainly thirteenth century. The tower is similar to that of Bywell St. Andrew's, and is the tallest and largest in Northumberland. It is 60 feet high. Externally it is $18\frac{1}{2} \times 18$ feet with walls 2 feet 9 inches thick. It is built of coursed ragstone, without buttresses, and for about three-quarters of its height is plain: then there is a slight offset with string course below the belfry stage, while above the belfry is a plain parapet. Some stones in the lower part as well as some quoin stones are Roman.

The interior of the ground floor was deprived of most of its interest in the eighteenth century, and there are no remains of the

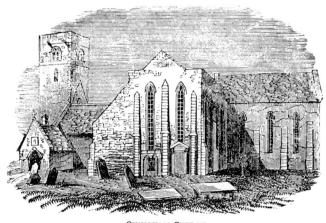

OVINGHAM CHURCH.

ancient tower arch which led into the nave. However an original window in the south wall has survived. There is no external entrance to the tower.

In the second stage there are windows on the east and west walls, the latter with arched lintel. The third stage has no openings but in the fourth on the west side is a narrow window with arched lintel.

The belfry has a double headed two light window in each face, all alike and similar to those at Bywell St. Andrew's. The parapet above is plain and modern.

The date of the tower is unknown but is probably early ninth century.

Ovingham Parsonage

The Vicarage

The east end is of fourteenth century workmanship and was built to house the Augustinian Canons from Hexham, along with the vicar. The remainder was erected in the seventeenth century although much altered in the nineteenth century.

Here Thomas Bewick received his education at a school run by the Rev. C. Gregson. His life here has been graphically described in his "Memoirs".

"I was for some time kept at reading, writing and figures – how long, I know not, but I know that as soon as my question was done on my slate, I spent as much time as I could filling with my pencil

Ovingha

The '
centurie
the Ne
Horsley
to the
was the
the Ovi
20th D
Ovingha
such an

OVINC

The
200 yar
the nar
to have
paid th
village.
in an c

PLANI

This
Roman
the Bro
here wa
who ca
scene.

"I no
nearly
my lef
I climb
in eve
fascina
strange

The

"At
wall 7
line; b
a farr
destro
13 ya
bramb

The
from
the ne

The
ficed

all the unoccupied spaces with representations of such objects that took my fancy; the margins of my books, and every piece of space and blank paper became filled with various kinds of devices or scenes I had met with; as soon as these spaces were filled I had recourse, at all spare times, to the gravestones and the floor of the church porch with a bit of chalk. At that time I had never heard of the word "drawing"; nor did I know of any other paintings besides the King's Arms in the Church, and the signs in Ovingham of the Black Bull, the White Horse, the Salmon and the Hounds and Hare. I always thought I could make a far better hunting scene than the latter; the others were beyond my hand. I remember once my master overlooking me while I was very busy with my chalk in the porch, and ridiculing me and calling me a conjuror. My father also found fault for "mis-spending my time with such idle pursuits"; but my propensity for drawing was so rooted that nothing could deter me from perservering in it; and many of my evenings at home were spent in filling the flags of the floor and hearth stone with my chalky designs. After I had long scorched my face in this way, a friend, in compassion, furnished me with some paper upon which to execute my designs. Here I had more scope. Pen and ink and the juice of the bramble-berry made a grand change, and I became completely set up; but of patterns or drawings I had none. The beasts and birds, which enlivened the beautiful scenery of woods and wilds surrounding my native hamlet furnished me with an endless supply of subjects."

Dyers of Ovingham

Ovingham Dyers

In Bewick's day Ovingham had its industries. Prominent was the dye works – Bewick's grandfather was an Ovingham Dyer. The mother of George Stephenson was a native of Ovingham and her father followed the same trade. He is represented with his employer, Thomas Dobson, in Bewick's woodcut of "The Ovingham Dyers". The Bleach Green, still to be seen, reminds one of the bleachers who found the water of the Whittle Dene so suitable for bleaching linen. Our drawing by Paul Brown shows the Green as it was fifty years ago.

The dyers in Bewick's drawing have been collecting urine from the houses. Urine was needed for curing leather.

facing stones remain on both sides. This grand exhibition must be seen no more. How little we value what is daily under the eye.

Here was a fine opportunity for measuring. The foundation was, in fact, below the surface of the ground and consisted of two courses of stones, each 6 inches thick, extending to the width of $6\frac{1}{2}$ feet. The second course set off 3 inches on each side, which reduced the foundation to 6 feet, and the third 3 inches of a side more, reducing the wall to $5\frac{1}{2}$ feet, its real thickness here.

The foundation is laid in the native earth, the bed is cemented with mortar. The soil being afterwards thrown up on each side of the Wall 2 feet high caused the foundation to be 3 feet deep.

I desired the servant, with whom I conversed, to give my compliments to Mr. Tulip and request him to desist, or he would wound the whole body of antiquaries. As he was putting an end to the most noble monument of antiquity in the whole island, they would feel every stroke. If the Wall was of *no* estimation he must have a mean opinion of me, who would travel 600 miles to see it; and if it *was* he could never merit my thanks for destroying it. Should he reply "The property is mine and I have a right to direct it as I please", it is an argument I can regret but not refute."

PLASHETTS

Plashetts Colliery is hidden away among the hills which feed the Belling Burn. The seams here were four feet thick being one of the oldest seams of coal in the carboniferous rocks. The village is first mentioned in 1717, the colliery in 1812. In the moorland north of Plashetts, at a place called Soney Rigg, was formerly one of the curious earthworks called Arthur's round tables. It is described as a circular area, five yards across, surrounded by a ditch and by seats cut out of the earth. In spite of its name the site is probably fairly modern. Near Plashetts is Haw Hill where the remains of a camp can be seen.

PRUDHOE

Prudhoe is usually associated with the famous medieval castle rather than "the ugly straggling colliery village". However in the Middle Ages the township, apart from the castle, was as important as Ovingham. Although coal mining is mentioned in 1434 and continued down to early in the nineteenth century the principal company was the Mickley Coal Company with its collieries at West Wylam. At Prudhoe there was a chantry dedicated to St. Thomas. It is first mentioned in 1340. In Prudhoe Grange there is an old doorway which may probably belong to the chantry although some historians say it comes from Ovingham. It is a fine piece of work with two colenettes on either side arched with roll mouldings. The hood-mould has nail-head decoration.

Prudhoe Castle

Prudhoe Castle is described in 1596 as "an old ruinous Castle in form not much unlike a shield hanging with one point upwards." It

Arch at Prudhoe Grange

stands upon a hill which rises abruptly from the plain of the Tyne. The site has been fortified from very early times and earthworks still remain outside the castle walls.

Among the Normans who came over with William the Conqueror was Robert de Umfraville, known as Robert with-the-beard. He was granted the district of Redesdale. Henry I added to the Umfraville possessions the barony of Prudhoe. Here, early in the twelfth century, Umfraville II built a castle of earthworks and timber on the general line of the existing ruins. The stone basement of the main gatehouse, with its twin-faced corbels, may have been the work of Robert's son Odinel since it looks like work of the first half of the twelfth century. Twice, in 1173 and 1174, the castle was unsuccessfully attacked by William the Lion of Scotland, who had a personal grudge against Odinel.

"Thus said King William: Then may I be accursed Excommunicated by priest, put to shame and discomfited. If I give the castle of Odinel a fixed time or respite. But I will cause him wholly to his joy and delight".

Immediately after these sieges the mound was levelled and a stone keep replaced the motte. This keep is the oldest in Northumberland apart from Norham. At the same time part of the curtain wall was rebuilt in stone. An interesting story is related about Odinel's rebuilding of the castle. "All his neighbours, the legend runs, had, either from love or fear, given him assistance in the work, except the men of

291

Wylam, a possession of the monastery of St. Oswin of Tynemouth, which had been freed from all contributions to castle-building by several royal charters. Neither the threats nor the persuasions of the king's officers had any effect. Odinel was so enraged that he sent for one of them who lived, without fear of God, in the city of Corbridge, and bade him seize the property of the Wylam peasants and bring it to the castle. This man took with him two officers named Richard and Nicholas, and proceeded at once to Wylam. According to the English law that had then been long established, a fine for neglecting to perform a customary duty like that of repairing a castle was first to be levied on the private property of the serfs, and only in case of this proving insufficient was recourse to be had to the Lord's demesne. The Corbridge official, however, announced his intention of laying hands on whatever first came his way, and it was in vain that his companions cautioned him not to interfere with the head of St. Oswin. They came to the pasture where the demesne oxen were grazing, but these, together with the ruddy youth and his barking dog who were looking after them, were by the power of St. Oswin made miraculously invisible and inaudible to the wicked distrainer". Cadwallader Bates.

The last of the Umfravilles who was baron of Prudhoe was one Gilbert who died in 1381. His widow married Henry de Percy, fourth Lord of Alnwick, and so Prudhoe castle came into the hands of the Percys in whose possession it has remained, with occasional attainders, to the present day.

The castle was considerably repaired and altered early in the nineteenth century. The plan above shows the castle before these alterations.

With its moat and gardens Prudhoe castle occupies three acres of ground. The position is very strong. On the north the escarpment of the ridge on which it stands is sixty feet high. On the south and east is a deep ravine through which a burn runs and on the west and south-west two broad moats complete the defence.

Approaching the castle from the south one crosses the dam which is on the east side of the mill-pond; on the right are the ruins of the castle mill. To the west was the pele-yard. The barbican is thirty-six feet long entered by a covered gateway. The barbican ended in a drawbridge which crossed the inner moat. An inner barbican leads to the gatehouse which is thus described in 1586.

The Gate is a Tower of Massy Worke on both sydes to the Topp of the Vault, above the Vault is the Chappell and above the Chappell a Chamber, which is called the Wardrobe, it is covered with lead but in greate ruine both in Leade and Timber.

The gateway has no portcullis and is an early example of the first half of the twelfth century. The chapel above the gate has the earliest known oriel window (1300), "one of the simplest and most graceful pieces of work of its kind". The passage through the gatehouse has a barrel vault and one of the corbels supporting the rib has two carved human heads.

The tower or keep is almost square with a forebuilding on the east. The walls are ten feet thick and for the most part are in ruins. It had three storeys.

The inner bailey has in the north-west corner a semi-circular tower with cross-loops in the basement and in the merlons of the battlements. Only the base remains of a similar tower in the south-west corner.

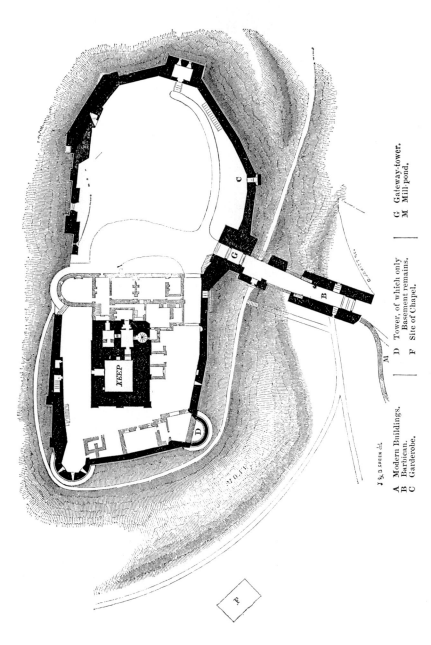

PLAN OF PRUDHOE CASTLE.

A Modern Buildings.
B Barbican.
C Garderobe.

D Tower, of which only
   Basement remains.
F Site of Chapel.

G Gateway-tower.
M Mill-pond.

EXTERIOR OF THE CHAPEL. 1300.

INTERIOR OF THE CHAPEL.

295

women at the Rideing-house (as the Wellington was originally called) with "their protector which they call'd their god, sitting, at the head of the table in a gold chaire, as she thought; and a rope hanging over the roome which every one touch'd three several times and what ever was desired was sett upon the table, of several kinds of meate and drinke, and when they had eaten, she that was last drew the table and kept the reversions. Anne Forster did swing upon the rope, and upon the first swing she gott a cheese, and upon the second she gott a beatment of wheat flower, and upon the third swing she gott about half a quarter of butter to knead the said flower withal, they haveinge noe power to gett water." Many more fantasies of the same kind were detailed at the Quarter Sessions at Morpeth. Robert Johnson, a servant of the owner of the house, Mr. Thomas Errington, deposed that at Christmas time, "being sheeling some oats, about two hours before the sunn-setting, all the geer, viz., hopper and hoops, and all other things but the stones, flewe down and were casten of and he himselfe almost killed with them, they comeing against him with such force and violence."

The Wellington Hotel ~ Riding Mill

The house in which Thomas Errington resided was built in 1660. In this year Thomas and his wife, on the restoration of the monarchy, left Newcastle to live in their new home. Under the Commonwealth Thomas had held many posts in the government of Newcastle.

Above the doorway, with its hood-mould, are his arms, Argent two bars and in chief three escallops azure impaling those of his wife Ann Carnaby, three roundels in chief azure, and two bars agent, together with the inscription T.B. 1660. Since the initials seem to have been recut at some later date the E was probably changed to B by mistake

298

or because later tenants were called Browell and Boutflower. The windows which were once mullioned also retain their hood moulds.

Manor House, Riding Mill   *From Dixon's Corbridge, 1912*

The Manor House as it stands today is a long-fronted two storied house on the north side of the road leading to Hexham. It belonged in the 18th century to the Smith family of Snow-hill in Benfieldshire. It was extended in the early 19th century. The right wing and the garden wall are castellated. Ralph Smith, who died in 1786 without any relatives, left the house and lands to Robert Surtees who had been his regular companion on the hunting field.

RIDLEY HALL

Ridley Hall is first mentioned in the reign of Elizabeth (1567) as the property of the Ridleys of Willimoteswick. In the later part of the seventeenth century it was acquired by the Lowes family and William Lowes, who was high Sheriff of Northumberland in 1773, built the mansion house described by John Hodgson in 1840. Of this building only the stable wing has survived. It has two arches with Gibbs surrounds. It is sometimes stated that the hall was built by an earlier William Lowes in 1743 but in *Notes of Haydon Bridge* we have the following entry: "August 20, 1789 – The foundation stone of Ridley Hall was laid by John Lowes, Esq., at a depth of nine feet below the surface. Mr. and Mrs. Lowes each made the workmen a handsome present."

"The situation of this house is cheerful and very charming, on ground retiring irregularly from the Tyne. Soft green slopes and a rich garniture of groves environ it on three sides; and on the south it has a broad and flat lawn, and the deep and thickly-wooded chasm of the Allen full in front". Hodgson.

The house was rebuilt in 1891 in the neo-Tudor style, Horatio Adamson being the architect. Some of the fireplaces and panelling were taken from other places including Mottisfont Abbey.

This view of the Newcastle to Carlisle railway is taken from near

Bardon Mill by J. Carmichael, 1838. On the right of the picture the buildings, in order are Ridley Hall (before rebuilding), Willimoteswick Castle, and Beltingham chapel. Near the chapel is the Georgian house still standing in Beltingham.

RIDSDALE IRONWORKS

Just south of West Woodburn by the A68 stands the ruins of an engine house which most travellers assume is a former pele tower. This is part of the Ridsdale Ironworks which was established in 1836. The site was chosen because of the proximity of the main raw materials needed – ironstone, coal, and limestone. Like the Hareshaw Ironworks at Bellingham it seems to have closed down about 1849. It was hoped to restore production when the Wansbeck railway was built but the growth of the Teesside iron industry made this impossible. In 1864 W. G. Armstrong dismantled two of the furnaces and removed them to his works at Elswick. Some of the pig iron used in the castings for the High Level Bridge at Newcastle was made here.

Size, 4 feet 8 inches by 2 feet 4 inches.

NVMINIB	Numinibus
AVGVSTOR	Augustorum
COH IIII GAL	cohors quarta Gallorum
EQ	equitata
FEC	fecit.

RISINGHAM (Habitancum)

Shortly after the erection of Hadrian's Wall it was decided, in order to control the area north of the wall, to re-occupy Dere Street. The operation was conducted by Quintus Lollius Urbicus in 139 AD.

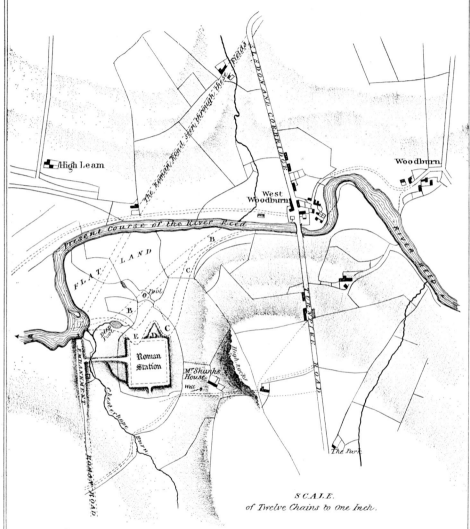

PLAN SHEWING THE SITUATION OF THE *ROMAN STATION HABITANCUM,* AT RISINGHAM, NORTHUMBERLAND.

High Leam

Woodburn

West Woodburn

The Roman Road, seen through these fields

WATLING STREET ROMAN

Present Course of the River Reed

RIVER REED

FLAT LAND

B

C

Pool

B

C

Dead Pool

E D

Roman Station

Mr Shanks House

Well

High rocks

ROMAN ROAD

Chesterhope Burn

EMBANKMENT

The Park

SCALE.
of Twelve Chains to One Inch.

A. *Foundation of a Bridge seen here.*
B B *Supposed Course of the River Reed when the Bridge and Station were built.*
C C *An outbreak of the River which threatened the destruction of the Station*

D *Large Wear made by the Romans to protect the Station.*
E *A second Outbreak of the River round the North end of the Wear and breaking into the Station.*

John Bell,
Gateshead.

It was then that Risingham was built. The garrison (the Fourth Cohort of Gauls, mounted) is commemorated on a remarkable sculptured slab now in the Library of Trinity College, Cambridge. The left panel shows Victory flying through space on a globe while the left panel shows the war-god Mars in panoply. Near the top of the slab are two human heads the one on the left being a three-headed Janus. Beneath Victory is a stork striking a fish, beneath Mars is a goose or cock. The stone is shown on page 301.

Size, 5 feet 11 inches by 3 feet 7 inches.

```
          . . . . .  ADIABENICO MAXI[MO]
    COS. III. ET M[ARCO] AVREL[IO] ANTONINO PIO
         COS. II. AVG[VSTO] . . . . . .
        PORTAM CVM MVRIS VETVSTATE DI-
LAPSIS IVSSV ALFEN[II] SENECI[O]NIS V[IRI] C[LARISSIMI]
CO[N]S[VLARIS] CVRANTE OCLATINI[O] ADVENTO PRO[CVRATORE]
     AVGG. NN. COH. I. VANGION[VM] . . . . .
      CVM AEMI[LIO] SALVIANO TRIB[VNO]
         SVO A SOLO RESTI[TVIT.]
```

[To] . . . . . Adiabenicus Maximus
consul for the third time and Marcus Aurelius Antoninus pious
consul for the second time august . . . . . .
this gate with the walls through age dilapidated by command of Alfenius Senecio an illustrious man
of consular rank under the care of Oclatinius Adventus the procurator
of our emperors the first cohort of Vangiones . . . .
with Æmilius Salvianus its tribune
from the ground restored.

Risingham is eight miles south of High Rochester where Dere Street crosses the Rede. Although not mentioned in the first Iter of Antonine its Roman name is known to be Habitancum from a later inscription. It occupies a site which was probably originally an island in a swamp on the edge of the Rede. The bridge across the Rede can still be traced by some tumbled stones.

At the end of the second century when the Governor of Britain Albinus withdrew large numbers of troops to the Continent, Habitancum was either abandoned or destroyed when the entire northern defences collapsed. However within a few years the Emperor Severus restored the wrecked forts and the Wall. A fine inscribed slab, dated 205-8 A.D., and here reproduced, comes from the south gate of Habitancum. It shows that the fort was completely rebuilt by the First mounted cohort of Vangiones, 1,000 strong. The defences of Habitancum are very fine partly because there was a supply of fine sandstone nearby, obtainable in large blocks. The fort was apparently left in ruins when Count Theodosius restored the Wall in 368 A.D.

Camden, in his Britannia, 1607 edition, refers to Risingham as follows:-

"There is also another towne beneath of ancient memory, which *Rhead* watereth, or rather hath now well neare washed away: they call it at this day *Risingham*, which is in the ancient English and German language, *The Giants Habitation, as Risingberg in Germany, the*

Deo Mogonti Cadenorum et Numini Domini noſtri Auguſti Marcus Gaius Secundinus beneficiarius conſulis Habitanci prima ſtatione pro ſe et ſuis poſuit

Giants Hill. Many shewes are there, and those right evident of antiquity. The inhabitants report that God Magon defended and made good this place a great while against a certain *Soldan,* that is, an *Heathenish Prince.* Neither is this altogether a vaine tale. For that such a god was there honoured and worshipped is plainly proved by these two alter stones lately drawn out of the river there . . ."

One of these altars is here reproduced from Horsley.

The translation reads:- "To the god Mogons of Cad . . . and to the spirit of our august Lord, Marcus Gavius(?) Secundinus, governor's staff officer, on completion of his first term of office at Habitancum paid his vow willingly and deservedly for himself and his staff."

(Horsley guessed that the word DEO should start the inscription. He was right because today the word can be traced with difficulty on the stone.)

The legend of Mogon has become attached to a remarkable sculpture called "Robin of Risingham". John Hodgson (1827) tells us that Parkhead Farm had become a mecca for visitors for here could be seen :-

"the remains of the celebrated figure, called ROBIN OF RISINGHAM, which was cut in high relief upon a huge block of 'slidden' sandstone rock, on the brow of the hill, a few yards to the west of the modern Watling-street. The stone itself was five sided, six feet on the base, eight feet high, five feet on the two sides to the right of the middle of its front, seven feet on the uppermost side to the left, and four on the lower: its thickness six feet.

The figure itself was about four feet high; had a panel above it about 29 inches long, and 20 broad, as if intended for an inscription; and a square block or altar opposite the right knee, probably left for the same purpose. When West Woodburn-bridge was building, the masons had cut wedge holes in this stone to board and quarry it for ashlars; but Mr. Shanks, the proprietor of Park-head, pointing to the crag from which it had fallen said: 'No: this hill of rock is at your service; but no man shall destroy my images.' His son, however, has taken away the figure as far down as the girdle, by cutting the stone into gate-posts. This act of spoilage, it is said, was done to prevent the curious from trespassing over a few yards of barren land, and from enjoying the pleasure of visiting 'the man in stone', who for so many ages had been the talk and wonder of the neighbourhood."

The action of Shanks need not surprise us today for even now there are many landowners and farmers who resent visitors to the Roman Wall and do their best to make their visit difficult.

Sir Walter Scott mentions the carving in his poem Rokeby.

> "Some ancient sculptor's art has shown
> An outlaw's image on the stone;
> Unmatch'd in strength, a giant he,
> With quivered back and kirtled knee.
> Ask how he did, that hunter bold,
> That tameless monarch of the wold,
> And age and infancy will tell
> By brother's treachery he fell."

He added a note that:-

"One popular tradition is, that it represents a giant, whose brother resided at Woodburn, and he himself at Risingham. It adds, that they subsisted by hunting, and that one of them, finding the game become too scarce to support them, poisoned his companion, in whose memory the monument was engraved."

The sculpture almost certainly represents a god worshipped by the Romans (For further detail see *Research on Hadrian's Wall* by E. Birley. 1961).

ROCHESTER

This small village has one of the most curious buildings in Northumberland. It is a little school with a porch built entirely of Roman stones brought from the Roman fort of Bremenium (High Rochester). Many of the stones can be traced back to their original use, especially the two rounded stones intended for "ballistae" Paul Brown's drawing

Rochester School

shows how the various stones were used in the original Roman fort. (The school has now been converted into a private house.) Near the church the Bagraw Burn runs under the road in company with the Roman highway called Dere Street and here can be seen a strange milestone which carries the word ELISHA. It is not an early Christian relic but simply tells us the distance to ELISHAW.

Not far from Rochester church between the Bagraw Burn and Dere Street is a temporary Roman camp almost 500 yards long but only 180 yards wide, large enough to accomodate a legion. High up the Rede is the prehistoric Woolaw camp. It is a Romano-British settlement with a rectangular enclosure with two entrances leading into two yards. Three hundred yards north west is another settlement near Burnhope originally consisting of eight huts with attached yards. The settlement is obscured by a number of later buildings "including one longhouse, possibly the 'Burdhop' destroyed by the Scots in 1584" (George Jobey. Prehistoric Northumberland). A little further is Bellshiel Bridge which is dominated to the north east by Bellshiel Camp. Although tillage has obliterated sections, the ramparts and ditch now measure each about nine feet wide. Its oblong shape measures roughly 500 by 400 yards.

G · D · N · ET
SIGNORVM
COH · I · VARDVLL
ET N EXPLORA
TOR · BREM · GOR
EGNAT · LVCILI
ANVS · LEG AVG PR PR
CVRANTE CASSIO
SABINIANO TRIB

Genio Domini nostri et
signorum
cohortis primæ Vardullorum
et numeri explora-
torum Bremeniensium Gordianorum
Egnatius Lucili-
anus legatus Augusti proprætor
curante Cassio
Sabiniano tribuno.

To the genius of our lord [the
Emperor] and
of the Standards
of the first cohort of the Vardulli
and the exploratory Bremenian
troop styled the Gordian,
Egnatius Lucilianus,
imperial legate and proprætor,
(under the inspection of Cassius
Sabinianus, the tribune)
[erects this altar.]

Unfortunately the area is now used by the Army and the huts and buildings mar the site while the artillery range nearby restricts walking.

Overlooking Bellshiel Camp is the sandstone hill of Bellshiel Law (1,068 feet). Here there is a cairn probably of the Bronze Age, 120 yards long and averaging 15 feet wide in which prehistoric flints were found. Lower down the hill is a group of rounded barrows.

The most outstanding historic monument here, however, is the great Roman fort of *High Rochester* called by the Romans *Bremenium.*

HIGH ROCHESTER (Bremenium)

Bremenium is one of the finest forts in Britain and is on a site of great strategic interest. The earliest Roman occupation of the site was represented by the turf rampart of an Agricolan fort. While Lollius Urbicus was Governor of Britain it was succeeded by a stone fort. A building inscription dated 142 A.D. shows he stayed here when on his way north to build the Antonine Wall in Scotland. It was reconstructed under Severus at the beginning of the third century, when the Scottish Wall had been abandoned, and became a place of great importance. Its occupation came to an end about 340 A.D.

The fort we see today is basically Severan with later alterations. It is almost square measuring 485 by 445 feet and covers almost five acres.

The fort at Bremenium is famous for its third-century artillery defences. On the ramparts large platforms were constructed for machines like the *onagri* (a smaller version of the ballista) whose power was derived from hair rope in torsion. From the north and west rampart these machines could be used against anyone advancing down Dere Street.

Size, 3 feet 6½ inches by 2 feet 4 inches.

Although the fort is now part of the village green of High Rochester there is a fair amount still to see. The west wall is the best preserved with a steep bank nine feet high and facing stones in places. The south gate is entered by a modern road and a guard chamber with wall 10 feet high can still be seen and the west gateway is complete to the springing of the arch.

The fort has provided many interesting inscriptions, almost fifty in all, of which we reproduce two outstanding examples:-

(1) *Venus with nymphs.* This relief is based on a classical scene, showing the goddess of beauty emerging from a pool formed by a woodland spring and preparing to dress her hair. Two nymphs with ewer and basin attend her. The Celtic artist was however unable to produce such a classical scene and the carving is crude. The stone is now at Alnwick Castle.

(2) *Building inscription of the 20th Legion.* The inscription reads *A detachment of the Twentieth Legion, styled Valeria and Victorious, made this.* Mars, the God of War is on the left and Hercules on the right. The boar between them is the symbol of the legion. Mars is dressed in full armour, bearing a spear and shield. Hercules is represented as fully grown and bearded with a massive muscular frame. He carries a club and a quiver full of arrows with a lion skin on his shoulders. Both figures are crudely carved but show great vigour. They are soldiers, not 'artists' sculptures.

750 yards south of the fort are the remains of a unique Roman monument. It is a circular tomb of which the base survives consisting of two courses of millstone grit. One stone in the lower course has

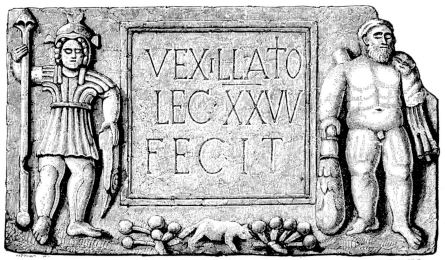

Size, 4 feet 6 inches by 2 feet 6 inches.

BREMENIUM

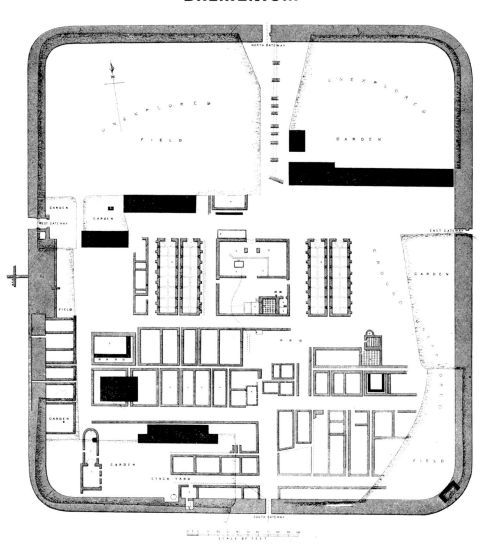

Plan of remains of the Roman Station at High Rochester excavated in 1852 and 1855. The black parts are modern farmhouses and buildings. + denotes buildings of which the internal area has been excavated.

311

Roman Tombs on Watling Street near High Rochester

been decorated with an animal's head. Cremated remains were found, an urn with bones (probably those of a Roman officer), and a coin of Severus (222-235). The tomb was discovered and excavated in 1850 by William Coulson, an Inland Revenue officer who was stationed at Bremenium to prevent whisky smuggling from Scotland. He found three other rectangular tombs whose stones have since been used to build a sheep-fold nearby.

A tombstone, now in Elsdon church, briefly records the official career of one Rufinus and his wife stating, that she herself was a woman of high social standing, being a senator's daughter.

Across the Sills Burn from Bremenium is Birdhope Camp. It consists of two camps one inside the other. The large camp was a temporary one and could hold a legion, the smaller camp, which is the better preserved, was probably occupied for a period when its occupants were probably engaged on engineering works in the neighbourhood. North of Birdhope along Dere Street are four more temporary camps which were revealed by air photography. Sills Burn South and North Camps have both been affected by agricultural work and are difficult to trace. Further on is the large camp of Silloans. Dere Street passes through it. Since Dere Street was the work of Agricola Silloans is one of the earliest dated camps in North Britain.

The next camp discovered from the air is Featherwood East, 4 miles north of Silloans, a large camp over 400 yards square with

High Rochester 1817

prominent ramparts. Nearby is Featherwood West built in the shape of a diamond. These two camps are in the most exposed site in Britain for Roman occupation. Nearby is the summit of Foulplay head (1,500 feet). From here to the border the only suitable place for a camp is Chew Green and here there are three temporary camps and two fortlets all crowded together.

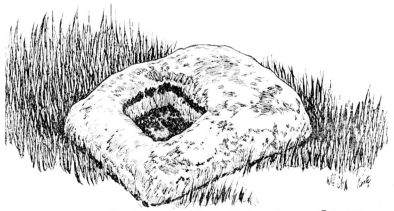

Outer Golden Pot, Chew Green.

Between Featherwood and Chew Green however is an interesting part of Dere Street. Here can be seen the sockets of two crosses which were probably Roman guide posts. They are called the Outer Golden Pot and the Inner Golden Pot. Roy, in his *Military Antiquities,* speaks of five or more of these stones remaining between Redesdale and Chew Green. The road near here is called Gammel's Path which means the Old One's Road. Ancient roads or earthworks are often thought by primitive peoples to be of demonic origin like the Devil's Causeway. The road here was frequently used by reivers (Thieves' Rode) and later drovers, and salt and whisky smugglers. It was also used as a rendezvous of the Wardens of the Middle Marches of England and Scotland when they met to punish offenders against the Border Laws. Often disputes were settled by single combat. Here Snowden a renowned Northumbrian swordsman slew the celebrated Scottish champion, John Grieve.

At the Border near Coquet Head the foundations of the tavern of Chew Green can still be seen.

(Chew Green is just outside the boundaries of Tynedale in Scotland).

ROMAN WALL

We have not written a special section on the Wall but the various forts and remains are covered under the following entries.

Brunton Turret	Greatchesters
Busy Gap	Halton Chesters
Carrawburgh	Hexham
Carvoran	Housesteads
Castle Nick Milecastle	Milking Gap
Cawfields Milecastle	Planetrees
Chesters	Sewingshields
Corbridge	Vindolanda
Fallowfield	Walltown

ROSE HILL BRIDGE

This stone bridge, which is 50 feet in height above the level of the water, carries the Newcastle to Carlisle Railway across the Poltross Burn which here divides the counties of Northumberland and Cumberland. Carmichael's view (1838) shows many interesting features in the neighbourhood of Gilsland.

The house, whose roof can just be seen to the left of the bridge, is the famous Mumps Hall which became famous from the novel *Guy Mannering.* The house on the right is the Station House.

RUDCHESTER HALL

About a mile and a half beyond Heddon along the military road we come to the Roman fort called Vindobala. Nearby is Rudchester

Hall, a picturesque old building. Rudchester means "the red camp" and when excavated the stones of the Roman camp were found to be reddened by burning. (The Testa de Nevill *c.*1250 gives the name as *Rucestre,* which Ekwall interprets as "Rudda's ceaster."

Rudchester Hall incorporates the remains of a late tower house once the home of the Rutherfords one of whom was described by Walter Scott as:-

A hot and hardy Rutherford
Whom men called Dickon Draw-the-Sword

Simon of Rudchester started to build his hall here in 1285. The Rutherfords acquired Rudchester in 1419. They were not an important or wealthy family but extremely litigious and were always going to law. One of them achieved fame by having thirty children by one wife and a later Rutherford had nineteen sons killed in the Civil War.

The present Rudchester Hall is to outward appearance eighteenth century and the remains of the medieval tower can only be distinguished by the thickness of the walls. In the house is a remarkable fireplace here illustrated. The inner fireplace with stone lintel and carved jambs has at the bottom a Roman Cohort and Centurial Stone from the Roman Wall which recorded the work done by the Third Cohort of the Century of Pedovius.

Fireplace at Rudchester Hall

The house is square built of four by two bays and two storeys high It was built about 1780 but the entrance door is probably c.1860. It lies south of the Roman fort overlooking the Tyne valley with attractive gardens. Originally it was a large farmhouse but is now a private residence with a new farmhouse and extensive old outbuildings next door. This Georgian house was built with original gothic windows (a great deal of the glass is original) and as such is rare for Northumberland.

One of the farm outbuildings has a blocked up door, which is of long and short work, typically Anglo-Saxon, but no firm proof of Anglo-Saxon origin. Among the outbuildings are two series of buildings around courtyards with brick arches (30 are surviving). The brick was probably locally produced although similar bricks (imported from the Low Countries) are used in the former Liberal Club in Pilgrim Street.

In the front of house (and shown in Paul Brown's drawing) is an Anglo Saxon window, uncovered some years ago. Its existence raises some questions which are difficult to answer with certainty.

Beneath the brow of the hill west of the Roman Camp is the Giant's grave, hewn out of solid rock, twelve feet long, four broad and two deep. Legend says it was a brewer's vat and the Romans used it to make a beverage somewhat like beer from the bells of heather.

Rudchester

The Giant's Grave

Since it contained bones when found its funeral use was also claimed. However it is almost certainly of Roman workmanship and was probably a settling tank connected with some Roman baths not yet discovered. It originally had a partition and the outlet hole can still be seen.

Dr. Charlton mentions that there was a "priest's hole or hiding-place" here, and relates the following incident connected with it:- "When Rutchester was searched for priests by Fenwick, the pursuivant in Elizabeth's time, Mrs. Rutherford, who was by birth a Swinburne, hid herself in this concealed chamber while her husband fled to the woods along the banks of the Tyne. But Fenwick was well up to his work. He felt certain from the suddenness of the attack and the surrounding of the house that the inmates had not all had time to escape, so he quietly took up his quarters there, till, on the third day Rutherford himself returned from the woods and gave himself up, as he knew well that his wife and daughter, having no time to gather provision, would be faint with hunger in their hiding-place."

(Quoted by Tomlinson)

RUDCHESTER FORT (Vindobala)

Rudchester, the fourth fort from the eastern end of the Wall, lies 6¾ miles from Benwell. It was garrisoned in the fourth century by the First Cohort of Frisiavones the name of a tribe from what is now the Netherlands. In the *Notitia* it is called *Vindobala*, in the *Ravenna* List *Vindovala*. In the second century the garrison was probably cavalry. Apart from brief mention by Camden the first description of the fort is by Robert Smith (1708):-

On the south side of the Wall, are visible ruins of a very large square Roman Castle, with foundations of several houses in the middle of the area: the square, as nigh as I can guess, may be about one hundred and fifty yards; and at the west part of the square are three or four plots of ground in the very Wall (which seems to have been five or six feet thick) for little Towers. This has also a Vallum round it, and joins close to the Wall.

The fort measures 515 by 385 feet and covers 4½ acres. Little is to be seen apart from mounds to the south of the Military road marking the west and south ramparts.

The building of the Military Road and the growth of agriculture in the eighteenth and nineteenth centuries led to systematic despoliation of the fort for its stone. The farm and house to the south and many field walls are built of Roman stones.

The first real exploration of the fort was carried out in 1924. Two of the main gateways were excavated, a large granary and part of the principia were revealed, and a hypocaust belonging to the Commandant's house was discovered.

The Wall joined the fort at the main east and west gates leaving the gate passages to the north. The Wall Ditch existed before the fort was built. The west gateway which led on to the berm of the Wall was walled up but the date is uncertain. The thresholds show no sign of wear but since it was rarely used by wheeled traffic the closure might have been late in the Wall's history.

The south gate had an unusual arrangement. The west guard chamber was entered from the north and faced into the fort probably to control traffic going out. The other guard chamber had its door leading onto the gate passage as was normal. Early on the west portal was blocked and changed into a guard chamber. At the same time the last portal was furnished with two inner doors.

When the Headquarter's building was excavated the wide middle chamber contained the usual strong room. Coloured plaster showed the room had once been decorated.

Size, 3 ft. 4 in. by 1 ft. 7 in.

DEO SOLI INVIC[TO]
TIB. CL. DECIMVS
CORNEL[IA] ANTO-
NIVS PRAEF[ECTVS]
TEMPL[VM] RESTIT[VIT]

To the god the sun unconquerable
Tiberius Claudius Decimus
Antonius of the Cornelian tribe
the prefect
this temple restored.

SOLI
APOLLINI
. . . .

To the sun
Apollo

. . . .

Size, 3 ft. 7 in. by 1 ft. 5 in.

Size, 4 ft. 1 in. by 1 ft. 6 in.

DEO
L[VCIVS] SENTIVS
CASTVS
LEG. VI. D[ECVRIO]? P[OSVIT][2]

To the god [Mithras]
Lucius Sentius
Castus
A decurion of the sixth legion erected
[this].

DEO INVICTO
MYTRAE P. AEL.[IVS]
FLAVINVS PRAE.
V. S. LL. M.

To the invincible god
Mithras Publius Ælius
Flavinus the præfect
most willingly
and fittingly
discharges his vow.

Size, 3ft. 6 in. by 1 ft. 8 in.

The Vallum passes some 240 yards to the south of the fort while the vicus lay to the south and south-west. The "Giant's Grave" 95 yards south of the south-west angle of the fort is probably connected with a military bath-house not yet revealed.

Five altars (one of them uninscribed) were found to the west of the Giant's Grave. Four are here reproduced. They belonged to the Mithraeum which was completely excavated in 1924. Two buildings were revealed both in the traditional style and shape. The date of the second building can probably be dated shortly after the destruction of Hadrian's Wall in 197 A.D.

319

SANDHOE HOUSE

Stands a little to the east of Beaufront in a superb position over-looking the Tyne valley. It was built by Dobson in 1850 in the Jacobean style of architecture. Tomlinson describes it as a "quaint modern mansion, containing a small theatre." A writer in the *Hexham Courant* some time before 1886 wrote:- "a quaint queer-looking building, in which the Elizabethan style of architecture prevails. Though the house has little to recommend it in its character as a gentleman's mansion, the situation is really a charming one, whilst the landscape beneath its front is one of unrivalled beauty. The lawns, terraces and fancy flower-pots are all laid out with exquisite taste, and both the rear of the hall and the village are embowered with arborescent plants." The small theatre is no longer there.

SETTLINGSTONES

This hamlet, three miles west of Newbrough, derives its name from an ancient boundary stone which once marked the estate belonging to Hexham church. The old lead mine here is first mentioned in 1690. Two miles up the Settlingstones burn near the Military Road can still be seen the reservoir which supplied water to this mine.

SEWINGSHIELDS

The farmhouse of Sewingshields is built entirely of stone from the Wall. The name is Old English meaning *shiels of Sigewine*. Turret 34b lies among the farm buildings and a centurial stone is preserved in the farm inscribed "The century of Gellius Philippus." West of the farmhouse on the north side of the wall once stood Sewingshields Castle. When Dr. Lingard visited it in 1800 or 1807 its walls were five feet high but a farmer later removed the vaults and the area was ploughed over. Hodgson tells us that in his time only a square lumpy mass of ruins overgrown with nettles could be seen near Broomlee Lough. In 1266 a manor house at Sewingshields belonged to Sir John de Holton but only in 1415 is it described as a castle in the hands of Robert Ogle. The list of 1541 says the old "tower" belonged to John Heron of Chipchase but was roofless and waste.

When Sir Cuthbert Radcliffe was Deputy-Warden of the East Marches he appointed two watchmen to stand at the *Sewynge shealles cragge from sonne sett untyll the sonne aryse* in order to give warning of any bands of raiders. In the sixth canto of *Harold the Dauntless* by Sir Walter Scott the old tower is referred to as *The Castle of the Seven Shields*. Here is his description:

". . . . No towers are seen
On the wild heath, but those that Fancy builds,
And, save a fosse that tracks the moor with green,
It nought remains to tell of what may there have been."

But a fine legend has been preserved by Hodgson in his *History of Northumberland*.

"Immemorial tradition has asserted that King Arthur, his queen Guenever, court of lords and ladies, and his hounds, were enchanted

322

in some cave of the crags, or in a hall below the Castle of Sewing-shields, and would continue entranced there till some one should first blow a bugle-horn that laid on a table near the entrance into the hall, and then, with 'the sword of the stone', cut a garter also placed there beside it. But none had ever heard where the entrance to this enchanted hall was, till the farmer at Sewingshields, about fifty years since, was sitting knitting on the ruins of the castle, and his clew fell, and ran downwards through a rush of briars and nettles, as he supposed, into a deep subterranean passage. Full in the faith, that the entrance into King Arthur's hall was now discovered, he cleared the briary portal of its weeds and rubbish, and entering a vaulted passage, followed, in his darkling way, the thread of his clew. The floor was infested with toads and lizards: and the dark wings of bats, disturbed by his unhallowed intrusion, flitted fearfully around him. At length his sinking faith was strengthened by a dim, distant light, which, as he advanced, grew gradually brighter, till all at once, he entered a vast and vaulted hall, in the centre of which a fire without fuel, from a broad crevice in the floor, blazed with a high and lambent flame, that showed all the carved walls, and fretted roof, and the monarch, and his queen and court, reposing around in a theatre of thrones and costly couches. On the floor, beyond the fire, lay the faithful and deep-toned pack of thirty couple of hounds; and on a table before it the spell-dissolving horn, sword, and garter. The shepherd reverently but firmly grasped the sword, and as he drew it leisurely from its rusty scabbard, the eyes of the monarch and his courtiers began to open, and they rose till they sat upright. He cut the garter; and, as the sword was being slowly sheathed, the spell assumed its antient power, and they all gradually sunk to rest; but not before the monarch had lifted up his eyes and hands, and exclaimed,

> "O woe betide that evil day,
> On which this witless wight was born,
> Who drew the sword – the garter cut,
> But never blew the bugle-horn!"

. . . Terror brought on loss of memory, and he was unable to give any correct account of his adventure, or the place where it occurred."

Half a mile north west of Sewingshields are two high points called the King's and Queen's Crag. Another local tradition is told about them.

"King Arthur, seated on the farthest rock, was talking with his queen, who, meanwhile, was engaged in arranging her 'back hair'. Some expression of the queen's having offended his majesty, he seized a rock which lay near him, and with an exertion of strength for which the Picts were proverbial, threw it at her, a distance of about a quarter of a mile! The queen, with great dexterity, caught it upon her comb, and thus warded off the blow; the stone fell about midway between them, where it lies to this very day, with the marks of the comb upon it, to attest the truth of the story. The stone probably weighs about twenty tons!"

North east of Sewingshields farmhouse is Fozley Moss. On an island in the swamp was once a prehistoric settlement.

SHIELD-ON-THE-WALL

Three miles west of Carrawburgh on the north side of the Military Road Milecastle 33 can be seen. Its north wall and gate are well preserved and parts of the south gate can be seen.

SHILLA HILL BASTLE

Is on the top of a low hill on the right bank of the Tarset. It is in poor condition. According to legend it was the home of Hodge Corby or Corbit Jack whose friend, Barty Milburn of the Comb, gave his name to the next tower.

SHITTLEHEUGH PELE

The shattered ruins of this pele tower stand above the road north of Otterburn (A696) up Redesdale near where it meets the Roman Dere Street. It is a conspicuous feature in the landscape. Shittleheugh is described by Hodgson as the "Mansion House of the Reeds" it is clear from the remains that additions were made to the original pele so that it formed the basis of a larger building. The massive stones used in the construction are a noticeable feature. Unlike most peles the door, with a lintel of a single huge stone, is in the long south wall and not one of the ends. The tunnels for the draw bars still remain and in front of the door remains of a porch can be traced. There are two loopholes in the ground floor which is vaulted in the usual fashion, and in the upper storey are three wall cupboards. There are foundations of two small buildings adjacent.

SHOTLEY CHURCH

The chapel of St. Andrew of Shotley lies three miles north west of Shotley Bridge on Grey Mare hill. It originally belonged to Blanchland Abbey. In 1680 it was in a sad state. The churchwardens tell us the church was *"all out of repair, our bells broken; a font of stone we have, but broken; we have no sentences of scripture; an almes box we want, and a chest with three locks; we have neither a reading nor letany deske; we have no pulpit-cloath nor cushion; we have no book of cannons nor homilies, nor register for christning, marrying, or burying, nor tables of the degrees of marriage prohibited."*

Two years later more complaints were made:

"We want a Bible, a register booke, a bier, and a black cloth; our churchyard walls are much out of repaire; the house belonging to our parson was burnt down in the late incumbent's days, and as yet unrebuilt."

In 1769 the chapel was enlarged and in 1892 altered and restored. It is a low cruciform building with round-headed windows and a bell-cote. In the churchyard is the famous Hopper Mausoleum. It was erected about 1752 by Humphrey Hopper of Black Hedley. Archbishop Singleton (1828) referred to this "immense structure, more conspicuous than the church itself . . . something in the taste, though far worse, than the gate of Burleigh and one of the gates of Caius College."

It is a square structure with six rudely carved statues in niches. Some niches have shell decoration. Above on each side an open broken pediment with two reclining figures. The family arms are on the south face. The dome has obelisks at the corners and is crowned with an open lantern. Of the two statues on the south face one is the martyred Bishop Hooper. The front of the Mausoleum is railed in. Black Hedley and Shotley Hall have figures from the Hopper Mausoleum.

SILVER NUT WELL

One mile south of the village, at Meadowhaugh, on the right bank of the Rede, and approached by a path from Old Town Farm, is the sulphur spring called Silver Nut Well. It is now merely a small piece of marshy ground. But once the bubbling water used to bring up from below hazel nuts perfectly preserved and coated with sulphuret of iron.

David Evans M.A.Rector.

SIMONBURN CHURCH AND RECTORY,
North.ᵈ
Published March 1835,by W.Davison Alnwick .

SIMONBURN

Simonburn, derived from "Sigemund's burn", is a picturesque village of the stream of that name which joins the North Tyne between Humshaugh and Wark. It consists of some rows of cottages around a village green. The parish was once the largest in the county, 100 square miles in extent and stretching thirty miles to the Scottish border. The Parish Church, according to tradition, was founded in the seventh century by disciples of St. Kentigern (Mungo). It is one of the finest churches in the county. Originally a thirteenth century building it was restored in 1762 by Robert Newton, architect of the Old Assembly Rooms in Newcastle, and in 1860 by Robert Salvin. Preserved in the church porch are fragments of a Saxon cross and other ancient carved stones.

A peculiarity of the church is the slope of the floor from west to east. In the church is the monument to Cuthbert Ridley (rector here 1604-1627) and his family with four defaced figures. Such early monuments are rare in Northumberland. In the churchyard a tomb-stone bears a strange epitaph.

"Tired of travelling through this world of Sin,
At length I'm come to Nature's common Inn:
In this dark place here, for to rest a Night,
In hopes t' rise, that Christ may give me Light".

John Wallis who wrote the *Natural History and Antiquities of Northumberland* (1769) was curate here and later at Bellingham.

The Georgian rectory was built in 1725, incorporating fragments of a house dated 1666 (as the back lintel states). Prior to this there was a fortified rectory called by Bowes a "lytle tower". It is a three-storeyed building with five bays and all windows are segment headed with heavily rusticated surrounds. The angles of the house have large quoins and the roof is hipped. There was also in 1541 a bastle at Hall Barns opposite to the church but no trace remains today.

Simonburn Rectory is famous for its eighteenth century lavatory, a magnificent three-seater, here illustrated.

Taking a lane westward from the green for half a mile one comes

to the fragmentary remains of Simonburn Castle defended on two
sides by steep ravines. All that can be seen today are the ruined vault
of a tower which has a turret projecting from the north-west face.
The castle is first mentioned in 1415 but there are traces on the site of
a "motte and bailey" of an earlier period. In 1541 it was recommended
as a post to be held by the Keeper of Tynedale with a garrison of 100
men. A legend that a treasure was hidden within its walls hastened its
decay since many people searched for it and so demolished most of the
building. In 1766 it was partly restored as an eyecatcher from the
gardens of Nunwick.

The Tithe Barn

The tithe barn at Simonburn is one of the rare ones to survive in
Northumberland. It stands in the rectory paddock as it has done
since medieval times. It is now a house but apart from the insertion
of windows it is but little changed. In 1806 the tithe value was estimated
as £2,000 a year. The parish was divided into seven in the early nineteenth century and today, after various sales of glebe-land, only twenty
acres remain.

About a mile south-west of the village is the picturesque waterfall
called Teckitt Linn. Near the fall is a rude grotto or cave, part made by
nature, part by art, with a stone seat and an aumbry. Here, it is said,
Wallis, the historian used to compose his work. Also near Simonburn
is Teckitt farm, the residence of the Ridleys in the fifteenth century,
and their arms still remain above the front door.

The rector of Simonburn makes an urgent midnight call

SLAGGYFORD

A mile from Knaresdale is Slaggyford. The first element means "muddy". According to tradition it was once a market town and had a fair, but began to decline when Alston obtained its charter.

Two miles further south is Kirkhaugh. The old church was replaced in 1868 by one with an extremely thin needle-spire. The vicar designed it himself dispensing with an architect. In the fields between Kirkside Wood and the School are two Bronze Age barrows. In the excavations of 1935 a golden ear-ring was discovered.

A mile to the south is *Whitley Castle* and a short distance beyond it is the Cilderdale Burn which is the south-west boundary of Northumberland. Alston is two miles further on.

SLALEY

The parish of Slaley was called *Slaveleia* in 1166; the Old English word means "a muddy piece of cleared land". Belonging to the barony of Bolbec it was held by a family taking its name from the place. It is a long straggling village just over five miles from Hexham. The church, founded in 1312, was rebuilt in 1832. A mile from the village on the Hexham road is an old inn called the *Traveller's Rest*. Its signboard has the following lines, found on a number of similar inns;

"When you go by and thirsty be,
The fault's on you and not on me;
Fixed here I stand and hinder none,
Refresh, pay, and travel on."

Midway between Slaley and Stocksfield at a place called The Bridges a stone slab is set into the stone wall beside the road. It is of Quaker origin and this is the area where the Quaker family of the Richardsons lived. The wording is as follows:-

FOR FRIENDS IN COUNCIL

Tis wise in conversation, To vary speech of present occasion, With experience of the past, Fact with argument, Tales with reason, Question with opinion, Jest with earnest, But tiresome to press discourse too far. 1901.

STAGSHAW BANK FAIR

One of the most famous north country fairs used to be held annually on 4th July at Stagshaw Bank near Corbridge. Before the days of railways it was a large cattle and sheep fair and at times 100,000 of the latter were on sale. Many of the sheep were brought by Highland drovers from Scotland. The fair was a great festival for the district. Rev. James Raine thus describes the scene.

Upon reaching Stagshaw Bank, a large tract of open ground, not far from Corbridge, inclining swiftly from the Roman Wall to the Tyne, we found ourselves in the midst of a great annual fair held on this declivity, chiefly for cattle, but in truth for goods of all kinds, 'things', as an old inventory at Durham has it, 'moveable or moving themselves'. At this place, which is the solitary field, at a distance from any population, there are great well-known periodical gatherings of buyers and sellers from the whole north of England, on the western or eastern coast; and the southern counties of Scotland send forth in abundance their men and goods to buy, sell, or be sold.

In a large pasture upon the slope of a hill, with a wide prospect, extending down the valley of the Tyne as far as Gateshead Fell, and in every other direction except north, having an almost unlimited view of a spreading tract of country, there were gathered together, without the slightest attempt at the order which is of necessity observed in markets and fairs held within the walls of a town, horses and cattle, and sheep and swine, and in short everything which is bred or of use in farming operations, with thousands of other things, which it would be no easy task to enumerate; and then there were people of all ages, from all quarters, and in all kinds of costume; the Scotchmen in his kilt, and the Yorkshireman in his smock-frock; and every variety of booth or hut for refreshment or dissipation. That we had stumbled on a fair of Roman origin may not, I think, be doubted. The situation of Stagshaw Bank is an extremely convenient one for gathering together at stated periods of the year the produce of thsi the eastern side of the island; and as long as the Romans were in possession of Britain, and there was an immense population along the line of the Wall from sea to sea, the natives would find a ready market for the produce of their fields and farmyards. The Wall, which runs at the distance of a mile northwards, would be a protection to the sellers of cattle and wares in that direction; and from the south they had nothing to fear.

A painting by Ralph Hedley shows the fair being proclaimed in the market place of Corbridge by the bailiff of the Duke of Northumberland The proclamation was as follows:-

These are in Her Majesty's name and in the name of the Most Noble ALGERNON GEORGE duke and earl of Northumberland, Earl Percy, earl of Beverley in the county of York, Baron Warkworth of Warkworth castle in the county of Northumberland, Lord Lovaine, baron of Alnwick in the said county of Northumberland, a baronet and one of the Lords of Her Majesty's Most Honourable Privy Council, Lord Lieutenant and Custos Rotulorum of the county of Northumberland and of the city and county of Newcastle-upon-Tyne, lord of this manor and fair, and the rights and privileges of the same, to strictly charge and command all manner of persons coming and resorting thereunto, well and decently to behave themselves in word and deed, and that they and everyone of them do preserve and keep Her Majesty's peace without offering any violence, making any riot, rout, or unlawful assembly or drawing any weapon, or shedding any blood during the continuance of this present fair, and that they nor any of them do use any unlawful buying or selling, or commit any misdemeanour whatsoever which may disquiet Her Majesty's peace and the civil government of this present fair, upon pain of such penalties and punishments as shall be inflicted upon them by the governor or officer of the said fair or manor, and that as well the buyer, seller, or exchanger shall repair to the clerks of the tolls and in their books record their names and surnames, together with the colour, marks, and ages of every horse, colt, gelding, mare, or filly, or any other sort of cattle, upon pain of forfeiting the same as shall be neglected to be tolled, and all other goods, merchandise, liquor, and so forth as do not pay their toll and stallage are under the same forfeiture. And it is further commanded that all manner of persons whatsoever, buying, selling or exchanging between party and party within the said manor and fair, do quietly and peaceably pay their tool and stallage due and accustomed to be paid, and if there should happen any controversy in the buying, selling, or exchanging between party and party within the said fair and manor, they may repair to the officer of the said fair, where they shall have justice in and by the Court of Pie Powder, according to the equity of their cause. And lastly know all men that his fair is to continue for and during the space of eight days next after this proclamation is read, and hereof all manner of persons as well foreigners as aliens and those of Her Majesty's subjects are required to take notice, as they and every one of them do tender their duty towards Her Majesty, and will avoid such penalties and punishments as are limited for the punishment of offenders. GOD save the QUEEN, and the lord of this manor and fair.

Writing in 1881 Robert Forster describes the fair as he knew it thirty years before. "This fair," he writes, "which was one of business as well as pleasure, was the largest held in England for one day and for business people came to it from all parts of the United Kingdom. Besides horses, sheep, cattle, and swine, various articles of merchandise were offered for sale, consisting of men's hats, boots and shoes, these articles generally filled several stalls, the former being mostly from Hexham, and a considerable quantity of the latter from Corbridge.* Jewellery and hardware stalls were prominent; saddlery and farming goods, such as hay rakes, forks, &c., were always plentiful; and always a large supply of cooperage goods, such as tubs, barrel churns, &c. Webs of cloth coarse and fine were shown to advantage on the green carpet by the side of the pond.† The far-famed gloves, known as the "Hexham Tans", suitable for all purposes and for all classes, always formed noticeable articles of sale. Care was always taken by some thoughtful business man to make provision for the better part of man's nature. A great variety of useful books were shown, suitable for the most profound thinker as well as useful for the general reader. On the south side of the Horse Fair, in the distance you saw a strong-made man somewhat elevated, with a crowd around him offering articles for sale; an approaching, we observe that it is Mr. C————, from the once famous Dog Bank, Newcastle, selling watches by auction, being for the most part forfeited pledges, the auctioneer assuring the public that each watch he offered was far superior to the one just sold, as once belonging to some squire or gentleman whose name was well known in the neighbourhood. This man regularly attended the fair for many years and had his share of business. Amidst all this whirl of busy life, the "little busy bee" was not forgotten, for there was always a good supply of "bee skeps," to meet the wants of those whose tastes were after the sweetness of honey in the comb. In all the articles named and others not named, the day being favourable, a good trade was done, in fact this was almost the only opportunity during the whole year that numbers of persons, especially from the outlying districts, had of obtaining them.

---

* Boots and shoes were subject to an official inspection by two cordwainers, annually appointed for this purpose at the court of the lord of the Manor, held in Corbridge, and called "searchers and sealers of leather". If upon inspection any of these goods were considered of inferior quality, they were condemned as such, seized and brought to Corbridge; often to be laid aside as lumber in the court room.

† From the Household book of expenses of Sir Francis Radcliffe, of Dilston:- "1678. May. My Lady Radcliffe to buy cloath att Whitson faire at Stagshaw, £10."

The stomach, that important part of humanity, was never once overlooked or forgotten; for the supply of immediate wants (outside the tents) there was an abundance. From a long row of gingerbread and orange stalls could be heard some dame crying out lustilily "boole up and buy a way", others were shouting at the top of their voice "London spice twopence a package," while others displayed along the length of their arm twenty-four squares of gingerbread offered at a shilling the lot; oranges, cherries, Barcelona nuts, &c., were plentiful. The vendors of all those articles whose names were many, each striving to make as good a day's work as possible, used all their skill to attract the attention of the public to the superior quality of their goods, "crack and try before you buy," with a measure half-filled with the bottom, was the ditty of the nut mongers, making the fair with other clatter, often mingled with the roar of Wombwell's lions, almost a Babel. It is stated by one who took notes on these occasions, that tons of gingerbread and ship loads of oranges were devoured on that day. In addition to what was consumed in the fair, immense quantities were carried home, for it was the custom for almost every one to do so, carrying it in their pockets or handkerchiefs (for there were no bags in those days), and this was called "their fair". The usual kind of drink was ale of which a considerable quantity was used;* as this was long before the days of teetotalism, few had any scruple to take as much at least as to quench their thirst, in fact no other beverage was thought of or provided; notwithstanding this, the writer is persuaded, all things considered, there was less intemperance than at the present time amongst similar gatherings.

To the thoughtless and giddy, this fair held out many temptations, all the little gambling arts which were then in use were in full swing; two of the most notable in this class, we notice.—That well-known character, the famous showman of the North "Billy Purvis", a man of many parts, attended regularly for nearly a generation. He had a booth, inside of which it is said he performed wonderful sleight-of-hand tricks, without the aid of apparatus. From the stage outside his booth, could be heard at a considerable distance, his stentorian voice shouting "come this way and see wor show", which at once let you know the whereabouts of "Billy," who with his painted face and gaudy dress, with his witticisms, drollery and gestures, always attracted great attention; poor Billy has long since ceased to walk on a broader stage than that of his booth, having laid down his load of life in Hartlepool, and his place knows him no more. Another well-known character, a queer little hunchback fellow, who was known by the cognomen of "wallop-a-way" attended equally with "Billy," his vocation always appeared to be a simple way of getting a few pence, and could hardly come within the range of gambling. He was a noisy little fellow; shouting all day long "a penny a throw, a penny a throw, miss my pegs and

---

* There were tents from districts extending to twenty miles or more in all directions, to which all parties from those said localities resorted; each tent being known by a large fly on which was the sign of the inn or public house the name of the owner, and the place it hailed from.

hit my legs." He always had a good number of lookers on, and did a good share of business principally amongst the juveniles; poor fellow, he has long since followed in the wake of "Billy," and his voice is heard no more. Many shows were there of different sorts, the most attractive being that of Wombwell's collection of wild beasts, &c. The writer well recollects when a youth his first look at this wonderful exhibition as being a grand sight, and recollects also a little incident which occurred at the time. A woman who was walking too near the side of the cages, of which in an upper apartment were kept a number of monkeys was eyed by one of them, which quietly pushing his long leg through betwixt the bars of the cage, and with his paw unceremoniously pulled off the crown of her bonnet, to the no little dismay of the good lady. At one time there were besides Wombwell's, two other large collections, owned by persons of the names of "Pit Cock", and "Polito," these exhibitions invariably secured a large attendance. Now to return to Corbridge from which we have somewhat (we trust not uninterestingly) wandered. On the afternoon of that day it used to be said that Corbridge could be easily taken. For business, persons attended the fair in the forenoon and those for pleasure in the afternoon; those who had been doing business returning again in the afternoon, when few only were left, as the old and infirm, the sick, and mere children, and a few others whose home duties necessitated their remaining. The exodus homewards commenced about five o'clock, which increased to about seven, when it became general; by eight o'clock, the great proportion of pleasure seekers as well as those of business were wending their way home, which many of them could not reach before morning; such is brief outline of the doings of the busy multitudes on that once great day, as Corbridge was the thoroughfare for nearly all who came from the south.

It is difficult to visualize the bustle of this great fair when you visit today the lonely spot where the immense gathering once took place."

STAGSHAW HOUSE

This house is a mile east of Sandhoe and is first mentioned in 1724. Rev. Francis Thompson was the owner in 1828 but about 1860 it was bought by the Straker family. S. F. Dixon tells us "that at one time a Mr. Ridley, who had been in Australia, lived there. He invented a reaping machine which was mounted on a waggon, the wheels of which were the propelling power of the machine. Only the heads of the grain were cut off, then they were rubbed out and filled into sacks all at the same time. The stubble and straw were burned, making a valuable fertilizer."

Stagshaw House overlooks the moor on which the famous Stagshaw Bank fair used to be held. Late in the nineteenth century the house was restored and enlarged.

STAWARD PELE

About eight miles west from Hexham on an impregnable site and in a picturesque situation stands the remains of Staward Pele. It could not have been built in a safer place. It is built high up on a tongue of rock with the river Allen on one side and the Harsingdale burn on the other. In the south the ridge narrows to six feet. One angle of the gate-house remains and the north wall of the main tower stands sixteen feet high, with traces of a Barmkin.

The pele is thought to date from the fourteenth century. In 1384 Edward Duke of York granted the property to the Friars Eremite of Hexham for a yearly rent of five marks. After the dissolution of the religious houses Staward Pele came into the hands of the Howards and Sandersons and afterwards became the home of John Bacon, a mining speculator who made a fortune out of the lead mines of Alston district. About the beginning of the eighteenth century Staward Pele was occupied by a man called Dickey of Kingswood who became notorious as a clever horse thief. He never used force but lived by his wits. A famous story is told of how he stole fat-oxen near Denton Burn, Newcastle and took them to Lanercost in Cumberland where

he sold them to a farmer who owned an excellent mare. This mare was soon in Dickey's possession. He fled towards Newcastle with the farmer in pursuit. Near Haltwhistle he met the farmer from Denton Burn looking for his cattle, and told him where the oxen were. He then sold him the mare in order that he could hasten to catch the thief. We can imagine what happened when the two farmers met.

Towards the end of the nineteenth century Staward-le-Pele was a favourite place for picnics. Often several hundred were gathered at the spot. Our engraving of 1885 shows several picnickers. Some strange names are found in this neighbourhood. There is *Sillywra* which as Hodgson remarks "has perhaps nothing remarkable about it, but a name of difficult derivation". Then there is *Ginglepot* which takes its name from the Echoing Pool in the River Allen. A path from Staward pele leads down to the river to a deep pool known as Cypher's Linn. Like all deep pools in Northumbria the place has a story of buried treasure. From the pool down river we come to Plankey Mill a favourite picnic spot where the river is crossed by a suspension bridge Planky Ford, nearby, was known in 1673 as *Planky Ford alias Nakedale*.

The farmhouse of Low Staward Manor was once the old manor house. The Earl of Derwentwater is said to have hid here shortly before the Jacobite revolt.

STOCKSFIELD

The pretty village of Stocksfield, although today a growing residential area, was in the medieval times overshadowed by the more important township of Bywell.

The lands of Stocksfield belonged in the Middle Ages to the prior and convent of Hexham and the name means "the field belonging to the "stoke" or "holy place". Tomlinson described it as a "pretty rural village, with a picturesque environment of wood and valley scenery."

Our photograph shows a communal oven about 1907. It was an open hearth oven built into wall of end house of the colliery row. It was used by the miners' wives in turn who fired the oven with their own coal and baked their bread and left the oven clear for the next neighbour. These ovens were a feature of Northumberland mining villages from the middle of the nineteenth century until early in the twentieth.

STYFORD HALL

The hall lies 2 miles south east of Corbridge. A Directory of 1886 describes it as "plain substantial building situated near the Tyne and surrounded by extensive grounds on all sides except the south, where a beautiful lawn extends to the river's bank." The three storeyed house was built or reconstructed towards the end of the eighteenth century. With its old walled gardens Styford Hall has an outstanding pleasant site.

Communal oven at Mickley Square, near Stocksfield

SWINBURN CASTLE

Swinburn Castle is first mentioned in 1346 but of this medieval fortress nothing survives. It is said to have stood on the lawn of the present house. The two tunnel vaulted basements to the east are sometimes claimed to be part of the old castle. In the list of 1415 it is recorded as belonging to the son of Roger Widdrington the founder. A wall around the castle is mentioned in 1479. In the Great Survey of 1541 it is described as a great tower with only the walls standing. About 1660 a manor house was built. It is two storeys high with nine windows on the upper floor. The hood-moulds have survived but the mullions have been removed. The house has been much altered. The massive chimney stacks on the west front are a striking feature. One of the door heads bears the date 1728 and the initials T.M.R. for Thomas and Mary Riddell.

SWINBURN CASTLE,
The Seat of Ra. Riddell, Esq.
Printed and Published by W. Davison, Alnwick.

Some time before 1760 the house we see today was built. Wallis (writing in 1769) tells us: "Mr. Riddell, the present owner of Swinburn Castle, married the daughter and sole heir of the late Horsley Widdrington of Felton, esq. His seat at Swinburn is of his own erection, out of the ruins of the old castle, after a very neat design." The wings were added in 1771. Hutchinson, writing in 1776, says:-

The modern seat of Mr. Riddell which arose from the ruins of Swinburn castle, an elegant stone building, covered with woods commands an extensive view, but it is over an open and ill-fenced tract. He is making rapid progress in the cure of this defect and multitudes of quick fences and plantations are arising, which in a few years will extinguish the disagreeable traces of that hostility and devastation which before the union marked this country with the melancholy memorials of warfare; and in their place give to the eye all the charms of rural opulence.

Swinburne castle is two and a half stories with a front of five bays and at the angles two canted bays which contain large rooms, two of which contain fine plaster ceilings. The entrance door has Tuscan columns and is connected with the window above which has a pediment. The staircase is lit by a Venetian window at the rear of the house. The fine ashlar work and beautifully coloured stone is noticeable. The Orangery and stables are both eighteenth century work.

337

In the park of Swinburn Castle is a remarkable standing stone or *menhir*. It is 11 feet high and 3½ feet in breadth. Associated with it are three or four *tumili* or burial mounds and some prehistoric terraces used for agriculture.

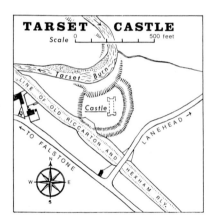

TARSET CASTLE

Little but a mound and ditch remains of this stronghold in the North Tyne valley. The site was of strategic importance from its command of the Tarset and Tyne fords and of the junction of two old traffic routes but it did not play an important part in history. The builder was John Comyn, a Scottish knight, who was granted licence to crenellate in 1267. It was burnt down by the Scots and the men of Tynedale in 1525. In the Survey of Border Castles made in 1541 the castle was described as "the Hall of the Lord Burrowe's inheritance, the which was burnt by the said Tyndalles sixteen years since, and more, at a tyme when Sir Rauffe Fenwick lay with a certain garrison in the tower at Tarset Hall for the reformation of certain mis-orders in the said country of Tyndaill". At the beginning of the century the walls were partly standing, of "about four feet thick, of the finest ashlar-work, and strongly cemented". It was defended by an outer wall, and a moat ten yards wide. "Its magnitude, strength, and antiquity", says Mackenzie, "have combined to impress the minds of the neighbouring people with the notion of its having been the dreadful habitation of a giant, and it is popularly believed that a subterannean road is cut out, even below the bed of the river, between this ancient stronghold and Dally Castle, which is distant about a mile to the south". Tradition asserts that along this passage "carriages have been heard to rumble, and then seen to emerge from the other end, drawn by headless horses". Strange to relate, during excavations in 1888 a well-built hewn stone underground passage was discovered but no plan was made and the stones were removed for building. The castle was a long narrow structure with a turret at each corner.

THOCKRINGTON CHURCH

A mile to the east of Colt Crag Reservoir on the crest of an outcrop of the Great Whin sill stands the lonely church of Thockrington, which from itx position is a landmark for miles around. There is only one farm in the vicinity and the approach is by a narrow moorland road.

The church is one of the oldest in the county and like Heddon, Kirk Newton, Seaton Delaval and Warkworth has a vaulted chancel. For more than 600 years the church belonged to the archbishopric of York. The Norman church consisted of a nave and apsidal chancel. The apse however seems to have collapsed, probably because its foundations on the slope of the hill were insecure. The shortened chancel was then reinforced by sturdy buttresses. The same had to be done later with the west end of the nave.

There is considerable Norman work to be seen, especially in the chancel, in spite of many restorations. The double projecting square bell-cote with its stone roof seems to have been "made up" from spare old masonry, probably in the seventeenth century.

There are some interesting sepulchral monuments in the churchyard. One is incised with a bugle (a forester's badge) and a sword. Another has a cross whose head is formed by four circles joined together with a book on one side and a sword on the other. A simple stone covers the grave of Lord Beveridge of Tuggal who is often called the Father of the Welfare State. His daughter lived at Carrycoats Hall nearby, hence the choice of Thockrington churchyard.

THORNEYBURN

A mile and a half from Tarset is the moorland village of Thorney-burn. At the same distance further west are the remains of a prehistoric fortification whose moat is still traceable. Near to it is an old pele called "Camp Cottage". Half a mile from Camp Cottage, occupying an elevated situation, is the hamlet of *Donkley Wood*, mentioned in the *Iter of Wark*, 1279 A.D., as being, in conjunction with Thorneyburne and Tarsethope, amerced in the sum of twenty shillings for decapitating a thief without awaiting the coroner's trial.

THORNEYBURN CHURCH,
William Elliot_Rector.   North.ᵈ
Published March 1825, by W.Davison, Alnwick.

The church of St. Aidan here was built in 1818 by H. H. Seward for the Commissioners of Greenwich Hospital and is similar to his churches at Greystead, Wark and Humshaugh. Our illustration was published in 1825. Archdeacon Singleton wrote the following interesting account of the parish in 1832:-

'The Rev. Edward Brice, A.B., rector. He was instituted in 1830 on the promotion of Mr. Elliott the first rector to Simonburn. He and his wife having passed most of their lives at Portsmouth and Plymouth (he having been chaplain to the ordinary in those ports) seem but little satisfied with the absolute seclusion of their very pretty rectorial house and garden. To be sure I saw it under a summer sun, whilst the poor lady detailed with horror her lively remembrance of two *Snow Blasts*!! They are moreover surrounded by waters, the Tarset with its steep and precipitous banks is to be forded, towards the north, and the broad and rapid Tyne is to be traversed towards the south. There is here a most charming and sheltered little garden. The church is new and good, and the house extremely comfortable. There are 17 acres of glebe. The usual congregation is composed of persons who come from the neighbouring hamlet of Greenhaugh in Bellingham parish; it amounts to about 40 on the average, and 15 communicants, the latter may seem disproportionate to the former, but it is the case in all the moorland parishes, where the remote and the aged and the failing make unusual exertions to attend the sacrament. There are two churchwardens, the registers begin in 1818. The books and vestments are good. The sacramental plate neat, consisting of a silver cup marked 'Thorneyburn Rectory', and a silver patten, rather deep and what silversmiths call Gadrone. The value of the living from the sad depreciation of the wool market does not surpass £130 p.a. . . . The neighbouring rectory of Greystead is of no greater value, and I am inclined to think the advice originally tendered to the commissioners of the Greenwich Hospital was very wise although unfortunately quite without success. They were advised 'to build a somewhat larger church at Greystead, and with the money destined for the erection of Thorneyburn and its appendages to build a bridge over the Tyne and afford the population of the northern side an opportunity of coming to church, whilst the whole district would have been benefited by the facility of intercourse, and the rector from both portions would have derived a more suitable and more decent maintenance.'

The old name of the site of the house and church was Drapercroft. The Commissioners had contracted for a place called Thorneyburn, and being too secure of completing their contract, had inserted the name in their Act. The purchase however was never completed, they bought Draper Croft, but to conform to the wording of their bill persisted in calling their rectory and its locality by the name of Thorneyburn.

The glebe and buildings for the two rectories and churches of Greystead and Thorneyburn cost £17,000!! I came to Thorneyburn in a four-wheeled carriage from Elsdon by High Green and the fearful descent of the Gate House and the Ford of the Tarset, and left it by crossing the Tyne at a ford a little below Greystead on my way to Bellingham."

THORNGRAFTON

Due north of Bardon Mill rises the heather-clad hill of Barcombe which overlooks the village of Thorngrafton (which is Old English meaning "farm by a thorn brake"). It is chiefly composed of sandstone well suited for building purposes, and is dominated by the *Long Stone* which stands on an eighteenth century base. A little below the summit of the hill is a prehistoric camp whose ramparts can still be seen showing the chieftain's house with pit-like dwellings for his followers and enclosures for the cattle. In the west corner of the camp was a Roman signal station with a magnificent view of the Roman Wall. Much of the stone for building the wall and the adjoining stations was quarried at Barcombe and "the tracks", say Dr. Bruce, "are visible by which the quarrymen transported the stone".

In one of these old quarries some quarrymen discovered in 1837 a bronze boat-shaped purse with a lid and spring lock, which contained sixty silver and three gold Roman coins. They were of great historical value since there were none after Hadrian's time and so the quarries could be dated. One of their number called Thomas Pattison was given the task of disposing of them. He showed them in the public houses of Hexham and they came to the notice of the Duke of Northumberland's agent who claimed them as treasure trove. The fascinating story has been told at length by Dr. Bruce but briefly we can record that Pattison refused to give up the coins, legal proceedings were taken against him and he was sent to gaol for one year. Shortly after his release he died, the imprisonment having affected him greatly. Twenty-one years after their discovery they were purchased from William Pattison by Mr. Clayton of Chesters for "fifty new bright sovereigns" and the purse can now be seen at Chesters Museum. The collection became known as the *Thorngrafton Find* since the place of discovery was on Thorngrafton Common. To the east lie Muckle and Whinnetley Moss, the former containing several rare plants.

TWICE BREWED

Before the construction of General Wade's Military Road the traffic between Newcastle and Carlisle was conducted on pack-horses. For part of the journey the carriers followed the old Roman way. At selected spots they used to camp out for the night and one of their favourite halting places was the Twice Brewed, or to give its correct title Twice Brewed Ale. The original inn is now the East Twice Brewed Farm. A new inn of the same name stands further to the west, and at the crossroads is a Youth Hostel called Once Brewed.

East Twice Brewed Farm.

William Hutton, in the year 1801, at the age of 78 travelled the whole length of the Roman Wall and wrote an account of his journey. Here is his amusing description of the Twice Brewed :-

"As the evening was approaching, and nature called loudly for support and rest, neither of which could be found among the rocks; I was obliged to retreat into the military road, to the only public house, at three miles distance, known by no other name than that of Twice Brewed.

'Can you favour me with a bed?'
'I cannot tell till the company comes.'
'What, is it club-night?'
'Yes, a club of carriers.'

A pudding was then turned out, about as big as a peck measure; and a piece of beef out of the copper, perhaps equal to half a calf.

Having supped, fifteen carriers approached, each with a one-horse cart, and sat down to the pudding and beef, which I soon perceived were not too large. I was the only one admitted; and watched them with attention, being highly diverted. Every piece went down as if there was no barricade in the throat. One of those pieces was more than I have seen eaten at a meal by a moderate person. They convinced me that eating was the 'chief end of man'. The tankard too, like a bowl lading water out of the well, was often emptied, often filled."

Most of the old inns along the Military Road closed down with the advent of the Newcastle and Carlisle Railway.

UNTHANK HALL

The present hall is of late nineteenth century work (1862) although a little of Dobson's work of 1815 may still survive. It is rarely mentioned in history except as the possible home of Bishop Ridley. But of the pele in which he was supposed to live nothing survives in the present building. Before he was burned at the stake in Oxford in 1555 he wrote to his sister:-

"Farewell, my beloved sister of Unthanke, wyth all youre children, my nephews and nices. Synce the departure of my brother, Hughe, my mynde was to have been unto them as a father; but the Lord God must and will be their father if they love him and fear him, and live in the trade of his law".

A chamber in the oldest part of the house was traditionally called "The Bishops Room". However Willimoteswick also claims to be his birthplace. The name Unthank is found in several places in the north east. The name seems to have been given to poor land which was "ungrateful".

VINDOLANDA

Vindolanda, the Roman fort and civilian settlement, lies behind the Roman Wall. In recent years important archaeological discoveries have been made here including the unique writing tablets and a vast collection of leather. In the old house of Chesterholm is the largest Roman museum in the north and near the civilian settlement a full scale reconstruction of sections of the wall can be seen.

Vindolanda was one of the original forts on the Stanegate. It was built on a plateau which except on one side is protected by nature. There were at least six forts here, four of wood and two of stone.

343

The remains we see today are of the last fort built a little before 300 A.D. It had four gates of which the north and west were the most important. The remains in the centre of the fort are those of the headquarters building.

However it is the civilian settlement which is of such great significance. It was built on land which is almost waterlogged and the dampness has helped to preserve the remarkable series of finds which have been made. There were two stone built settlements. The first was erected about 163 A.D. and abandoned in the middle of the third century. A few decades later another settlement of inferior quality was built which lasted until the end of the fourth century.

Of the buildings to be seen in the settlement three are of interest.
1. The Military Bath-house which is well preserved.
2. The *Mansio* or inn for travellers. It was of great importance since Vindolanda was on the Roman road called the Stanegate.
3. The corridor house, the largest civilian building yet discovered.

In the waterlogged ground, which was ideal for the preservation of articles left there, a fantastic collection of writing tablets has been found which are slowly being translated and providing important historical information. For Britain a unique collection of textiles has been discovered along with vast quantities of leather. These can be seen in the large well equipped museum.

To many visitors the great interest of Vindolanda lies in the excavations which are taking place. The site is not a museum piece but a working area where archaeologists can be seen pursuing their trade.

Writing tablet from Vindolanda (courtesy Vindolanda Trust)

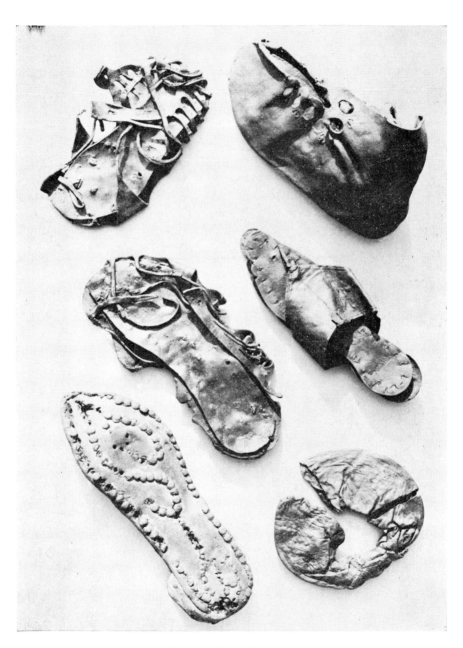

Footwear from Vindolanda

Roman milestone near Vindolanda

WALL

The small hamlet of Wall with its sandstone-slated houses has had an uneventful history apart from being ravaged by the Scots in 1315, 1467 and 1546. It was overshadowed by the much larger and important village of Acomb. It is however known today for its popular hotel named after the builder of the Roman Wall – Hadrian.

WALLTOWN

The village of Walltown or rather what is left of it lies on the Roman Wall one mile north east of Greenhead. Here is a spring surrounded by masonry called "King Arthur's Well". Tradition, quite erroneously, says that here Paulinus baptized King Egbert. Here among the rocks can be seen patches of chives said to have been planted by the Romans. Camden tells us:- "There continueth a settled persuasion among a great part of the people thereabout, and the same received by tradition, that the Roman soldiers of the marches did plant here eveywhere in old time for their use certaine medicinable hearbs, for to cure wounds; whence is it that some empirick practitioners of chirurgery in Scotland, flock hither every year in the beginning of summer, to gather such simples and wound-herbes; the vertue whereof they highly commend as found by long experience, and to be of singular efficacy".

The tower here in 1542 belonged to John Ridley, the brother of the martyr but only mounds in the field denote its site. The present farmhouse was built with stones from the tower. Hodgson said he saw in an old part of the house a lintel with the initials T.M.A. and the date 1713. Near Walltown are some of the finest views of the Wall particularly to the east towards Allolee Farm and to the west are some finely preserved sections particularly near the Nine Nicks of Thirlwall.

WALWICK GRANGE

Walwick Grange is one mile south west of Chollerford Bridge on the banks of the North Tyne. In 1740 it was advertised as to let in the Newcastle Courant and described as "a handsome new house very well furnished". In 1757 John Errington was in occupation and in that year had a lawsuit with the earl of Northumberland because he had refused him the right of a carriageway over "his grounds called the Chesters, leading from the village of Humshaugh to the village of Newborough." Wallis (1769) describes it as "a modern structure, built on to an old tower, in a low situation on the brink of the North Tyne, upon a rock", belonging to Anthony Errington. A view of the house was painted by T. M. Richardson, Jun. in 1839 (Laing Art Gallery) and in the following year John Hodgson wrote: "Here the tall wind-raked chimnies, that surmount the house; and the old gardens, orchards and terraced walks that overhang the right bank of the North Tyne, on calm and sunny days, gaze on their own interesting features in the dark, ale coloured waters of the river of late years since the place became the residence of the agent to the duke of Northumberland, the approach to the house, and the condition of the contiguous ground have been so greatly improved, that the trimness of the garden and the agriculture of the farm are models for example."

WALWICK HALL

Walwick is finely situated on the Roman Wall west of Chollerford. Walwick Low Hall is first mentioned at the beginning of the eighteenth century. Called Walwick Hall in 1828 it was the seat of Matilda Bulman. Bulmer's Directory of 1886 informs us the owner was J. M. Ridley.

WARDEN

Near the suspension bridge crossing the Tyne is the village of Warden. Hodgson describes its situation as "very sweet under the shelter of Warden Hill on the north". It is situated in the fork formed by the junction of the North and South Tyne which are both fordable nearby. The name is derived from the Old English "weard dun" which means "Watch Hill". Warden Hill is occupied by a large Iron Age hill fort whose ramparts and ditches cover two acres.

The church here is famous for its Saxon tower (although doubts have been expressed as to whether it is pre-Conquest) which is the smallest in Northumberland. Externally it measures 16 by 13 feet with walls 2 feet 10 inches thick. The quoins are large Roman stones. The tower has four stages internally, three of which have windows

of Saxon type externally and Norman inside. The fourth story, the belfry, was greatly altered in the eighteenth century and battlements added. The face was renewed and set back. The church was almost "entirely rebuilt" in 1765.

WARDEN BRIDGE

At West Boat near Warden was an ancient manorial ferry. It was replaced by a suspension bridge in 1826 erected under the direction of Captain Samuel Brown, R.N. The suspension bridge was replaced early in the present century but the old toll house on the south side is still there. On the north side is the old Boat Inn. Our photo shows the suspension bridge about 1904.

The Boat Side Inn at Warden Bridge was built in 1857. The bridge was erected in 1903. However the inn (or beerhouse as it was described) catered for traffic across the earlier Chain Bridge and before that for the ferry boat.

Warden Railway Bridge is about two miles west of Hexham and carries the Newcastle to Carlisle railway across the South Tyne. The original bridge, here illustrated, by J. W. Carmichael, was a timber superstructure on piers of stone. It consists of five openings of fifty feet span each.

Boat Side Inn ~ Warden.

Chain Bridge at West Boat, 1899

WARDREW HOUSE

Half a mile from Gisland Spa on the opposite side of the River Irthing is Wardrew House. Here was Wardrew Spa. Hutchinson, in 1776, described Wardrew as "famous for its Spaw. The waters have been analized, and require not my pen to repeat their virtues, so well known to the public. The conveniences for a few visitors are narrower, but commodious enough; the situation is retired, not much of the romantic; the walks are solemn, and the whole scene befits a mind that carries its ideas and meditations to distant regions; for there are few objects present which either elevate or entertain. Calmness and tranquillity are the effects such sameness of subject insinuates to the mind; and indolence, with that degree of ease stiled negligence, succeed to take the place of pleasure".

Wardrew House was built in 1752 on the site of an older building. It is a plain house of stone. The poet Burns visited it in June 1787:- "Left Newcastle early and rode over a fine country to Hexham to breakfast, from Hexham to Wardrew, the celebrated spa where we slept." It was here that Sir Walter Scott first met his future wife, Charlotte Spencer. The country around has some very rare flowers and plants which inspired Scott to write his poem: *To a Lady with Flowers from a Roman Wall*, 1797.

> *Take these flowers which, purple waving,*
> *On the ruined ramparts grew,*
> *Where, the sons of freedom braving,*
> *Rome's imperial standard flew.*
> *Warriors from the breach of danger*
> *Pluck no longer laurels there;*
> *They but yield the passing stranger*
> *Wild-flower wreaths for Beauty's hair.*

One of the windows of Wardrew House had a pane of glass signed by Sir Walter but it was removed by one of its owners, Mr. Hodgson Hinde, to discourage visitors.

WARK

In a beautiful setting the village of Wark, although now of little importance, was once the capital of North Tynedale. Traces of the Norman motte and bailey castle built here are still to be seen in a field called the Mote hill. It is first mentioned in 1399 but by 1538 we are told "Wark has no stone standing, though so necessary to bridle Tynedale". The motte was levelled to build the present farm which has a Tudor door-head as its sole relic of antiquity. Wark was held in demesne by the kings of Scotland. Records of two courts held at Wark by the kings of Scotland's justices in 1279 and 1293 have survived. Here is one extract.

"William, the parson of Corbridge, was taken for a burglary in the house of Hugh of Burton, and was committed to prison at Wark, and convicted at the assizes. But as the bishop of the diocese had no "attornatus" there to claim his clerk, the said William was remitted to prison, from which he afterwards escaped, and fled to the church at Simonburn, where he was kept till he was claimed by Lambert, vicar of Warden, and taken to the prison of the Bishop of Durham, where he soon after died".

The name Wark is derived from the Old English *weorc* meaning fortification.

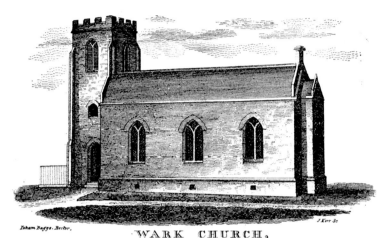

WARK CHURCH,
North TyneNorth.
Published Dec.ʳ 1823. by W.Davison Alnwick.

WELTON HALL

Welton Hall lies close to the Whittle Dene Reservoirs on the line of the Roman Wall. It consists of an ancient pele tower, a Jacobean mansion, and a modern house. The name Welton (early Waltenden) means "Wealt's Valley". It was once a place of some importance. To the musters of 1538 it sent forty-one able-bodied men. Although part of the barony of Prudhoe it was given, about 1189, to the Priory of Tynemouth. In 1694 the last of the Weltons sold the estate to Sir William Blackett of Wallington for £4,260.

The ruined fifteenth century pele tower is built of Roman stones taken from the nearby wall. It has a tunnel-vaulted basement with a low and narrow entrance. Attached to the tower is an L-shaped manor house. Most of it seems to be of 1614 as the date above the doorway informs us. The picturesque front has a magnificent two-storeyed bay with mullioned and transomed windows.

"Old Will o' Welton, whose initials appear on the tower, was celebrated for his great strength. One of his feats of prowess is said to have been exhibited when age had deprived him of sight. This blind Samson, sitting outside the tower, called a plough-boy to him, and asked him to let him feel his arm as he wished to find what sort of

353

Doorway of Welton Hall

bones folk had now-a-days. The lad, apprehensive of his grip, held forth, instead of his arm, the iron plough coulter, which Will, forthwith, snapped in twain, pensively observing, "Men's banes are nought but girsels (gristles) to what they were in my day!"

There is a room in the hall which is said to be haunted by the ghost of Lady Welton who was murdered by "Long Lonkin" the freebooter. (See Nafferton Tower).

WESTER HALL

William Smith built a house a quarter of a mile west of Haughton Castle in 1730. Only a door lintel with his name and date remains incorporated into the nineteenth century house which replaced it.

However the early house had a walled garden of which the garden house in the south west corner has survived. It is a square brick building on the garden side with pyramid roof crowned by a fine weather vane. The upper storey was a pigeon loft. The ground floor was a room with a door on the south. Both are surmounted by extraordinary scrolly pediments and primitive human heads. Such baroque garden ornamentation is rare in Northumberland.

WHITELEY SHIELD BASTLE

The farm of Whiteley Shield is in the hamlet of Carr Shield on the river West Allen. The ruined bastle still remaining is illustrated here.

WHITFIELD

The village of Whitfield lies four miles south of Bardon Mill overlooking the river East Allen. The name "white" is used to denote "dry open pasture ground in opposition to woodland and black-land growing heath". The manor of Whitfield was granted by William the

Whiteley Shield Bastle.

Lion, king of Scotland to the canons of Hexham. At the dissolution of the monasteries it came into the hands of the Whitfields who for long had been the tenants of Hexham Abbey.

Whitfield Hall lies just over a mile to the south on the bank of the river. Originally it was a fortalice built in the time of Henry the Sixth. It was enlarged in the seventeenth century. But in the middle of the eighteenth century the Whitfield family were in serious financial difficulties and sold their estate to William Ord of Fenham who rebuilt the house in 1785 from plans by Newton of Newcastle. In 1856 a storey was added, and further alterations were carried out in 1968.

Writing in 1840 John Hodgson thus describes the changes made on the Whitfield estate when the wealthy Ord family took it over:

"At this time, the roads through the parish were mere track-ways, and the principal employment of the people was the conveyance of lead ore to the neighbouring smelt-mills, in sacks, on the backs of ponies. There was not a cart in the country. The farms were very small – seldom above £20-a-year, and the dwelling-houses and farm-offices upon them of the most wretched description. Of these the present owner pulled down between 78 and 80; and has replaced them with large and substantial farm-houses and commodious offices; besides building numerous cottages, workshops, and mills for grinding corn, and sawing timber. The *turnpike road* through the parish was first made under authority of an act of parliament passed in 1778; but since 1824, under the provisions of another act, its line has been very greatly improved, and at present its fine order allows a stage-coach and daily post to pass along it for above seven miles through the estate. The *highways* of the parish have also been very much improved of late years, both in line and surface; extensive inclosures, and plantations formed; much general improvement made in the land, especially in draining; and indeed, the whole face of the country, the habits, manners, clothing, and food of the inhabitants entirely changed within the last half century".

His idyllic description of the hall is worth repeating: "The house overlooks a fine park, interspaced with luxuriant groups of forest trees; and has before it the Monk-wood, full of hollies, and growing on a bold and rocky declivity, at the foot of which, between shady banks, the West Allen, in winter, rushing over foaming lins and a stoney bed, raises her voice to the roar of the storms; or, hushed in summer, tunes her song to the breathings of genial winds, and the notes of the woodland choir. Its site is on a dry ridge or knoll, between the Allen and the Oxclose burn, and the view from the terrace, down the two united streams, through groves and hedge-rows, and over the Bear's-bridge, the Inn, and far below, is charmingly sweet and cheerful. Indeed at every turn about the house and park, and by the sides of 'the bonny burns' Nature and Art have kindly accorded in forming endless combinations for the admirers of rural beauty to wander among and adore".

To the west of Whitfield is the strangely named Ding-Bell-Hill. The early name was Ving-Vell-Hill. Whether this is a corruption of Wine-Well-Hill (fron a spring of fine water) or Ding-Bell-Hill (the church is ½ mile away) is doubtful.

Half a mile to the east is Old Town, once part of Whitfield, where there are vestiges of several old peles. The Whitfield Lead Mills once stood near the meeting of the East and West Allen. They were built by the London Lead Company and were called the *Cupola Mills* from the form of a reverbatory furnace used there. The name survives in the *Cupola Bridge*.

The river is crossed at Whitfield by the Blueback Bridge which takes the road climbing up to Allendale Town. At the beginning of the century a cyclist was killed here when he lost control on the steep hill. A memorial commemorates the accident. The modern church dedicated to the Holy Trinity was built in 1860. No public houses are allowed on the Blackett-Ord estate so the people of Whitfield have to travel for a drink. The nearest place is "The Cartsbog" on the road to Haydon Bridge.

WHITFIELD CHURCH and RECTORY

Whitfield Rectory

One mile above the present village of Whitfield is the old church of St. John's and the rectory. The church is small and the rectory large with five bays and two storeys. One hundred and fifty years ago

357

the opposite was the case. Our illustration shows the church and rectory at that time. A few years earlier the rectory was more primitive. The dwelling apartments were on the second floor, approached from the outside by stairs and the cattle were stabled below.

WHITLEY CASTLE

This is a Roman fort, not a medieval castle. Its ancient name is unknown and it lies close to Whitley Castle Farm. John Warburton an Inland Revenue Officer who visited Northumberland *c.* 1715 wrote:- "Whitley: a discontinued village on arising ground near ye meeting of ye River Gelt and Tine, and in several hands, in which is ye ruins of an old castle". It was the Roman fort to which he referred, without knowing its origin.

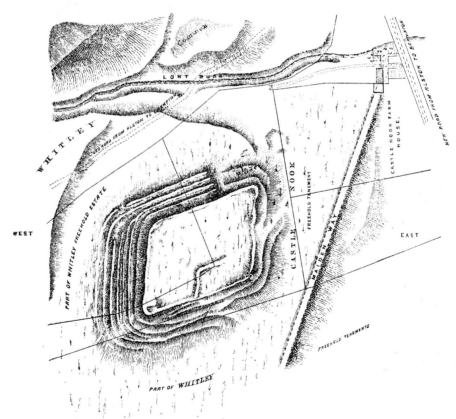

ROMAN STATION *at* WHITLEY *in* NORTHUMBERLAND

WHITTLE

Little is left of the township of Whittle. Its chief feature being the wooded valley of the Whittle Dene which to the north is dammed to

form the Whittle Dene Waterworks. In the Middle Ages the mill was
the most important spot in this valley. The water in the burn is very
soft and clear and used to be celebrated for its power of bleaching
linen-cloth.

WHITTLE DENE RESERVOIRS

The Whittle Dene Water Company formed in Newcastle in 1845.
The Prospectus declared:

*There are few advantages which a large and populous town can possess
more important than a copious supply of water, suitable alike for drinking
and for general domestic purposes. Not only is it essential to the health,
comfort and convenience of the inhabitants at large but it is conducive,
in the highest degree, to habits of sobriety and cleanliness in the working
classes, especially when it is conveyed into their own houses and supplied
at all times without restriction. The benefits, however, which an abundance of good water are calculated to confer, have never yet been
extended to the towns of Newcastle and Gateshead, and so loud and
universal are now the complaints of the bad quality of the water obtained
from the river Tyne for the use of the inhabitants that there is every
inducement to seek elsewhere for a purer source of supply than that
river is capable of affording . . . The smaller streams which occur in the
immediate vicinity of Newcastle and Gateshead are all either deficient
in quantity or defective in the quality of the water . . . Fortunately,
however, there exists, within a practicable distance of Newcastle, a
stream called Whittle Burn, which is situated in the neighbourhood of
Ovingham and is free from all these objections and a project has
recently been formed for obtaining from that source the much-needed
supply of pure water.*

The idea was certainly not too early. In the same year Dr. Reid had
reported that only one twelfth of the inhabited houses in Newcastle
had water laid on and the principal source of supply, the river at
Elswick, was polluted by the discharge from the common sewers.

"The master mind", according to a contemporary document, "who
directed the movement was that of Mr. William George Armstrong
whose hydraulic inventions were just beginning to attract attention."

The capital of the company was £120,000 and the Secretary was
William Armstrong and with little opposition they went ahead
building a reservoir near the village of Horsley. They estimated their
reservoir would have enough reserves to last ten months but they had
miscalculated. In 1853 there was a drought. They had to draw supplies
from the river at Elswick. The worst cholera epidemic on Tyneside
followed.

In the twelve years following 1845 eight reservoirs were constructed
at Whittle Dene. In 1863 the name was changed to the present
Newcastle and Gateshead Water Company. The water supply was
still inadequate and in 1871 the East Hallington Reservoir was constructed, Colt Crag in 1884, Little Swinburn in 1886 and West
Hallington in 1889. After several years' work Catcleugh Reservoir

was completed in 1904. All these reservoirs are mentioned in our book.

Whittle Dene Reservoirs cover 150 acres and contain 500 million gallons.

WHITTONSTALL

The village of Whittonstall is three miles south west of Stocksfield· It occupies an exposed position on the summit of a hill which separates the valleys of the Tyne and Derwent. The name (*Quictunstal* in 1242) means the "farmstead with the quickset hedge". In the early thirteenth century Hugh de Baliol allowed part of Whittonstall "to be assorted, cultivated, built upon and enclosed by a ditch and a hedge". This grant was probably the origin of the village of Newlands near Ebchester. The church, dedicated to St. Philip and St. James was completely rebuilt in 1830. The only fragment of the thirteenth century church is a beautiful early English corbel. The church stands immediately to the west of the old course of Watling Street (Dere Street) which passes through the graveyard.

Willimoteswick Castle.

WILLIMOTESWICK CASTLE

The ruins of the old border stronghold of Willimoteswick (also called Willimontswyke) stands on a slight eminence a short distance from the village of Bardon Mill. The strange name means Willimot's dwelling and has nothing to do with the guillemots which are supposed to have frequented the marshes nearby. The ruins of the tower are incorporated into the farmhouse which has been built on the site. The castle was the chief seat of the ancient family of the Ridleys and the birthplace of the Protestant martyr who was burnt at the stake before Balliol College, Oxford, in 1555. Thirty years after, on the decease of Nicholas Ridley, at the time sheriff of the county, two men and a woman were committed to prison by Sir John Foster on suspicion of having caused his death by witchcraft. An inventory of Nicholas Ridley's goods made at the time records the following:- Twenty pairs of double linen sheets, ten pairs of 'strakinge' sheets, ten pairs of 'harne' sheets, six 'wishons', six 'worset wishons', six candlesticks, a new cupboard, a 'hurle' bed, a new 'presser', seven chests, two 'carping' cloths, two cupboard cloths, four new sacks, the 'Boke of Marters', and a Bible.

During the Civil War the Ridleys espoused the Royalist cause and their estates were forfeited in 1652 and passed into the hands of the family of Lowes, who derived their name from the Forest of Lowes, of which they were the lords.

WILLIMOTESWYKE (TOWER AND MANOR HOUSE) FROM THE N. 1884

The history of the castle is obscure. It is not mentioned in the list of 1415 but in 1541 it is described as "a good tower and stone house adjoining thereto, of the inheritance of Nicholas Ridley, and kept in good reparations".

The entrance tower to the castle is an imposing building with walls seven feet thick. The top storey is corbelled out on three projected roll-mouldings. The windows are small but some higher up are mullioned with hood-moulds probably added in the seventeenth century.

WILLIMOTESWYKE FROM THE EAST, 1860.

Willimoteswick Castle ·· The Entrance ··

The entrance archway is tunnel vaulted. The upper hinge-pin of one of the gates and the holes for the sliding bar which closed them can still be seen. On the right is a newel staircase leading to the battlements. One of the rooms contains the original capacious fireplace almost eleven feet wide.

Of the old house only two odd oblong and very narrow towers remain rising above the recent buildings. Although they have corbelled battlements they appear to have been intended as lookouts.

WYLAM

The township of Wylam (a Saxon name meaning "Wila's homestead") lies on the north bank of the Tyne. The County History (1926) describes the village as "situated on a southern slope, well sheltered, and though composed chiefly of ugly modern cottages yet they are draped in creepers and brightened by thriving little gardens, which give it a cheerful appearance". From the twelfth century it belonged to Tynemouth Priory. Here the monks had a special residence. Whether this was a fortified house in the true sense of the term is doubtful. The remains, in the form of a tunnel-vault of sixty feet by nineteen feet, are incorporated in the present Wylam Hall. Wylam House or sporting house, as it was called, was used by the monks of Tynemouth as a place of rest and recreation. It was destroyed by the Scots early in the fourteenth century and restored by Prior Whethamstede in 1405.

Besides a medieval vaulted ground floor Wylam Hall has a seventeenth century doorway, here illustrated and "a cosy seventeenth century room, panelled in black oak, from the floor to the ceiling". (Archaeologia Aeliana 1914).

Most of the building we see today dates from about 1880 with a wing of 1914. It has recently been modernized and converted into flats.

After the Dissolution of the Monasteries the township was broken up and passed into several hands, the chief holder eventually being the Blackett family who resided at Wylam Hall.

The coal mine is first mentioned in 1292. During the sixteenth and seventeenth centuries it was in the King's possession for many years. In 1611 his surveyor examined the overman and a hewer in the colliery. They said that "there is only one pit wrought there, in the occupation

Wylam by R. P. Leitch 1862

of Timothy Draper esquire. The pit is about 16 fathoms deep, the seam is one yard thick, the coal good, and may continue twenty years, and be worth £10 yearly, if there be vent for them, as now is. There is no waste and they do not know of any other mines likely to be discovered in these grounds. It finally came into the possession of the Blacketts. In 1825 Mackenzie describes the colliery:-

The coal is worked on the south side of the Tyne, conveyed under the river, and drawn up here; and from hence sent by locomotive engines by a rail-way to Lemington, a distance of about 5 miles. Each engine draws ten wagons, that carry eight chaldrons of coal, or 21½ tons, which is above two tons and one-tenth to each wagon. Sometimes a dozen or more wagons are dragged by one engine. A stranger is struck with surprise and astonishment on seeing a locomotive engine moving majestically along the road, at the rate of 4 or 5 miles an hour, drawing along from ten or fourteen loaded waggons; and his surprise is increased on witnessing the extraordinary facility with which the engine is managed. This invention is a notable triumph of science. Here are also a number of cinder ovens, in which the small coal is prepared for the use of manufactories. Wylam coal is chiefly consumed in steam-engines, for which it is found well adapted.

Christopher Blackett, the owner of Wylam colliery was the first northern coalowner to show an interest in the locomotive. He had experimented in 1804, without success, with an engine after the design of the Cornish engineer, Trevithik. It couldn't be used on the Wylam waggonway but was used as a fixed engine in a Newcastle iron-foundry. In 1812 he tried a second engine on his waggon-way, which was so designed as to work with a toothed driving-wheel upon a rack-rail. In these experiments he was assisted by William Hedley, the viewer of the colliery.

William Hedley (1779-1843) was born at Newburn. He went to school at Wylam where he was taught by a mathematician called Watkins. At the age of 22 he became manager of Walbottle colliery and afterwards at Wylam.

"He first became interested in the use of steam engines around 1810, at which time horses were expensive due to the demands of the wars with the French. This situation was seriously threatening the profitability of Hedley's mine and a closure seemed imminent. Hedley thought a great deal about the problem. At first he experimented with oxen instead of horses but they proved unsatisfactory. He then turned his attention to steam engines, which had lately became popular.

"The locomotives then in use relied on some form of cog system or chain to link the carriage with the rails, for it was widely believed that without such an arrangement an engine by itself would ' . . . only draw after it on a level road, a weight equal to its own.' These systems were very inefficient due to the enormous frictional loss of power at the junction of carriage and rail. Hedley realised that the basic premises of design were misguided and that the use of a smooth wheel on a smooth rail would be much more efficient. It was a simple idea which all other designers and engineers had overlooked, but its worth had yet to be proved.

"In great secrecy, working only at night, Hedley started to experiment. He built a carriage with smooth wheels which could be turned by means of cranks operated by men. There were two cranks on each side of the carriage and the operators stood on small platforms above the ground. Using a short track of smooth rails, and experimenting with various weightings of the carriage and with various loads, Hedley demonstrated to his own satisfaction that his novel system was workable

He was obviously aware of the importance of his invention because he promptly patented it. The patent is dated 13 March 1813.

"Hedley's work was aimed at improving the profitability of his colliery, and so he quickly started to put the results of his experiments into practice. He engaged Thomas Waters of Gateshead to undertake the construction of the locomotive, which was powered by a steam engine of 6″ bore. It was soon nicknamed 'Puffing Billy', presumably after its designer." (*B. Shurlock. Industrial Pioneers of Tyneside.*)

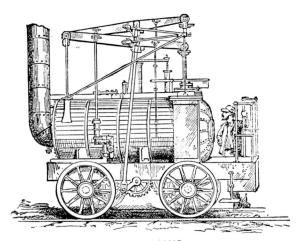

PUFFING BILLY, 1813.

The first model was not very successful but a second lighter model worked extremely well and proved that smooth wheels on the locomotive, Hedley's major invention, could work.

Although George Stephenson is usually credited with the invention of the locomotive men like William Hedley made major contributions.

George Stephenson, of course, was born at Wylam on July 9th 1781, in a cottage which stood beside the waggonway from Wylam to Lemington. It is a red-tiled two-storey rubble building called High Street House, so called because it was near the old post-road or "street" between Newcastle and Hexham. The lower room in the west end of the house was the home of the Stephensons. Its floor was of clay, its walls unplastered, and bare rafters above. The horse drawn waggons on the wooden ways in front of the house were probably one of the first sights to be seen by the young Stephenson. However his parents left when he was a little child and his life was spent chiefly at Newburn.

In 1948, a century after Stephenson's death, the cottage where he was born was given to the National Trust by the North-East Coast

Interior of the house at Wylam, where George Stephenson was born

below: Exterior view of the house

Institution of Engineers and Shipbuilders. In 1929, the centenary of the success of the Rocket at Rainhill, a metal plaque, with a relief of the Rocket, was unveiled on the front of the house.

Holeyn Hall, on the north of Wylam township, was also the home of another Tyneside inventor. Here Sir Algernon Charles Palmer lived for many years.

Boat House Inn . Wylam.

Acknowledgements

We have not included a bibliography in this book. It would be too long. However certain books have been of great assistance. The most important is the *Northumberland County History* followed by Bruce's *Roman Wall* (various editions), and the *Lapidarium Septentrionale* (1875). Several volumes of *Archaeologia Aeliana* have produced information and illustrations. Many other books are mentioned in the text. The Carvoran Measure is reproduced by permission of the Trustees of the Clayton Collection (Chesters Museum). Photographer Terry Hay.